Uganda:
A Nation in Transition
Post-colonial Analysis

Godfrey Mwakikagile

Uganda: A Nation in Transition: Post-colonial Analysis

Godfrey Mwakikagile

First Edition

ISBN 978-9987-16-035-8

New Africa Press
Dar es Salaam, Tanzania

Contents

Introduction

THIS work is a study of Uganda as a nation during the post-colonial era.

It looks at the problems the country faced during its first years of independence including the constitutional crisis following the abolition of the kingdoms; the demand by the Buganda kingdom for federal status and its refusal to accept a unitary state; the ouster of Kabaka Mutesa II from the presidency and his subsequent exile to Britain; the paradoxical nature of the demand by Buganda kingdom for federal status under a unitary state and of having a hereditary ruler, Mutesa, the king of Buganda, serving as president of a country that was not under a monarchy.

It also looks at the difficulties in achieving national unity in a country divided by ethno-regional loyalties including kingdoms and other traditional centres of power;

the division between Buganda and the rest of the country; the division between the north inhabited by Nilotic ethnic groups and the south that is predominantly Bantu; the role of the military and security forces, dominated by northerners, especially the Langi and the Acholi, in tilting the balance of power in favour of northern leaders during Obote's reign; the 1971 military coup in which President Milton Obote was overthrown and which led to the rise of Idi Amin to power; the reign of terror under Amin and how the centre of power shifted in favour of his people from the northwest; the 1980 general elections which led to Obote's return to the presidency, plunging the country into a civil war that came to be known as The Bush War; and the rise of Yoweri Museveni to power and his status as the longest-serving president in the country's post-colonial history.

It has its shortcomings and may not be a comprehensive study of Uganda during the post-colonial period. But it addresses most of the major events which have taken place and which have affected the lives of most Ugandans since independence. For that reason alone, it can serve a useful purpose as an introduction to the study of Uganda during some of its most turbulent years in the post-colonial era.

Chapter One

Uganda after Independence:
Obstacles to National Unity

AMONG the three East African countries of Kenya, Uganda, and Tanganyika which united with Zanzibar in 1964 to form Tanzania, Uganda faced the biggest threat to national unity soon after independence.

The threat came from the Buganda kingdom which did not want to be an integral part of Uganda. It wanted to reclaim its status as an independent kingdom which it enjoyed before colonial rule. It was forcibly united with the other kingdoms and traditional centres of power by the British to form Uganda.

Dissatisfaction among the Baganda, under their king known as *kabaka*, led to demands for independence for the kingdom. The demands amounted to secessionist threats. Their complaint was simple. They did not want to be an integral part of Uganda. They wanted to have their own country.

The secessionist threats were swiftly neutralised by Uganda's first prime minister, Milton Obote, who led the country to independence. He was greatly resented by the Baganda because of his determination to assert control over their kingdom in order to maintain national unity at any cost.

Uganda was also faced with a strange paradox soon after independence. It involved the *kabaka*, king of the Buganda kingdom, a federalist at best and separatist at worst, serving as president of Uganda which was established as a unitary state.

It was Obote himself, leader of the Uganda People's Congress (UPC) and the country' first prime minister after independence, who was responsible for this situation out of political expediency.

He approached Kabaka Mutesa II to form an alliance between the Uganda People's Congress and the kabaka's party, Kabaka Yekka which was solidly Baganda in membership, in order to keep the Democratic Party led by Benedicto Kiwanuka out of power. The *kabaka* became the president of Uganda and Obote remained prime minister.

However, the office of president did not have any executive functions. Real power was in the hands of the prime minister who was the head of government and appointed cabinet members as well as other government officials including ambassadors.

But how could a king serve as the leader of a country that was not a monarchy? Buganda was a monarchy. But Uganda as a country was not. It was a unitary state. And how could someone who sought federal status for his kingdom with the rest of the country be president of a unitary state?

Obote himself resolved this contradiction shortly thereafter when he abolished all the kingdoms and expelled the king of Buganda from the presidency of Uganda to consolidate his position and lay a solid foundation for a highly centralised state.

But it was a solution that soured relations between the people of the Buganda kingdom and the national government for years until Yoweri Museveni became president of Uganda and restored all the kingdoms although only as cultural institutions without any political power.

Some people in Buganda wanted federation for Uganda instead of having a highly centralised state which almost had absolute control over the whole country because power was concentrated at the centre under the national government.

But this concession by some Baganda nationalists – who considered their kingdom to be a nation within a nation but who probably knew they would not succeed in seceding – was also rejected by the national leaders, especially Obote.

The national leaders felt that a federal form of government posed a threat to national unity in a country that was divided along ethnoregional lines with very strong traditional centres of power, especially the kingdoms of Buganda, Bunyoro, Ankole, Toro and the princedom of Busoga whose demands for autonomy could lead to demands for independence.

In fact, the first government formed at independence was no more than a coalition of these regional blocs and various interest groups, including religious ones – Protestant, Catholic and Islamic – which did not even have a common nationalist agenda besides a few leaders who advocated unity at the national level transcending ethnicity and regionalism.

All those divisions and rivalries persisted and became an enduring phenomenon in Ugandan national life years after independence only in varying degrees of intensity.

Compromises to form the first government at independence entailed inclusion – in the cabinet – of some of the leading politicians from the kingdoms and other parts of the country.

Prime Minister Obote came from the north. His stronghold was among his fellow tribesmen, the Langi (also known as Lango) in Lango District. He was also supported by their neighbours, the Acholi.

Mr. Grace Ibingira came from the Ankole kingdom and was also a member of parliament for Ankole West. He also served as justice minister and secretary-general of the ruling Uganda People's Congress (UPC) which drew its greatest strength and support from different parts of the country – especially in the north and in the west – outside Buganda where the dominant party was the Kabaka Yekka whose membership and leadership was almost exclusively Bugandan; while that of the Democratic Party led by Benedicto Kiwanuka, who also came from the Buganda kingdom, was predominantly Catholic.

It was also Grace Ibingira who designed Uganda's national flag.

Other prominent members in the first cabinet (1962 – 1971) who came from different parts of the country included Felix Onama from West Nile District – home of Idi Amin – in northwestern Uganda. He first served as interior minister and later as defence minister. As defence minister, both the military and the police were under his jurisdiction. He also once served as secretary-general of the ruling Uganda People's Congress (UPC).

Others included George Magezi from Bunyoro kingdom, Dr. Emmanuel Lumu, from Buganda kingdom, Cuthbert Obwangor from Iteso, Mathias Ngobi from Busoga, John Babiiha from Toro kingdom, John Lwamafa from Bukiga, Adoko Nekyon from Lango, Alex Ojera from Acholi, N. M. Patel, an Indian; J. T. Simpson, an Englishman; Sam Odaka from Musamia, John Kakonge from Bunyoro, Shaban Nkutu from Busoga, Joshua Wakholi from Bugisu, Lameck Lubowa from Buganda, Max Choudry from Karamoja, and others.

They also represented all the major religious groups in Uganda: Protestant, Catholic, and Muslim.

Yet the cabinet was not a monolithic whole. Its composition was deliberately structured to represent competing and even conflicting interests, local and regional as well as religious, without a single unifying ideology. Its members ranged from the most reactionary to the most revolutionary; from idealists and visionaries to realists and pragmatists; from liberals to conservatives; tribalists to nationalists and pan-Africanists, and so on.

The ruling Uganda People's Congress under Obote faced a formidable task of not only establishing a strong central government; it had to contend with ethnic and regional rivalries – especially among the traditional kingdoms – and instill a true sense of nationalism and patriotism in the people who did not consider themselves to be one. Other countries such as neighbouring Tanzania did not face those problems on the same scale Uganda did. As President Julius Nyerere stated at the annual conference of the Uganda People's Congress in Kampala, Uganda, in June 1968:

"When you consider that one of the really serious tasks facing political parties in Africa is the removal of of outmoded and useless institutions, and their replacement with modern institutions of government capable of producing the fruits of independence for the people of Africa, and bearing in mind the problems the UPC had inherited in this respect, I want to suggest quite seriously that the UPC faced a greater problem of institution transformation than any of her sister parties in Eastern Africa, and that therefore the UPC has been more successful than any of her sister parties of the Mulungushi Club – and certainly more successful than TANU." –

13

(Julius Nyerere, quoted in Colin Legum and John Drysdale, eds., *Africa Contemporary Record: Annual Survey and Documents 1968 – 1969*, London: Africa Research Limited, 1969, p. 233).

While some of the prominent politicians from the kingdoms sought to maintain the territorial integrity of Uganda even if under a highly decentralised federal structure, although they supported Obote in his determination to build a unitary state, the Buganda kingdom sought secession. The kingdom tried to secede even before independence and wanted to attain sovereign status separate from the rest of Uganda.

But that was not the kind of political arrangement Ugandan leaders who led their country to independence wanted to have. They did not want any part of Uganda to secede. And they did not want the country to have a weak government. What was needed, according to Obote and other national leaders, was a strong central government which could keep the country together. As Professor Saadia Touval states in his book *The Boundary Politics of Independent Africa*:

"Uganda's unity has been threatened both before and after independence by separatist sentiments among the important Baganda people who possessed, until 1966, a measure of autonomy in their Buganda kingdom." – (Saadia Touval, *The Boundary Politics of Independent Africa*, Cambridge, Massachusetts, USA: Harvard College, 1972, 1999, p. 30).

Buganda threatened to secede in the fifties. And about two years before independence, it again threatened to secede. That was in 1960. Other kingdoms in Uganda also posed a threat to national unity, only in varying degrees.

Secessionist sentiments among the Banyoro of Bunyoro kingdom were partly fuelled by the Baganda who had territorial disputes with them. What are known as "the lost counties" were transferred from the Bunyoro kingdom to the Buganda kingdom by the British during the advent of colonial rule.

Also, the fact that Buganda was the most powerful kingdom in Uganda played a role in encouraging the Banyoro in their quest for greater autonomy and even for independence to avoid being dominated by the Baganda if they remained an integral part of Uganda. They believed that after independence, Uganda would be dominated by the Baganda who were also the most highly educated people in the country.

Their quest for autonomy was also compounded by nationalism among the Banyoro themselves who did not consider themselves to be a part of Uganda. As James Minahan states in his work, *Encyclopedia of The Stateless Nations: Ethnic and National Groups Around the World*:

"Ganda domination and the Lost Counties controversy initiated the growth of modern Nyoro nationalism.

The movement began as an anti-Ganda popular movement. The Nyoro also saw the British as their enemies, powerful protectors of their ancient rivals in Buganda.

In 1921 Nyoro nationalists formed a political group called Mubende-Bunyoro, which quickly became the kingdom's most popular political party; its demands included the return of the Lost Counties and secession from British Buganda. The British treated the kingdom as conquered territory until 1933, when the king (*omukama*) finally signed a protectorate agreement.

The territorial dispute between Bunyoro and Buganda acquired renewed importance when Britain prepared Uganda for independence. In 1961 the *omukama* refused to attend a constitutional conference until the British authorities resolved the conflict.

The Ganda refused to negotiate, setting off a serious

crisis as Bunyoro moved toward secession and prepared for war.

British mediation produced an agreement to hold a plebiscite in the disputed area, finally allowing Uganda to achieve independence in 1962. The Kingdom of Bunyoro reluctantly agreed to accept autonomy and a semifederal status within Uganda.

In 1964 the inhabitants of the Lost Counties voted to return to Bunyoro. The conflict again became a crisis when the Ganda government refused to accept the results of the plebiscite.

Nyoro soldiers gathered in Hoima and prepared for war, but the dispute quickly lost importance as even more serious threats menaced the kingdoms. The Ugandan government, dominated by non-Bantu northern tribes, instituted laws to curtail the kingdoms' autonomy. In 1966 the government abrogated the autonomy statutes and in 1967 abolished the kingdoms as administrative units." – (James Minahan, *Encyclopedia of The Stateless Nations: Ethnic and National Groups Around the World*, Westport, Connecticut, USA: Greenwood Publishing Group, 2002, p. 1429. See also, cited by James Minahan, V.W. Nyakatura, *Anatomy of an African Kingdom: A History of Bunyoro-Kitara*, 1973; Clarence Apuuli, *A Thousand Years of the Bunyoro-Kitara Kingdom*, 1981; and Phares Mutibwa, Lawrenceville, New Jersey, USA: *Uganda Since Independence: A Story of Unfulfilled Hopes*, Africa World Press, 1992).

Minahan goes on to state:

"Nyoro nationalists enthusiastically supported the overthrow of the hated government (of President Milton Obote) in 1971 by a young army colonel, Idi Amin Dada.

Amin's new government, a brutal dictatorship dominated by Amin's small northern Muslim tribe, soon lost all support in Bunyoro. In 1972, Nyoro leaders,

16

sickened by the excesses of the Amin regime, called for Bunyoro secession, but the movement lost momentum as Amin's henchmen systematically eliminated its leaders.

The infamous Amin regime, finally overthrown in 1979, gave way to a series of weak, unstable Ugandan governments. A large resistance movement arose among the southern Bantu peoples of the former kingdoms of the southwest, led by Yoweri Museveni, an ethnic Ankole. After years of bush warfare, Museveni took control of Uganda in 1986 and created the country's first Bantu-dominated government.

Relative peace and democracy permitted the rebirth of Nyoro nationalism, based on demands for the restoration of the kingdom. A more radical minority advocated the secession of Bunyoro from Uganda, arguing that the kingdom's inclusion in the multi-ethnic state had brought it only terror, death, and destruction.

In July 1993 the government allowed the partial restoration of the kingdom and the enthronement of a new Nyoro king, Solomon Iguru, a descendant of Kabarega and the 27th monarch of the Bito dynasty. In September 1993 nationalists demanded the restoration of the kingdom's traditional boundaries, including the Mubende area of Buganda, the Lost Counties.

The first national elections in 16 years were held in Uganda in April 1996. The majority of the Nyoros supported President Museveni, fearing the chaos and violence of the north of the country. The vote generally split along regional lines in Uganda, with the Bantu south supporting Museveni, while the Nilotic north supported opposition leaders.

For decades the Nyoros had been among the poorest of the peoples of Uganda, but in the 1990s they experienced a resurgence due to a new emphasis on cash-crop production by small-scale farmers. New prosperity and the partial restoration of the kingdom fueled demands for greater autonomy and for real political power for the new *omukama.*

Presently, the king is a cultural leader, with no political or administrative power, but under his patronage the Nyoros are striving to salvage and maintain their age-old culture and kingdom....

In May 2001, the kingdom government took control of two palaces, royal burial grounds, and other cultural sites in the region from the Ugandan government. The monarchy has begun to reunite the Nyoros, who have had no unifying symbol since 1967." – (James Minahan, *Encyclopedia of the Stateless Nations*, ibid., pp. 1429 – 1430).

Although the kingdom is politically powerless, there are probably many Nyoros who still would like to regain their glorious past when they lived as an independent people under their own leadership.

There is latent nationalism among many people not only in Bunyoro but in other traditional kingdoms as well, although the majority have, even if grudgingly, probably accepted their status as an integral part of the modern nation of Uganda. But a resurgence of nationalism – micro-nationalism, sub-nationalism or proto-nationalism – among them can not be entirely ruled out in the future on a continent where ethnicity remains a potent force in national life.

Toro, an offshoot of Bunyoro, is another kingdom which has experienced nationalist awakening among its people through the years who consider their homeland to be a separate entity although the majority, as in all the other kingdoms, acknowledge that they are an integral part of Uganda. But there has always been an undercurrent of sub-nationalism among the Toro like in other traditional societies and jurisdictions which constituted viable entities once ruled by their own people as nations or micro-nations until the British came and united them to form a bigger country that came to be known as Uganda.

It was also the British colonial rulers who encouraged nationalist aspirations among the Toro although they at the same time wanted to maintain Uganda's territorial integrity for administrative purposes to facilitate colonisation:

"Encouraged by the British, who believed that Ugandan independence was still decades away, the kingdom became the focus of Toro nationalism and identity. In 1953 the Toro royal government demanded federal status and the extension of the Lutoro language to all the kingdom's schools, even in the non-Toro Ruwenzori district.

The issue of Toro nationalism intensified as independence for Uganda neared in the late 1950s. Toro nationalism grew in an effort to keep the revenues from the Kilembe Copper Mine for themselves, and over what they perceived as lesser treatment for their *omukama*. Activists demanded that the *omukama* of Toro be granted the same privileges as the *kabaka*, the king, of Buganda, Uganda's largest and most powerful kingdom." – J. Minahan, *Encyclopedia of the Stateless Nations*, ibid., p. 1912).

Inextricably linked with Toro aspirations for autonomy and even for independence if possible is the Rwenzururu secessionist movement in the Ruwenzori – or Rwenzori – mountains in southwestern Uganda on the border with the Democratic Republic of Congo (DRC).

The Rwenzururu region is home to the Bakonjo and the Bamba, the dominant ethnic groups in the area who strongly resisted integration into the Toro kingdom by the British colonial rulers. As James Minahan states:

"The rapid growth of Toro nationalism parallelled the growing nationalism of the Konjo and Amba, in a reaction to increasing assimilation.

The two mountain peoples demanded separation from Toro and the creation of a separate Ruwenzori district within Uganda. The threat to the kingdom's territorial integrity raised Toro demands for recognition as an independent state before future relations with Uganda were regulated. On the eve of Ugandan independence the kingdom adopted a new constitution that ignored the Ruwenzori people's demands for official recognition of the kingdom's three peoples (Toro, Konjo, and Amba).

In 1962 the Toro accepted semifederal status within the newly independent Ugandan state. Toro nationalists, somewhat mollified by official recognition of the kingdom, blocked Konjo and Amba efforts to separate in a distinct district.

In early 1963 the mountain tribes rebelled, and on 13 February 1963 they declared independence as the Republic of Ruwenzuru, basing their claims to the entire Toro kingdom on historical possession and assertions that the Toro had migrated to the region from Bunyoro and should return to their original homeland.

Uganda's independence government, dominated by northerner Milton Obote, had little sympathy for the traditional Bantu monarchies in the southern districts. In 1967 the Obote government abolished the kingdoms as centers of local nationalism and separatism, and in 1970 the Ruwenzori rebels were finally defeated.

The Ugandan government (was) overthrown in a coup led by Idi Amin in 1971....Initial Toro support of Idi Amin in the belief that he would restore the kingdom quickly disappeared. Princess Elizabeth of Toro formed part of Amin's administration, but she was later framed and dismissed.

Persecution of the Christians fueled a revival of Toro separatism as Amin excesses accelerated (Amin was a Muslim). A strong secessionist movement in Toro ended in 1972 with the murder or disappearance of the majority of Toro's leadership." – (Ibid., p. 1913).

Although Toro secessionist attempts were suppressed

by Obote and later by Amin, there was no guarantee that they would not be rekindled in the future.

One of the main reasons for secessionist sentiments among many people in the different kingdoms was centralisation of power and dictatorial rule.

There was also, among southerners, opposition to domination of the national government by northerners, especially the Langi and the Acholi. Obote, a Nilotic not a Bantu, was a Langi. The army and security forces were also dominated by northerners. Obote himself had become unpopular in the south especially after he abolished the kingdoms, all of which were in southern Uganda.

After his ouster by Amin in 1971, he returned to power in 1980:

"In 1980 Obote again took control of Uganda but met with stiff resistance in the southern Bantu regions. A Bantu supported resistance movement, led by Yoweri Museveni, rallied the peoples of the former southern kingdoms. Obote's efforts to destroy the rebels led to a great... loss of life....

Museveni finally took control of devastated Uganda in 1986, forming the country's first government controlled by the southern Bantus.

The relative freedom (under Museveni), after two decades of terror and destruction, rekindled Toro nationalism. The land issue, involving claims to territories taken from Toro during the colonial period and turned over to rival tribes, became the focus of the growing national movement.

In July 1993, with the Museveni government approval, the Toro kingdom was partially restored, and Patrick Olimi Kaboyo in 1995 was crowned as the twelfth king of Toro in Fort Portal. The monarchy became a cultural expression, without its former political and administrative powers.

The Konjo and Amba of Bundibugyo District initially

21

refused to relinquish the former royal lands they had occupied, but in March 1994 senior members of the Ruwenzori movement acknowledged the new king, officially ending the conflict that had begun three decades before. The Ruwenzori rebellion resumed in the late 1990s.

The Ugandan government's emphasis on cash crop production in the 1980s and 1990s aided economic recovery. Devastated during the 1960s and 1970s by civil wars and brutal dictatorships, the Toros had slipped back to a premodern existence. The economic resurgence parallelled the cultural and political revival of the kingdom.

Rebel groups in the Ruwenzori Mountains mounted raids on Toro towns in the western districts in early 2000, disrupting the tourism and farming industries. The rebels, mostly based among the Ruwenzoris, sought to separate the mountainous west from the Toro. Reaction to the threat to split their ancient kingdom raised nationalist tension in the kingdom to levels not seen since the early 1960s.

Toro nationalism, led by the Protestant minority, at the turn of the twenty-first century was less separatist than federalist. Many saw the king and the traditional legislature as the logical extension of Ugandan federalism. A completely restored Toro within a Ugandan federation would safeguard the Toro culture and traditions, while federalism and regional autonomy would support the moderate nationalist demands against the more radical aims of the small militant minority.

Many Toros support nationalism on the belief that had the kingdom seceded in 1962 as a member state of the British Commonwealth, they would have escaped the devastation, ruin, and massacres of the Amin and Obote years.

Increasing violence between the Toros and migrants from other areas of western Uganda, particularly the Kigas, became a serious problem in 1997 – 98, and by early 2002 had destabilized many of the rural areas. Many people fled to the relative safety of the towns and cities." – (Ibid., pp. 1913 – 1914. See also Kenneth Ingham, *The Kingdom of Toro in Uganda*, 1975; Emmanuel K. Twesigye, *African Monarchies and Kingdoms of Uganda*, 1995; Thomas P. Ofcansky, *Uganda: Tarnished Pearl of Africa*, 1996).

As we have just learned, there were other secessionist attempts in the southwestern part of the country, besides Toro, before and after independence in the sixties and in the following years.

In June 1962, just three months before Uganda won independence in October, the Bakonjo and the Bamba severed ties with the Toro and declared they were not a part of the Toro kingdom. They had their own identity and history, culture and customs. They also suffered oppression and discrimination under the Toro for years and demanded to have their own separate territory, the same demand they made in the fifties.

The British rejected their demand. The Bakonjo and the Bamba responded by launching guerrilla warfare.

It was low-intensity armed resistance and continued even after Uganda won independence. Their nationalist movement was named Rwenzururu. It was secessionist and wanted to establish a kingdom for the Bakonjo and the Bamba.

On 30 June 1963, the Bakonjo and Bamba nationalists declared independence and named their new country the kingdom of Rwenzururu. Isaya Mukirania became king.

But the kingdom did not last long and was brutally suppressed by the Ugandan army. Toro soldiers in the army played a key role in neutralising the Bakonjo and Bamba secessionists.

However, the secessionists regrouped. They resurfaced years later and posed a great threat to national unity from 1979 to 1982. The government of President Obote reached an agreement with the secessionists. They agreed to abandon secession and accept autonomy for their region.

The odds against them were overwhelming. Unlike the Baganda, the Banyoro and the Ankole, the Bakonjo and the Bamba were not, even when combined, a very large community to be a viable entity had their demand for secession been accepted in order for them to establish an independent state. And there was, of course, the powerful machinery of the state – the central government – to suppress them.

But that did not dissuade them from pursuing their goal, an aspiration that is more common among larger groups. As Professor W. J. Argyle states in *Tradition & Transition in East Africa: Studies of the Tribal Element in the Modern Era*:

"It is, of course, true that size has usually influenced a group's chances of winning and maintaining independence, that ultimate test of nationhood, and it is also true that the most conspicuous attempts to seize independence have been made by large tribes like the Ibo, the Kongo, the Luba, the Lunda, the Ganda. Yet similar bids have been made by much smaller groups.

The Konjo and the Amba of Uganda cannot number more than about 150,000, but in 1962 some of them began a rebellion, followed by the declaration of an independent state and an appeal to U Thant for United Nations' protection against the forces of the Uganda government (Stacey, 1965, p. 81; and *infra*, p. 252ff.).

No doubt many of those who took part in this rebellion saw it merely as a chance to free themselves from the domination of the hated Toro. For its leader, Mukirane, and for his closest followers, it meant something more which would have been recognizable to European nationalists.

Its origin went back to a 'Bakonjo Life History Research Society' – partly inspired by an outsider, Mr

Stacey – which Mukirane later turned into a political movement and renamed the 'Rwenzururu Secessionist Movement.' – (W. J. Argyle, in P. H. Gulliver, ed., *Tradition & Transition in East Africa: Studies of the Tribal Element in the Modern Era*, London: Routledge and Kegan Paul Ltd., 1969, pp. 52 – 53).

He goes on to state:

"After the rebellion had begun, Mukirane set up a rudimentary administration in the mountains with himself self-proclaimed 'President' of the new state of Rwenzururu, which had its own national flag and anthem. A statement justifying the secession included many of the classical nationalist complaints and demands: too few schools and scholarships for Konjo and Amba children; hardly any Konjo or Amba teachers and priests; an unfair allocation of land and of the products derived from it; discrimination against Konjo and Amba in appointments to the bureaucracy.

Such pretensions on behalf of so small a people seem bizarre enough, and it is not surprising that Mr Stacey came, reluctantly, to the conclusion that Mukirane was mad.

Yet was he any madder than, say, the leaders of the Basque nationalists? There are only about three times as many Basques as there are Konjo and Amba,[7] but numbers did not prevent them from demanding and obtaining from the Spanish government in 1932 the same degree of local autonomy as had previously been given to the Catalans, a much larger group.

During the Civil War, Basques took the next step and set up the Republic of Euzkadi with a provisional government headed by a President (Thomas, 1965, pp. 81, 83, 370). The Republic was, of course, suppressed by General Franco's armies, but Basque nationalism and separatism still survive today, and Basques are still being imprisoned for advocating them. Nor are the Basques a unique case in Europe.

The populations of Albania and Esthonia were probably both under a million when they achieved national independence, and that was one argument which their larger neighbours used against their national aspirations. Unless we wish to identify ourselves with Russians, or Serbs, or Greeks or Italians, we surely have no reason to accept the argument. By the same token we cannot, on the grounds of size alone, deny the nationalism of many small groups all over Africa today.

In fact, it has already been implicitly conceded by a few authorities. Not long ago Post (1964, p. 67) pointed out that 'if a nation is conceived as having a common culture, language, and historical experience, as the eighteenth- and nineteenth-century European writers held, then the closest approximation to national sentiment in West Africa must be the 'tribalism' so often denounced by the nationalists.'

What I have done in this paper is to extend the scope of Post's generalization to cover other parts of Africa and to document it by apt illustrations." – (Ibid., p. 53 – 54).

The nationalist aspirations of the Bakonjo and the Bamba, two small tribes or ethnic groups in the Ruwenzori mountains in southwestern Uganda, is one such apt illustration of the legitimate aspirations of an oppressed and neglected people using the language of nationalism – taken for granted by larger groups – to articulate their demands.

Their demands may have seemed unrealistic, given the overwhelming power of the state to crush rebellion and because of the small size of their stateless nation that had yet to be realised. But they were no less legitimate.

The Bakonjo and Bamba secessionists made another attempt to achieve their goal when they launched a rebellion under the banner of the National Army for the

Liberation of Uganda (NALU) in the late eighties and early nineties when Museveni was president of Uganda.

The secessionists had a lot of support among their people. According to a survey conducted by Makerere University in 2008, 87 per cent of the people in Rwenzururu wanted to have their own kingdom. Museveni's government acceded to their demand and declared the Kingdom of Rwenzururu as a cultural institution – but without political power.

Charles Mumbere became the *omusinga* (king) of the Rwenzururu kingdom in October 2009. His authority is strictly social and cultural. Political power is in the hands of the national government. His father, Isaya Mukirane, was the leader of the secessionist movement which was mostly Bakonjo. He was acknowledged as the king of Rwenzururu and was killed when his son Charles Mumbere was only 13 years old.

But Museveni's government also stated that no such kingdom had existed in the past and there was no historical justification to the claim by the secessionists that they were reclaiming lost glory.

Ankole is another kingdom whose sub-nationalism was an obstacle to national unity through the years before and after independence.

One of the four kingdoms in the country, all in the south, Ankole first sought to maintain its status as a sovereign entity during colonial rule just the other kingdoms attempted to do. But it failed to do so and was forced to accept curtailment of its authority by the British colonial rulers.

Suppression of Ankole nationalism did not achieve its goal. Instead, it had unintended consequences. It fuelled nationalist sentiments and aspirations among the people of the kingdom.

Latent nationalism has always existed among the Ankole and the people of the other kingdoms even during the most brutal periods in Ugandan history. It could not be neutralised. And like all the other kingdoms, it has been profoundly affected by the changes which have taken place in Uganda through the years and was one of the first victims of centralisation of power soon after the country won independence from Britain in 1962.

Although the central government exercised control over the country, it also created instability because the kingdoms did not fully accept the new national rulers who had assumed power after independence. As Professor Edward Kannyo, a Ugandan, states in the *International Handbook of Human Rights*:

"The roots of political and social instability in Uganda lie in the fragmentation of the polity at the time of the attainment of political independence in 1962. This fragmentation is traceable to political, administrative, economic, and cultural processes which developed during the colonial regime.

Like virtually all the other African states, Uganda is a creation of the nineteenth-century European colonial expansion. It encloses dozens of cultural and linguistic groups which had previously lived independently of each other. Within the space of sixty years, they were arbitrarily brought under one politico-administrative system.

The colonial regime was a bureaucratic authoritarian system and did not provide for full-fledged political participation by the indigenous peoples at the national level. In Uganda, meaningful African political participation was restricted to local administrative levels which varied in size and form of government.

The kingdoms of Buganda, Bunyoro, Ankole, and Toro enjoyed higher degrees of administrative autonomy than the other parts of the colony. Among the kingdoms, Buganda stood out through its greater size, its greater administrative autonomy and, more particularly, its attachment to the '1900 Agreement' signed with the British government which provided for a higher degree of political autonomy and was regarded as a covenant by the Buganda government, and the resultant special consideration which the colonial regime always showed to the Buganda monarchy.[4]

The restriction of effective African political participation to local levels during the colonial regime was compounded by the uneven socioeconomic development of the country. Buganda took the lead in the development of modern education, commerce, and the cultivation and marketing of export cash crops.

The relative lag of the other parts of the country, compounded by the desire of important segments of the political elites in Buganda to seek independence outside the colonial territorial framework, as decolonization looked imminent, led to resentment on the part of political leaders from other areas which must on balance be considered as having been an obstacle to the evolution of strong national political leadership on the eve of political independence[5]." – (Edward Kannyo, Chapter 18, "Uganda," in Jack Donnelly and Rhoda E. Howard-Hassmann, eds., *International Handbook of Human Rights*, Westport, Connecticut, USA, 1987, pp. 386 – 387. See also, cited by E. Kannyo: 4. The *Kabaka* (king) of Buganda was the only ruler accorded the honorific 'His Highness.' See D. Anthony Low and R. Cranford Pratt, *Buganda and British Overrule*, London: Oxford University Press, 1960; 5. Cf. Ali A. Mazrui, 'Privilege and Protest as Integrative Factors: The Case of Buganda's Status in Uganda,' in *Protest and Power in Black Africa*, ed. Robert I. Rotberg and Ali A. Mazrui, New York: Oxford University Press, 1970, pp. 1072 – 87; David E. Apter, *The Political Kingdom in Uganda*, Princeton, New Jersey: Princeton University Press, 1967; Tarsis B. Kabwegyere, *The Politics of State Formation*, Nairobi, Kenya: East African Literature Bureau, 1974; Nelson Kasfir, *The Shrinking Political Arena*, Berkeley: University of California Press, 1976; Samwiri R. Karugire,

A Political History of Uganda, Nairobi, Kenya: East African Literature Bureau, 1980; Grace S. Ibingira, *The Forging of an African Nation*, New York: viking Press, 1973).

There were other factors which contributed to the fragmentation of the Ugandan polity and accentuated ethnic and regional differences and rivalries as well as social cleavages which continued after independence and impeded efforts to achieve genuine national integration. As Professor Kannyo goes on to state:

"Another major colonial legacy has been rivalry based on conflict between Protestant and Roman Catholic political elites.

This rivalry originated in the late nineteenth-century struggles between the French (Catholic) and English (Protestant) Christian missionaries, backed by their respective countries, for control of the kingdom of Buganda, which became the nucleus and heart of the future Uganda. It was reinforced by the dominant role which the missionaries came to play in the provision of primary and secondary education for their followers.

When national political parties were formed in the 1950s, they came to reflect these religious rivalries. Thus, the Democratic Party (DP) was identified with Roman Catholic elites who sought to redress their discriminatory underrepresentation in national and local administrative bodies, while the Uganda People's Congress (UPC) was, though to a lesser degree than was the case with respect to the DP and Catholicism, identified with the Protestant elites who sought to preserve their overrepresentation.

In the period immediately before and after the attainment of political independence, the major claims articulated by the contending political parties and groups involved the institutional character of the postcolonial state, that is, unitarism vs. federalism and the closely

30

related issue of the terms on which Buganda would be incorporated in an independent Uganda; the redress of socioeconomic inequalities between regions and districts; and the representation of different religious groups in elite political and administrative positions. The resultant pattern of politics was extremely complex.

Broadly speaking, in the period 1961 – 1966, politics revolved around the overlapping and yet conflictual relationships between (1) the two major political parties, the UPC and the DP; (2) the four kingdoms of Buganda, Bunyoro, Toro, and Ankole; (3) the district of Busoga, whose dominant elites wanted to convert it to a kingdom; and (4) the other districts of the country which did not have monarchical institutions and comprised the majority of the population of the country. The dominant elites in these various institutions competed for power and influence at certain times and over certain issues and collaborated at other times and over other issues. The same pattern applied within the institutions themselves.

The four kingdoms were united in their determination to preserve their monarchical institutions and a certain degree of political autonomy. However, in the period leading up to the political independence of the country, the leaders of Bunyoro, Toro, and Ankole would often join with the leaders from other political groups to oppose any attempts on the part of Buganda to secede from the country or to acquire any status which exceeded their own. In addition, Bunyoro had a direct quarrel with Buganda over some border territories which the British had transferred from Bunyoro to Buganda at the beginning of the colonial regime.

The elites in Busoga sought to convert their district into a monarchical unit and to emulate the institutions of the Buganda and Bunyoro kingdoms, with which the region shared important cultural and historical links. As for the rest of the districts in the country, the main goal was to maintain as much parity of status as possible with the

31

kingdom areas.

It was against this complex background that the UPC and the DP competed for control of the postcolonial state. Both parties were united in their desire to preserve the inherited state in its colonial boundaries. In spite of some rhetorical ideological disputes within the UPC between 1964 and 1966, there were no serious class ideological differences between the two parties. The best one can say is that the UPC contained more people who espoused a more radical interpretation of African nationalism and who advocated a more neutralist foreign policy posture than the DP. However, these individuals were far from being dominant within the party.[6] Both parties were compelled to make compromises with the strong prevailing ethno-cultural sentiments.

The two most contentious issues which the political leaders faced at the time of independence were the degree of autonomy which would be enjoyed by the Kingdom of Buganda and the other kingdoms and the question of who would be head of state. The 1962 Independence Constitution provided for a complex political structure granting a high degree of regional autonomy for Buganda, lesser autonomy for the kingdoms of Bunyoro, Toro, and Ankole, and even lesser autonomy for the 'Territory' of Busoga. The rest of the country had a unitary relationship with the central government.

As had happened in other former British colonies, when Uganda became independent, the British monarch became the head of state and was represented in that ceremonial position by a governor-general who, in this as in other cases, was the last British governor. However, it was clear that this was a temporary arrangement and within a year, the question of who would replace the governor-general arose. This was an emotional issue for the various political groups. As George W. Kanyeihamba has recalled:

While there was agreement on this change the problem was to find the right candidate. The kingdoms would not accept a commoner to occupy the important position of Head of State and thereby become, in importance, greater than their Kings. Buganda went further, no one even if he be King, could be Head of State unless he was the Kabaka [King] of Buganda Himself. The non-kingdoms districts were not silent either. Unused to the regions of Kings they would not accept one of them to be Head of their Independent State.[7]

A compromise solution was found. The head of state would be chosen from among the traditional rulers. However, in order to satisfy the nonkingdom areas, the position of 'constitutional head,' a type of surrogate king, was created for these districts. Any one of these leaders would be eligible for the position of head of state. The head of state was to be known as 'president.' There was also to be a vice president, and both offices were to be held for a term of five years and were to be elected by the National Assembly on a secret ballot.

The *Kabaka* of Buganda became the head of state and the *Kyabazinga* (king) of Busoga – who was also the UPC vice president – became vice president of Uganda. To quote Kanyeihamba again: 'The Baganda were jubilant, the other Kings happy and the rest of the country satisfied for now there was a possibility that each region was in a position to become produce a President.[8]

It is almost certain that this solution would have failed eventually. The replacement of the *Kabaka* of Buganda as head of state, which would have been demanded to give a chance to another ruler, would have been strongly resisted in Buganda. Moreover, the creation of nontraditional 'king surrogates' outside the kingdom areas was not universally popular and had given rise to conflicts within some districts." – (E. Kannyo, ibid., pp. 387 – 389. See also, cited by E. Kannyo, in his chapter notes: 6. Cf. Mahmood Mamdani, *Politics and Class Formation in Uganda*, New York: Monthly Review Press, 1976, pp. 189 – 227; 7. George W. Kanyeihamba, *Constitutional Law and*

Government in Uganda, Nairobi, Kenya: East African Literature Bureau, 1975, p. 67; 8. Ibid., p. 68).

A look at Uganda during its first years of independence in the sixties and in the following decades clearly shows that a number of factors have made it very difficult for the country to achieve unity the way, for example, neighbouring Tanzania has in spite of the fact that it has a very large number of tribes or ethnic groups: about 130.

Tanzania also has substantial numbers of Christians and Muslims – 33% to 35% for each – unlike Uganda which is predominantly Christian. Yet it has managed to avoid ethnic conflicts and rivalries in a way Uganda has not been able to. It has also achieved religious harmony between Christians and Muslims.

The British colonial government in Uganda played a major role in accentuating social cleavages and in fostering ethnic rivalries.

The Buganda kingdom which formed the nucleus of what was to become the country and nation of Uganda – it even gave the country its name, "Uganda" from "Buganda" – was favoured by colonial rulers over the other kingdoms. This kind of favouritism fuelled hostility towards Buganda among many people in the other kingdoms who felt that they were not considered to be as important as the Baganda.

It also laid the foundation for a future secessionist movement among the Baganda who felt they were entitled to rule the whole country after independence; if they could not, they would secede.

There was also a major dividing line between the north and the south. The British focused their attention on the southern part of Uganda in terms of development while virtually neglecting the north. The result was hostility between the two regions fuelled by economic inequalities.

The north remained underdeveloped. Educational opportunities were virtually non-existent in the region while the south had almost all the schools including institutions of higher learning such as Makerere University College founded in 1922.

Religious differences between Protestants – who were mostly Anglican – and Catholics in Uganda aggravated the situation when political competition also assumed a religious dimension, even though this problem was not as serious as ethnoregional rivalries. But it did play a role in impeding progress towards national unity especially when the members of the Democratic Party, which was predominantly Catholic and was led by Benedicto Kiwanuka who came from the Buganda kingdom, made a concerted effort to undermine Prime Minister Obote who was a Protestant and a northerner.

And as in almost all the other African countries, ethnic and regional loyalties have always played a major role in Ugandan politics, clearly demonstrated even during the first years of independence.

The ethnic and regional dimension in Ugandan life and politics was also partly a product of British colonial rule. While the south had the largest number of educated people, in fact one of the largest in East Africa if not the largest during that period, the north provided soldiers.

The largest number of soldiers and members of the security forces during colonial rule and after independence were northerners, mostly Acholi and Lango – or Langi. Obote himself was a Lango.

The imbalance persisted after independence. But it also greatly benefited Obote who, as a northerner, had solid support from the army and other security forces during his term in office until he was overthrown by Idi Amin, a fellow northerner although from the northwest, in January 1971.

But without the support of the army which was then under the leadership of Amin who had been promoted by Obote to that position, Obote may not have been able to survive in office. And he would not have been able to neutralise and oust the *kabaka*, Edward Frederick Mutesa, from the presidency even though the title was more ceremonial than functional; power was in the hands of the prime minister, Obote, during that period.

Although Uganda has survived as a nation, it has had to contend with various forces which could have torn the country apart, especially along ethnoregional lines because of the rivalries among the various ethnic and regional groups which have championed regionalism or micro-nationalism, seeing themselves as nations within a nation. As Professor Joshua Forrest states in his book, *Subnationalism in Africa: Ethnicity, Alliances, and Politics*:

"In Uganda, decades of subnationalist ferment, religious and political strife, and militarized autocracy created a context of intense instability that long preceded Museveni's installment as president.

During the colonial period, powerful ethnoregional leadership structures with direct precolonial roots were strengthened, while the British artificially created several smaller kingships.

The Buganda kingship, with solid links to its precolonial antecedent, was accorded unusual privileges and considerable autonomy.[22]

Immediately prior to Uganda's 1962 independence elections, the traditional Ganda leadership, fearful of losing their privileged position, declared that Buganda would secede from Uganda. However, constitutional negotiators enticed the Ganda to acquiesce by promising autonomy and special status for Buganda within a quasi-federal framework.

The western kingdoms of Bunyoro, Toro, and Ankole, along with the very small kingdom of Busoga, were granted nearly as wide a berth of autonomy, despite the fact that the Ankole and Toro kingdoms had been virtually invented by British administrators.[23]

The resultant political stability proved relatively short-lived. In the early 1960s, parliamentary maneuverings by a variety of opponents of Prime Minister Obote considerably weakened his political power. By 1966, the Ganda king Kabaka Mutesa II, who had been granted the largely titular but symbolically significant post of Ugandan president – Prime Minister Obote ran the country – formed a political alliance with parliamentarian backbenchers who opposed Obote's rule.

This proved a strategic error: Obote then preempted Mutesa, removing the king and his political allies from their government positions and subsequently deciding to rescind the formal autonomy that had been granted to the Buganda kingdom as well as to the aforementioned western kingdoms.[24] Buganda reacted by rejecting the authority of the Ugandan national government.

The ending of autonomous status for the kingships exacerbated the level of state-ethnic tension. Subnationalism in Buganda now became strengthened, as Ganda elites, bureaucrats, and ordinary people coalesced both politically and culturally. Territorial and ethnic assertion here converged with popular enmity toward Obote, so much so that Obote felt it unsafe to set foot inside Buganda.[25]

The Bugandan autonomy movement persisted through the Idi Amin and second Obote regimes, serving a potent reminder of the fragility of the political basis on which the integrity of the Ugandan nation-state rested."[26] – (Joshua B. Forrest, *Subnationalism in Africa: Ethnicity, Alliances, and Politics*, Boulder, Colorado, USA: Lynne Rienner Publishers, Inc., 2004, p. 220. See also, cited by Joshua B. Forrest: 22. Crawford Young, *The Politics of Cultural Pluralism*, Madison, Wisconsin, USA: University of Wisconsin Press, 1976, p. 227; 23. Frank van Acker, "Ethnicity and Institutional Reform: A Case of Ugandan Exceptionalism?" in *Politics of Identity and Economics of Conflict in the Great Lakes Region*, ed. Ruddy Doom and

Jan Gorus, Brussels: VUB University Press, 2000, p. 165; Donald Rothchild, *Managing Ethnic Conflict in Africa: Pressures and Incentives for Cooperation*, Washington, D.C.: Brookings Institution, 1997, p.68; 24. Young, *Politics of Cultural Pluralism*, pp. 150, 265; 25. Ibid., pp. 264 – 266; 26. van Acker, "Ethnicity and Institutional Reform," p. 152).

But Buganda was only a part of the problem, although the major part of it in terms of posing a real threat to national unity. However, other parts of the country had the potential to cause instability and even promote regional fragmentation. As Professor Forrest goes on to state:

"Meanwhile, long-term economic neglect helped to fuel the generation of separatist movements in the northern and western regions.

During the colonial as well as the postcolonial era, the largely rural northern and western regions remained mostly outside the state-centric development rubric.[27] Frank van Acker uses a district-by-district analysis of road-building and electrification projects to convincingly depict the long-term structural economic neglect of the north and west.[28]

Northern discontent stemming from economic inequity generated uprisings, protests, and demands for autonomy by northern and western region traditional leaders. In combination with Gandan subnationalism, this helped to ensure that Uganda would continue to spiral steadily toward internal fragmentation.

The inability of the Ugandan central government to grapple effectively with rural challenges was made especially clear by the rise of the Rwenzururu separatist movement, which sought autonomous rule based on traditional leadership structures for the Konjo and Amba peoples.

The Konjo and Amba were under the jurisdiction of the

Toro kingdom, which was cooperating fully with the Ugandan state. The subnationalists aimed to free themselves of both the kingdom and the nation-state. Tensions led to battles in 1963 – 1964 between the Konjo and the Amba on the one hand, and Toro and Ugandan army units on the other; the latter effectively suppressed the rebels.

However, the Rwenzururu movement reconsolidated over time, and in the wake of the power vacuum left by the collapse of Idi Amin's regime in 1979, it was again able to pose a serious subnationalist threat.[29]

The second Obote administration pursued negotiations with Rwenzururu leaders and reached a settlement in 1982 according to which Konjo and Amba elites agreed to abandon outright secession in return for 'a degree of autonomy'; the appointment of Konjo and Amba to administrative posts; and the provision of economic benefits, such as motorized vehicles, shops, and student scholarships, that would be assigned for distribution by the traditional leaders of these two groups.[30]

The Rwenzururu movement had forced the state to grant power and goods to traditional leaders for the sake of political stability.

In reaction to the monarchical restorations of the 1990s, the Rwenzururu movement was revived yet again, this time with its leaders insisting on separatism. De facto Konjo and Amba control over their claimed districts had already been achieved"[31] – (Ibid., pp. 221 – 222. See also, cited by Joshua B. Forrest: 28. van Acker, "Ethnicity and Institutional Reform," p. 151; 29. Rothchild, *Managing Ethnic Conflict*, p. 90; 30. Ibid.; 31. van Acker, "Ethnicity and Institutional Reform," p. 165).

Ethno-regional loyalties and rivalries have always been a part of life in Uganda. That is one of the main reasons why subnationalism has equally been an enduring phenomenon in the country although in varying degrees, at different times.

But it is marginalisation of the groups and regions which have been kept on the periphery or which don't consider themselves to be a part of the mainstream which has really fostered this sentiment.

Had there been equality, meaningful participation in the political process and in the government as well as equitable redistribution of the nation's resources, for all the groups and regions, a lot of this clamour for separation, secession and greater regional autonomy to the detriment of national unity would not have been heard as loudly as it has been through the years.

Even after Yoweri Museveni seized power and tried to build a broad-based national movement to involve people and groups from all the regions of the country, there were still those who felt they were being ignored or deliberately excluded from the political process and other areas of national life because they challenged the president or dared to openly say there is no true democracy in Uganda except for Museveni and his supporters.

Dissatisfaction with the central government, lack of opportunities for members of some groups who feel they have been marginalised, curtailment of freedom, and the government's determination to concentrate power at the centre, have contributed to tensions in a country where many people, probably the majority, have not yet transcended ethnoregional loyalties for the sake of national unity.

Other factors such as lack of economic opportunities, regional disparities in education and income, sociocultural differences, tribalism and other forms of discrimination simply because you are different or you are not one of them, and mistrust of the national government regardless of who is in office, have all contributed to these tensions which have manifested themselves in different ways through the years but with the same tragic consequences: dividing the nation, pitting one group against another, and encouraging regional fragmentation. And as Forrest states:

"Recent tensions reflect the radicalization of monarchists who now insist on complete autonomy and fully independent powers for the Kabaka.

At the same time, a proliferation of new claimants to unrecognized kingships in the restive north and west, especially on the part of the Alur and the Teso, signal further instability, and Lango activists are calling for their own autonomous state.

Adding to this instability is the fact that two of the four officially restored kingships – Ankole and Toro – have now been effectively rendered moribund by the intensity of popular opposition to those kingships within their respective regions.[39]

In these ways, the monarchical reinstallments and the president's attempt to create a stable quasiconsociational political system both reflect and expose the very real limitations to state power and to the integrity of the nation-state.

Uganda's rural regions have repeatedly defied incorporation; they represent elusive redoubts within which the state vainly seeks to fasten its political girders, even when it does so by utilizing relatively loose mechanisms of government control." – (Ibid., pp. 224).

It is clear that Uganda faced serious problems in her attempts to achieve national unity soon after independence. One of the major problems was the quest for greater regional autonomy which would have greatly weakened the national government had this goal been achieved by the kingdoms of Buganda, Bunyoro, Toro, Ankole, and the princedom of Busoga which at different times had tried to elevate its status to become a kingdom like the rest.

But the biggest threat to national unity was secession. However, this phenomenon was not peculiar to Uganda.

41

There were other African countries which were also threatened by secession.

In East Africa, Kenya also had to contend with separatist tendencies in the Coast Province whose inhabitants wanted to unite with Zanzibar because of the cultural and historical ties they had. The ties were forged during Arab rule among the people in the coastal regions of Kenya and Tanganyika and on the islands of Zanzibar and Pemba. Like their Arab rulers, the people were also overwhelmingly Muslim, a unifying bond that transcended ethnicity and regional loyalties.

There have been other separatist demands in East Africa. The Somali of the North Eastern Province of Kenya, what was once known as the Northern Frontier District, and of the Ogaden region in Ethiopia have always wanted to unite with their kith-and-kin across the border in Somalia. Their brethren in Somalia have expressed the same desire to unite all Somalis who live in Greater Somalia. Greater Somalia is an area composed of Somalia itself, Djibouti, and the regions in neighbouring countries inhabited mostly by Somalis: the Ogaden in Ethiopia, and northeastern Kenya.

In Zambia also, there were secessionist threats among the Lozi of Barotse kingdom in the western part of the country which is the Western Province. There were also separatist tendencies in the Southern Province among the Tonga and the Ila who straddle Zambia's border with Zimbabwe and Mozambique.

In Congo-Leopoldville, there were strong secessionist tendencies among the Bakongo in the fifties. And after the country won independence, secessionist demands continued not only among the Bakongo but also among the members of other ethnic groups in all of the country's provinces. The strongest demands came from Katanga Province which seceded only 11 days after Congo won independence from Belgium on 30 June 1960.

Another province, South Kasai, seceded on 8 August

1960 and its leader, Albert Kalonji, declared himself king of the new country.

In the Ivory Coast, there was an uprising among the Sanwi in 1959 in their attempt to secede and establish an independent state under a monarchy.

The Tuareg of northern Mali refused to recognise the national government in Bamako and attempted to secede in 1963. Even before independence, they demanded independence for their region. They told the French colonial rulers Mali should be partitioned so that they can have their own country. They were ignored.

In April 2012, following a military coup in Bamako which caused disarray in the nation's capital, leaving a power vacuum, the Tuareg took advantage of the situation to achieve their goal. They seized the entire northern half of Mali and declared independence. They named their new country the Islamic Republic of Azawad. According to a BBC report, " Mali Tuareg Rebels Declare Independence in the North," 6 April 2012:

"A rebel group in northern Mali has declared independence for a region it calls Azawad, after seizing control of the area last week.

The National Movement for the Liberation of Azawad (MNLA) made the statement on its website, adding that it would respect other states' borders.

The MNLA is one of two rebel groups to have gained ground in the area after Mali's government was ousted in a coup.

The African Union has condemned the declaration as 'null and void.'

Former colonial power France and the European Union have also said they will not recognise Azawad's independence....

The army seized power on 22 March, accusing the elected government of not doing enough to halt the two rebel groups - the MNLA and an Islamist group opposed to independence, which wants to impose Islamic law, or Sharia, across the whole country.

'Brink of disaster'

The declaration comes as rights group Amnesty International warned that Mali was on the brink of a major humanitarian disaster in the wake of the rebellion.

It demanded that aid agencies be given immediate access to the country after days of looting, abduction and chaos in the northern towns of Gao, Kidal and the historic city of Timbuktu, which have all been taken by the rebels.

On Thursday the MNLA rebels declared a 'unilateral' ceasefire after the UN Security Council called for an end to the fighting in Mali.

A statement posted on the rebel website on Friday proclaimed independence, adding it would respect existing borders with neighbouring states and adhere to the UN Charter. The statement also called for recognition from the international community.

'We completely accept the role and responsibility that behooves us to secure this territory. We have ended a very important fight, that of liberation... now the biggest task commences,' rebel spokesman Mossa Ag Attaher is quoted as saying by the AFP news agency.

The Tuareg people inhabit the Sahara Desert in northern Mali, as well as several neighbouring countries and have fought several rebellions over the years, complaining that they have been ignored by the authorities in distant Bamako. But the Tuareg are not the only people who live in the area they claim as Azawad.

Islamists and Tuareg

Journalist Martin Vogl in Bamako says there are two main interpretations for why the MNLA made its declaration now.

Firstly, he says it could be intended to forestall a possible intervention by the West African regional body, Ecowas and secondly to show that it, rather than the rival Ansar Dine group, is in charge of the north.

But he also points to problems with the proclamation, such as the absence of a referendum to prove a popular mandate, as well as reports that the Islamist rebels may control more areas than the MNLA.

Ecowas military chiefs met on Thursday in Ivory Coast. Afterwards, they said they had discussed a proposed force's rules of engagement and would await a response to their suggestions from the region's heads of state. A 2,000-strong force has been put on standby, while France has promised logistical support.

The MNLA was formed last year, partly by well-armed Tuareg fighters returning from Libya, where they had backed former leader Muammar Gaddafi.

But the UN has voiced alarm at the presence of Ansar Dine, which has links to an al-Qaeda franchise which operates in the region.

Correspondents say that Western powers are more concerned by a growing Islamist threat throughout the region than a Tuareg issue which is considered a political internal problem.

The MNLA could possibly expect greater autonomy rather than independence if it came back to negotiations and helped fight the Islamists, they say.

Mali has been in disarray ever since the 22 March coup enabled the rebels to secure territory in the north.

People are continuing to flee the area and buses to the capital have been packed with people desperate to get out. Reports say the situation in the northern town of Gao, in rebel hands, is particularly tense.

The Algerian government also says seven of its staff were kidnapped by unknown gunmen in Gao. The consul and six colleagues were forced to leave their diplomatic mission at gunpoint.

The Algerian government says it is doing all it can to find them.

Ecowas has closed Mali's borders to trade, frozen its access to funds at the central bank for the region's common currency and slapped travel bans on the coup leaders and their supporters.

The coup and Tuareg rebellion have exacerbated a humanitarian crisis in Mali and some neighbouring countries, with aid agencies warning that 13 million people need food aid following a drought in the region."

Although Tuareg separatists came nowhere close to achieving their goal in the sixties and in the following decades, they remained a source of instability in Mali, especially in the north where they continued to campaign for autonomy and independence sometimes by violent means.

Ghana under Kwame Nkrumah also had to contend with separatist threats among the Ashanti in the central region. They posed the biggest threat to national unity.

The Ewe in the east also posed a threat. There was an irredentist movement among the Ewe in the Volta region seeking to unite the Ewe of Ghana and Togo who had been separated by the boundary between the two countries during colonial rule.

There were also separatist demands among the Dagomba and members of other ethnic groups in northern Ghana, a region that was once known as the Northern Territories.

Nkrumah effectively neutralised all those threats by establishing a highly efficient centralised state with power concentrated at the centre just as Obote did in Uganda, Jomo Kenyatta in Kenya and Kenneth Kaunda in Zambia although in varying degrees.

It was fear of the domino effect: once one region or province goes, the rest will go and become independent states. That is why many African leaders were very suspicious of those who demanded regional autonomy. They feared such devolution of power to the regions or provinces could eventually fuel demands for secession and even lead to secession in some cases. And as Touval states:

"The ethnic composition of the African states has been an important influence in shaping governmental attitudes and policies on boundaries. Boundaries may be likened to the external shell of the state. Since the majority of African states have not yet attained internal cohesion, it is in their interest to preserve this shell intact.

In many cases, the maintenance of the status quo has come to be associated with the self-preservation of the state. It was feared that, were the right to secede granted to any group or region, such a grant could stimulate secessionist demands from additional regions or groups, and thus threaten the disintegration of the state. The danger of such disintegration has been vividly exemplified by the secessionist movements that have sprung in several states....

The interest of states in preserving the status quo is reflected also in the qualms many states have shown about annexing regions or tribes from neighboring states." – (Souval, ibid., pp. 30 and 31).

The only leader in Ugandan post-colonial history who attempted to claim some land from neighbouring countries was Idi Amin who, in October 1978, annexed about 700 square miles of Tanzanian territory in Kagera Region in the northwest bordering Uganda. Tanzania fought back and drove out Amin's occupying forces. Amin also claimed parts of western Kenya and southern Sudan without success.

Most African leaders, including Ugandan, want to maintain the borders inherited at independence.

The problems most African countries face are internal,

not external. One of them is ethnic and regional rivalries. Uganda is one of the countries on the continent which have had to contend with this problem since independence. And it has not been fully resolved as different groups continue to demand autonomy for their regions from national leaders who are determined to maintain a highly centralised state as the best guarantee for national unity.

Most African leaders articulate the same position on a continent where they fear their countries can easily disintegrate along ethnoregional lines if extensive devolution of power to the regions is allowed in order to defuse tensions and resolve ethnic and regional rivalries.

That is why decades after independence in the sixties, most African countries have not adopted a federal form of government which would have enabled regions or provinces to have autonomy, reducing the power at the centre over the rest of the country. They have remained highly centralised states with no prospect for devolution of power to the regions.

Chapter Two

Post-colonial Uganda: National consolidation

UGANDA has gone through major changes since independence in the sixties. They have mostly been violent.

The first one involved the removal of Kabaka Mutesa II in February 1966 when his palace on Mengo Hill in Kampala was attacked by soldiers led by Idi Amin. It was alleged that Kabaka Mutesa had ordered some weapons and that the weapons were being kept in the palace.

The Kabaka himself conceded in his book, *Desecration of My Kingdom*, that he did indeed seek weapons from Britain as president of Uganda but the British government turned down his request.

What were the weapons for? Even the prime minister, Milton Obote, asked him that question. And he had no authority to order the weapons because his title, as president, was only ceremonial. Real power was in the hands of the prime minister who was the head of the government. Kabaka Mutesa was not an executive president.

Obote denied ordering the attack on Mengo Hill and implied Amin exceeded his authority when he used violence during the siege of the palace. As he stated in an interview with Ugandan journalist, Andrew Mwenda, which was published as part of a series in the *Daily Monitor*, Kampala, Uganda, in April 2005 a few months before before he died in October the same year:

"I did not order an attack on Lubiri in 1966.

On February 9th, Muteesa called the British High Commissioner and asked for massive military assistance. When I asked Muteesa why, he said it was a precaution against trouble. I asked him, 'Trouble from whom and against whom?' He just waved me to silence.

Although he was president, head of state and commander in chief of the armed forces, Muteesa did not have powers to order for arms.

Later, I sought the advice of my Attorney General, Godfrey Binaisa QC. He told me that given what Muteesa had done, I had to suspend him from being president of Uganda; the only way I could was to suspend the constitution itself....

Regarding the attack on the Lubiri, I regret it only in as far as I was the head of government. I had nothing to do with it.

I was having a luncheon at Kampala Lodge with Bulasio Kavuma, Badru Kakungulu and Elidad Muwonge of Bugerere when we heard at about two o'clock, a bomb at Lubiri.

We later found out that it was Idi Amin's soldiers who

were bombing Lubiri. I called for Amin, he came and we discussed it.

Amin tried to justify his action saying that the men who were in the Lubiri wanted to overthrow the government, wanted to overpower the army. I did not accept that one. I ordered him to return the troops to the barracks, which he did.

By this time, the battle of Mengo was over, although many authors have said the battle went on into the night. Unfortunately Mutesa was my friend." – (See Appendix II: Obote Speaks).

If Obote did not order the attack on the palace (Lubiri), who did? Since it was supposed to be a matter of national security, was it his first cousin, Akena Adoko, head of the intelligence service – General Service Unit (GSU) – who was also the second most powerful man in Uganda after Obote himself, who ordered the attack? Or was it Amin, on his own, who decided to use violence? He was the commander of the army.

The General Service Unit was founded by Obote's government. Obote also had a paramilitary force, the Special Force Units. Most of the members of this private army came from his tribe and home region. They were mostly Langi (Lango). The Special Forces Units worked closely with the army and the police.

In his book, *Desecration of My Kingdom*, Kabaka Mutesa II contends that it was Obote who ordered the attack on the palace:

"It was not yet dawn – about 5:30 in the morning – when I was awakened suddenly by the sound of gunfire: quite near, I reckoned, certainly inside the wall that surrounds my palace and grounds....

Troops from the Uganda Army were attacking my palace on the orders of the Prime Minister, Dr. Obote. So much was clear. Nor should it have been in the least surprising. We had been suspecting such a move for weeks, and I myself had been surprised when nothing happened the previous evening. Yet I was filled with a sense of outrage now that it was happening....

Many people from the city, Kampala, and the villages had come up and waited round the palace the previous day, not from knowledge of imminent disaster, but instinctively, uncertain whether they were giving or receiving protection....

There seemed to be an endless follow-up supply of enemy soldiers, many of whom were occupied with destroying my rooms. I think they believed their own stories about hidden supplies of arms, and even indulged in fanciful ideas that a king must have hoards of treasure buried beneath his palace....

Once I was overwhelmed with emotion, and foolishly returned to the palace garden alone. There I selected a looter and shot him out of honest rage. I felt calmer and somewhat uplifted as I made my way back." – (King Freddie, *Desecration of My Kingdom*, quoted by Crawford Young, *The Politics of Cultural Pluralism*, Madison, Wisconsin, USA: The University of Wisconsin Press, 1976, p. 151. See also King Freddie, *Desecration of My Kingdom*, London: Constable & Co., Ltd. 1967, pp. 1 – 3).

The attack on Mengo was one of the most tragic incidents in Uganda's post-colonial history. It had far-reaching consequences which reverberated through the years.

There were some casualties. But there is a dispute on the number of people who were killed. Some reports say about 1,000 people were killed. They were mostly civilians. Kabaka Mutesa escaped and fled to Britain where he died in London three years later when he was 45 years old.

The most violent phase the country went through involved Amin during his eight-year reign of terror after he seized power from Obote in a military coup in January 1971. His rise to power was the most dramatic development in the country's history up to that time. It had tragic consequences for Uganda and beyond and the country has not yet fully recovered from his brutal reign.

There have been other changes, including constitutional, such as the abolition of kingdoms in 1967 and their restoration in 1993 by President Yoweri Museveni although only as cultural institutions without any political power as in the past. But the biggest changes have involved transfer of power from one government or regime to another.

Also, when Obote returned to power in 1982, his resumption of office had serious implications and tragic consequences for the country.

Another major change came in 1986 when Museveni took over the country after waging guerrilla warfare against the government. He won the war and the country entered another phase.

Uganda has witnesses some of the worst excesses of African leadership in its 50 years of independence. It has yet to see the best its leaders have to offer.

Like other African countries, its history during the post-colonial era is one of broken promises and unfulfilled hopes. It is also one of horrendous tragedies, mostly a product of state-sponsored terror.

When the country won independence from Britain in October 1962, it had all the attributes of a potentially successful nation including a significant number of highly educated people, although they were mostly Baganda from the Buganda kingdom. But they were still Ugandans destined to play a major role in the development of their country.

The British also left an infrastructure which facilitated economic growth after independence, although the infrastructure was skewed in favour of the southern part of the country.

But it was Obote's government which laid the foundation of modern Uganda during the first few years of independence until his ouster in 1971. His government built roads, schools and hospitals across the country; increased economic growth and income for the average Ugandan; and expanded manufacturing and boosted export trade.

Uganda also had an abundance of natural resources many African countries did not have; it still does. In fact, Uganda and a number of other African countries had a higher per capita income than some southeast Asian countries did. Yet those countries, the Asian tigers, are now some of the most developed in the world; a point underscored below:

"In 1965, Nigeria was richer than Indonesia, and Ghana richer than Thailand. Today Indonesia is three times richer than Nigeria, and Thailand five times richer than Ghana.

In 1965, Uganda was richer than South Korea. And in 1967, Zambia also was richer than South Korea. Zambia had a per capita income of $200, and South Korea, $120. After 30 years, South Korea's gross domestic product per person was more than $10,000 in 1998, and Zambia's $400.[4] Yet, by African standards, Zambia is considered to be one of the richest countries on the continent in spite of all the misery, hunger and starvation ravaging this country endowed with abundant minerals and arable land more than enough to feed its entire population....

African countries have become international beggars. And they have been begging since independence in the sixties. Yet, some of these very same countries had the potential to develop and outstrip their southeastern Asian counterparts which are now known as the Asian tigers because of their brilliant economic performance. And the contrast is glaring.

In the sixties, the southeast Asian countries were as

poor as or poorer than some African countries which are now on international welfare, dependent on donors for their very survival. They include 'prosperous' ones today such as Uganda. As Ugandan President Yoweri Museveni said in a speech to the United National General Assembly in February 1997, in 1965 Uganda was 'more prosperous than South Korea and Nigeria more prosperous than Indonesia.'[8]

So what happened?

It is also worth remembering that the year 1965 when Nigeria was richer than Indonesia, Ghana richer than Thailand, and Uganda and Zambia richer than South Korea, was around the same time when all those African countries had just won independence from Britain; which means it was *not* the African governments which made those countries prosperous when compared to their southeast Asian counterparts. It was the British colonial governments which did that.

Ghana won independence in March 1957, Nigeria in October 1960, Uganda in October 1962, and Zambia, formerly Northern Rhodesia, in October 1964; hardly enough time - by 1965 - for the new African governments to have made any appreciable impact on their countries' economies to achieve significant progress within so few years and outstrip the southeast Asian nations." – (Godfrey Mwakikagile, *Africa is in A Mess: What Went Wrong and What Should Be Done*, Pretoria: New Africa Press, 2006, pp. 12 – 13; 19 – 20.

See also from chapter notes for Chapter One:

4. "Africa's Democratic Despots," in *The Economist*, January 3, 1998; Reginald Dale, "Finally, Some Good News From Africa," in the *International Herald Tribune*, December 13, 1996, p. 15; Yoweri Museveni, in a speech to the UN General Assembly, February 1997, cited by Tom Stacey, "African Realities," in *National Review*, May 19, 1997, p. 30; Godfrey Mwakikagile, *Economic Development in Africa* (Commack, New York: Nova

Science Publishers, Inc., 1999), pp. 3, and 99.

8. Yoweri Museveni, in a speech to the UN General Assembly, February 1997, cited by Tom Stacey, "African Realities," in *National Review*, May 19, 1997, p. 30).

The Ugandan economy performed reasonably well during the sixties. But all those gains were reversed during the seventies when Idi Amin was in power. He destroyed the economy. It was not until the mid-1980s that the economy started to improve after major economic reforms were introduced and implemented, with the biggest gains made under Museveni.

The economic ruin of the seventies under Amin was preceded by a crisis of legitimacy for the state under Obote in the sixties.

Obote consolidated his position, with the army dominated by fellow northerners tipping scales in his favour, after he expelled Kabaka Mutesa. But he was far from being accepted as the legitimate leader of Uganda especially in the south where he had abolished the kingdoms. He was greatly resented by the people in the former kingdoms, especially Buganda, for stripping their traditional rulers of power and taking their position as the leader of the former kingdoms which were an integral part of Uganda of which he was the leader.

But his ruling party, the Uganda People's Congress (UPC), also enjoyed significant support in the former kingdoms – except Buganda – because it was broad-based and inclusive, embracing people from all parts of the country unlike political parties in the Buganda kingdom – the Democratic Party (DP) and Kabaka Yekka (KY) – whose membership was solidly Baganda. And he enjoyed strong support in the north, his stronghold and homeland.

Yet his government had to resort to coercive tactics to achieve its goals because of the strong opposition it faced especially in the south. Ethnicity continued to play a major role in national life and in the government. It was also used as a bargaining tool and as a weapon to extract concessions from the government. Obote also used it to consolidate his position, for example, by offering leading Baganda politicians cabinet posts and other high-ranking jobs in the government.

By including some of his opponents in the government, he demonstrated the imperative need for compromise as a cardinal principle in politics and in the conduct of national affairs. And ethnic and regional considerations were a central component in the successful administration of the country.

There was a need for regional balance in the government although it was not fully implemented in all areas. Obote felt that it was necessary to build national consciousness in place ethnic loyalties if Uganda were to survive and develop as a country and as a cohesive whole. But the crisis of legitimacy for his leadership especially in the south continued to be a major problem for his government. As Dr. Juma Anthony Okuku, a lecturer in political economy at Makerere University, Kampala, Uganda, states in his paper, "Ethnicity, State Power and The Democratisation Process in Uganda":

"The post-colonial practices of the mainstream nationalists, who inherited the national state, saw the reproduction rather than the deconstruction of ethnicity in Uganda's body-politic....

The post-colonial practices enhanced rather than deconstructed ethnic consciousness....

The post-independence government led by Milton Obote, 1962 – 71, had a number of assumptions. First, the task of nation-building called for uniting all the forces of society. To him, diversity of ethnic identities was inherently negative and obstructive to successful nation-building and development. As Obote stated in 1963:

The tribe has served our people as a basic political unit very well in the past. But now the problem of people putting the tribe above national consciousness is a problem that we must face, and an issue we must destroy. (Hansen, 1974: 63).

This set the stage for the clash between the UPC, a republican party, and KY, an ethnic chauvinist and monarchist party devoted to the preservation of the special status of Buganda Kingdom in the post-colonial setup." – (Juma Anthony Okuku, "Ethnicity, State Power and The Democratisation Process in Uganda," Discussion Paper 17, University Printers, Uppsala, Sweden, 2002, p. 15).

Even before independence, Obote warned against the preservation of the monarchy in the Buganda kingdom, contending that it would militate against national unity, as would the preservation of the other traditional centres of power in other parts of the country. According to *Africa Contemporary Record: Annual Survey and Documents*:

"President Milton Obote's first decade in parliament was celebrated in August/September 1968.[1]

In almost his first speech in the Uganda Legislature on 6 May, 1958, the almost unknown young radical nationalist from Lango (he was 32) in a criticism of colonial policies had said:

If the Government is going to develop this country on a unitary basis, how on earth can the Government develop another state within a state?

Does the Government really think that, when self-government comes to this country, the state of Buganda will willingly give up the powers it has already got now, in order to join with other outlying Districts or provinces? I do not think so.

Now, ten years later, Dr. Obote had not only seen the accuracy of his prophecy; he had also become the instrument for breaking the power of the State of Buganda, as well as sweeping away much of the country's Old

Order.

For him, 1968 was a decisive turning point: his leadership was under challenge, and with it his plans for unifying Uganda within a modernising political system.

Uganda's basic political problems at independence in 1962 were dominated by the rigid and strongly-based determination of the Kingdom of Buganda to maintain its distinctive identity – either by achieving a political ascendancy over the rest of the country as was largely the case in the heyday of Buganda's overlordship, or through secession.

Thus Buganda's politics had two parallel drives: the thrust to leadership for control of the modern political system, and the thrust towards separatism.

Because Buganda lies at the heart of modern Uganda's economy and metropolitan development, and since its people – the Baganda – were the best-educated and most sophisticated among the Ugandans, its threat to those who opposed it was formidable: more especially since the modern young Kabaka – a tough, shrewd and entirely inflexible leader – was strongly backed by the Buganda parliament, the Lukiiko, and supported by a closely-controlled system of rural government through a hierarchical chieftaincy system dependent on the Kabaka; these were buttressed by a close-knit system of Palace politics.

All these threads of Buganda's power and authority were brought together in the Kabaka's hands on Mengo Hill – the seat of his palace and local parliament above Kampala." – (Colin Legum and John Drysdale, eds., *Africa Contemporary Record: Annual Survey and Documents 1968 – 1969*, London: Africa Research Limited, 1969, p. 230. See also, cited above: 1. A commemorative pamphlet, *Dr. Obote's Decade – Ten Years in Parliament* was published by the Milton Obote Foundation, Kampala. It contains his speech to parliament on 6 May 1958 quoted above).

Obote inherited the ethnic configuration of Ugandan politics left by the British and whose biggest beneficiaries were the Baganda. His attempts to control the dynamics of ethnicity and change the social order and political landscape were fiercely resisted by the Baganda and, to a lesser degree, by the members of the other kingdoms.

Even attempts to resolve disputes by constitutional means were opposed by Buganda when the monarchy felt resolution of the disputes would not be in the best interest of the kingdom. One of the best examples was the case of the "lost counties" which once belonged to Bunyoro but which were given to Buganda by the British for the role the Baganda played in helping the colonial rulers to take over Bunyoro. As Okuku states:

"One explosive political problem the government handled constitutionally was the long-standing dispute between the Buganda and Bunyoro Kingdoms over the so-called 'lost counties.' These were counties that belonged to the Bunyoro Kingdom before the onset of colonialism but were given to the Buganda Kingdom as appreciation for its assistance in the conquest of the Bunyoro Kingdom by the British.

The colonial government left it to the government of the newly independent state to settle this issue through a referendum. The referendum was held in 1964 as was required by the independence constitution. The population in the two counties voted overwhelmingly for their return to the Bunyoro Kingdom.

This democratic solution to the problem of ethnic conflict provoked instead ethnic antagonism between Buganda and Bunyoro on the one hand, and the central government and the Buganda Kingdom, on the other. The Buganda Kingdom was not content with the way the dispute was handled by the government of Milton Obote. This resulted in a strain between the Buganda Kingdom and the central government culminating in the breakup of the UPC/KY alliance formed at independence (Karugire, 1988: 184).

The ethnic conflict, militarism and authoritarianism that followed between 1964 and 1971 during the Obote I regime had this tension as one of its sources. The leadership on both spectrums of the 1964 wrangle was rather antagonistic and confrontational, a recipe that democratic practice is not made of.

The 1966 crisis, which resulted in the violent overthrow of the independence constitution, was a culmination of *three* political developments. First, the breakup of the UPC/KY alliance, second, the leadership wrangle in UPC, using the Congo gold scandal[2] as an excuse to overthrow Obote. This resulted in Obote's detention of his own cabinet ministers for the plot and third, the unilateral suspension of the Independence Constitution in 1966.

Using authoritarian methods in what was essentially a civil conflict that could have been handled politically compounded the problem. The long-term effect of this was to exacerbate ethnic mobilisation and destroy any chance of democratic solutions to such cleavages. Because the opposition to Obote came from mainly Bantu politicians, the crisis came to take on a North-South dimension.

While it is true that Obote was trying to break up the heaviest concentration of power in the land in order to safeguard his position and perhaps concentrate on the nation-building objective, instead of using democratic means, he did so through the use of ethnicity. The treatment of Buganda between 1966 and 1971 lent little credibility to his declared intentions of reducing the significance of the ethnic factor in Uganda's politics.

The Baganda were still regarded as so hostile and unreliable that the region was kept in a state of emergency throughout this period (Hansen, 1974: 66 – 71). Suppressing the Kingdom of Buganda and the imprisonment of Southern politicians without trial simply politicised ethnicity in the country's body politic. Obote's partisan authoritarianism played a key part in keeping ethnic consciousness alive in the country waiting for an opportunity to re-assert itself....

The Congo gold scandal refers to allegations by an opposition parliamentarian in 1965, that the prime minister, Milton Obote, his defence minister, Felix Onama, and army commander, Idi Amin, were involved in smuggling gold and ivory from eastern Congo. The Uganda army had been sent to aid the Lumumbist rebellion led by Mulele Congo in its military operations." – (J. A. Okuku, "Ethnicity, State Power and The Democratisation Process in Uganda," op. cit., pp. 15 – 16).

Ethnicity continues to play a role in Uganda politics and in life in general fifty years after independence despite professions to the contrary by some people, especially national leaders who, in their rhetoric, emphasise the imperative for national unity and talk as if ethnic considerations don't play a major role across the spectrum – social, political, and economic.

What may sometimes be overlooked when examining the ethnic factor in Ugandan national life is the fact that even if the kingdom of Buganda did not exist, Ugandan nationalist leaders – Obote and his colleagues – would still have faced a formidable task in their attempt to unite the country.

There were other kingdoms, as well as other traditional centres of power, which even by themselves – individually or collectively – did make the task of nation building difficult because they did not subscribe to the national ethos of one Uganda espoused by Obote and his compatriots.

The advantage the national government had was coercive power, including military power, the kingdoms did not have. Even Buganda, the most advanced and most powerful among the kingdoms, did not have the military might to resist let alone defeat the national army and security forces, as was tragically demonstrated when Kabaka's palace was attacked and destroyed, as the king fled in a humiliating way.

But in spite of their military weakness, the kingdoms were a formidable force in the political arena with or without the combined strength of other traditional societies which were also opposed to the central government in Kampala. As Colin Legm and John Drysdale state in their co-edited work, *African Contemporary Record*:

"Although Buganda offered the toughest problem to the modernising nationalists, it was by no means the only difficulty they had to face.

Each of the other three kingdoms – Toro, Ankole and Bunyoro – and the Princedom of Busoga had their own well-structured political systems; each was suspicious of the modern political centre at Entebbe. Also they had traditional rivalries – especially between Buganda and Bunyoro – this, however, had advantages for the nationalists since it helped prevent southern Kingdoms – mainly Bantu-speaking – developing an alliance of traditional interests.

Also, in the centre of the country, are two large areas, Teso and Lango, which – having entered into the modernising economic and education system at a fairly early stage – constitute important political units; but they lack the strong tradition of centralised leadership.

To the North – among the Nilotic peoples stretching to the frontiers of the Sudan and the Congo – are scores of scattered ethnic groups who fared least well under colonialism, and who got into the modernising process several decades behind the Southerners. Bringing them forward rapidly was an obvious priority for their own leaders; but those who undertook this task were in danger of being accused of wishing to favour 'the North' – with its

Islamic contacts – against 'the South' – with its Christian traditions and Bantu cultures. Both these elements were conveniently exploited by politicians in the North and the South." – (Colin Legum and John Drysdale, *Africa Contemporary Record*, op. cit., pp. 230 – 231).

All those different traditional societies in different parts of the country made integration very difficult. They knew they were all an integral part of the modern nation of Uganda. But they wanted to remain separate to manage their own affairs and even pursue goals – ethnic and regional – which were in conflict with national interests.

Although the national leaders tried to bring the different parts of the country together in order to build one cohesive nation, ethnic and regional loyalties continued to play an important role across the spectrum; a phenomenon that has haunted Uganda since colonial times.

Even when some leaders seemed to be determined to transcend ethnicity and regionalism, the problem continued to resurface. In fact, no government of Uganda – civilian or military – during the post-colonial era has been able to insulate itself from this problem.

Obote himself was not entirely immune from that. Some of the most highly prominent or sensitive posts in his government were given to fellow northerners including his relatives. For example, he chose his first cousin, Dr. Akena Adoko, to be the head of the intelligence service which was known as the General Service Unit (GSU). Adoko was the second most powerful man in Uganda after the president. Another cousin of Obote, A.A. Nekyon, was a cabinet member and one of his closest advisers.

However, most of the senior posts in the government were held by southerners, not by northerners as some critics of Obote have alleged, a dominance attributed to the high level of education among southerners contrasted with northerners. Yet, it is equally true that ethnicity was an influential factor even in the government of Obote who espoused principles of meritocracy and truly nationalist policies embracing everybody. And as Okuku states:

"In spite of the various regimes' apparent aversion to ethnicity in Uganda, they have rested on distinctly ethnic political foundations and reproduced themselves on the basis of definable, and in most cases, narrow ethnic alliances. The ultimate result of authoritarianism, militarism and the stifling of civil society organisations was that it did not get rid of ethnicity and regionalism and construct a nation-state....

The other part of the state where the political leadership failed to transform its ethnic base was the military. The introduction of militarism and the mobilisation of ethnicity in the military, impacted negatively on political development in Uganda.

During both Milton Obote's regimes in the 1960s and the early 1980s, Idi Amin's regime in the 1970s, and including Yoweri Museveni's since 1986, militarism was and has been employed as a means of capturing and maintaining power. As a result, the resolution of the problem of ethnicity through democratic means in the foreseeable future has been postponed.

The scourge of military power that looms throughout Uganda's post-independence period was introduced in Uganda's politics between 1964 and 66. Between 1964 and 66, democratic solutions were abandoned and Obote resorted to militarisation of the country's politics as a strategy for crisis management (Okoth, 1995: 123). The loss of the 1964 – 65 power struggle between the Prime Minister, Obote, and the President, *Kabaka* Mutesa, within the UPC/KY ruling coalition, resulted in the retreat of Mutesa into enclave, chauvinistic Ganda ethnicity and aggressive, militarist ethnicity on the part of Obote, with a reliance on the army which was dominated by the northerners.

By 1967, th army had been dragged into Uganda's

politics, thereby eroding the relative degree of democracy and pluralism that had prevailed in the country between 1962 and 1966.

Militarisation only exacerbated the ethnic question. This is because the army had been used in a showdown with an ethnic group in the 1966 invasion of Kabaka's Lubiri (King's Palace). The army could no longer be regarded as an organ that was neutral in an ethnic sense (Hansen, 1974: 66).

The deliberate recruitment of the Specialised Paramilitary Corps into the Obote regime along ethnic lines lent little credence to his fight against ethnicity. Obote initiated a massive expansion of a Special Paramilitary Corps, Special Force, and created a lavishly equipped intelligence service, the General Service Unit, GSU, under the command of Akena Adoko, his cousin, and recruited almost solely from his own ethnic group, the Langi (Hansen, 1974: 88).

The result was the rise of an ethnically organised state. Obote failed to resolve the contradictions inherited from the colonial political economy.

Every regime in Uganda since then, Yoweri Museveni's National Resistance Movement (NRM) included, has used ethnicity in the military and other state organs to retain power." – (J.A. Okuku, "Ethnicity, State Power and The Democratisation Process in Uganda," op.cit., pp. 18, 19 – 20).

Idi Amin also used his ethnic base to seize power in 1971. When he overthrew the government with the help of the British and the Israelis, he used soldiers in the army who came from the West Nile District, his region in the northwestern part of Uganda. Soldiers – the Langi and the Acholi – from the north-central part of northern Uganda, Obote's home region, remained loyal to the president and even contemplated a counter-coup to reinstate him. But it was too late.

There is no question that all Ugandan leaders have used and have benefited from ethnicity or ethnic and regional loyalties at one time or another only in varying degrees. But, although Obote was one of those leaders, it is also true that his government was not filled with northerners even if it seemed to be controlled by them mainly because the army and security forces, dominated by fellow northerners, tipped scales in his favour.

Even as late as 1968, six years after independence and not long before he was overthrown about two years later, most government jobs, especially in the civil service, were filled by southerners. And the cabinet reflected regional balance, north versus south. According to *Africa Contemporary Record 1968 - 1969*:

"A recurrent feature of political controversy in Uganda is the allegation that under President Obote there had been a persistent attempt to impose Northern domination on the rest of the country; this allegation is used to buttress the cause for a 'Bantu alliance' among the Southerners.

Sometimes it is also argued that there is a secret understanding between Uganda's Northerners to ally themselves with the Luo political forces of Kenya led by Mr. Oginga Odinga: this is frequently referred to as 'Rule by the O's' since so many Nilotic names – Obote, Odinga, Onama – begin with O.

What these allegations fail to explain is that the overwhelming majority of senior posts in Uganda are filled not by Northerners, but by Southerners; and that the composition of Obote's Cabinet reflects more or less the same ratio of Southerners to Northerners as existed before the crisis of 1966.

It is possible that pressures of the Northerners – latecomers to modernisation – for a fair share of the posts in the central government might help to explain the suspicions about 'a Northern push.' – (Colin Legum and John Drysdale, *Africa Contemporary Record*, op.cit., p.

235).

However, what happened two years earlier in 1966, with strong ethnic overtones, did set the stage for what was to take place in the following years and decades in terms of political changes in Uganda.

The 1966 crisis which led to the ouster of Kabaka Mutesa was a turning point in the history of Uganda. As the king of the Buganda kingdom, his ouster, especially by a government led by a northerner and by soldiers who were also predominantly northerners, had serious ethnic implications and repercussions across the country and throughout the post-colonial period.

Almost every major change or political event that has taken place in Uganda in the following decades can be traced to that critical moment. Here is how the events unfolded:

"Unlike most African countries, religion has played a role in Uganda's modern political development – mainly between Protestants and Catholics. Latterly, too, the Muslim factor has been introduced.

In the politics of pre-independence the nationalist forces were divided and thus weakened; the traditionalists were strong but divided, and so less effective than they might otherwise have been. This enabled the running to be made by the Democratic Party (DP), led by Mr. Benedicto Kiwanuka, which appealed nationally to the Catholic vote.

His temporary majority in the Legislature was a challenge to both the nationalists and Buganda. To defeat him Obote's Uganda People's Congress (UPC) entered into a political alliance of convenience with its arch political enemy, the Kabaka of Buganda.

To both sides this uneasy alliance offered temporary advantages; first, to rid themselves of Kiwanuka's DP; second, to manoeuvre against each other from a base of shared power at the centre – with the Kabaka as President (the Royal Republican), and Dr. Obote as Prime Minister.

Neither side had any illusions about each other's intentions.

At first it seemed that Obote's nationalist forces had the better end of the deal; but in 1966 the pendulum swung unexpectedly against Obote when he discovered that an influential group within his own Cabinet were not only working secretly against his leadership but had entered into a convenient alliance of their own with the Kabaka.

This produced the familiar post-independence crisis shattering the brief period of relative stability. Obote struck back fast and had to retain his initiative: what happened in the succeeding months is directly relevant to understanding the situation which Obote faced in 1968.

22 February, 1966. Prime Minister Obote ousts Kabaka as President; suspends the Constitution; arrests five of his leading Ministers – Grace Ibingira, Dr. Emmanuel Lumu, George Magezi, Balaki Kirya and Mathias Ngobi. He announces: ' We are introducing a new era and new issues in Uganda's politics. It would be unfortunate to go back now to a government at Mengo controlled by the Kabaka.'

15 April, 1966. A temporary Constitution is introduced with an Executive President, abolishing the Prime Minister. Obote assumes the Presidency.

20 May, 1966. Lukiiko demands Uganda's expulsion from Buganda Kingdom by 30 May.

20 – 23 May, 1966. Considerable violence in Buganda.

24 May, 1966. Obote again takes the initiative, sending a small group of his forces to investigate reports that the Kabaka has imported arms into Mengo. After a sharp skirmish, Kabaka escapes and Mengo Hill is occupied. State of emergency declared in Buganda.

1 May, 1967. President loses two of his closest Ministerial colleagues – his cousin, Mr. A.A. Nekyon, who is the President of the National Association for the Advancement of Muslims; and Mr. Godfrey Binaisa, the senior Buganda politician in the Cabinet, who gives ill-

health as the reason for resigning as Attorney-General.

9 June, 1967. President announces policy to abolish all four Kingdoms and to turn Uganda into a Republic.

22 June, 1967. National Assembly is converted into Constituent Assembly to discuss a new Constitution.

10 July, 1967. President dismisses Mr. Cuthbert Obwangor, his Minister of Planning and Economic Development, a prominent nationalist politician from Teso, following a public disagreement over the new Constitution.

8 September, 1967. Constituent Assembly passes the new Constitution and Public Order Act against the protests of the Opposition. It provides for an Executive President, a Republic, abolition of the status of the four Kingdoms, the division of Buganda into four Administrative Districts in line with the rest of the country, central control over Local Administration, and a Preventive Detention Act.

President Obote, having survived the crises within his own ruling UPC and in the Kingdoms, was faced in 1968 with the huge task of making the Constitution work and of carrying out the revolutionary changes initiated by the creation of new institutions.

His main challenge still came from Buganda; but despite many alarms about a Buganda uprising – stoked up by the Kabaka and his Court in exile in London – they remained passive, though by no means won over to the new order. Nevertheless, the Baganda in the Cabinet and in senior positions in the civil service remained loyal to the President; and a number of Buganda politicians came over to join the UPC." – (Ibid., pp. 231 – 232).

The constitutional challenges Obote faced in the late sixties, and the acrimonious debate that ensued over the constitutional overhaul, led to other developments. Obote was accused of being intolerant of criticism and of instituting a dictatorship. There were also charges of censorship.

Critics said the government was too sensitive to criticism and was unwilling to tolerate dissent, although Obote himself was open to criticism and even debated leading academics such as Professor Ali Mazrui.

Mazrui taught political science at Makerere University during that time. Obote once asked him if he knew the difference between being a politician and being a political scientist.

It was also during that period that some of the most highly influential people in Uganda were arrested on charges of sedition. One was Abu Mayanja, a veteran of the independence struggle. He was one of the founders of the leading political party in the country in the fifties, the Uganda National Congress (UNC) together with Obote, Ignatius Musaazi and others, and served as its first secretary-general.

In the April 1968 issue of *Transition*, he criticised the 1967 Uganda constitution, thus incurring the wrath of the government which brought sedition charges against him. He was acquitted of the charges but was re-arrested under the Emergency Powers Act which became effective on 1 November the same year.

Another prominent figure who was arrested was Rajat Neogy, editor of *Transition*, a highly influential scholarly journal published in Kampala and considered to be the most intellectual magazine ever published in Africa:

"A new Emergency Powers Act, effective on 1 November (1968), empowered the appropriate Ministers to make regulations for securing the defence of Uganda, public safety, effective government, maintenance of public order, enforcement of the law, and the maintenance of necessary supplies and services.

The regulations cover the detention or restriction of people and deportation of non-citizens, the performance of labour or services, and the possession of property. They also provide for amending or suspending any law,

71

including the prohibition of strike action.

A member of Parliament, Mr. Abu Mayanja, and Mr. Rajat Neogy, editor of the magazine *Transition*, were arrested in November and charged with publishing and printing a seditious publication. The charges referred to a letter which appeared under Mr. Mayanja's name which repeated what the writer called 'a rumour' at the appointment of Africans to the Uganda Judiciary had been held up mostly for tribal reasons. The prosecution alleged that this brought into hatred or contempt the President, Dr. Obote.

These two arrests provoked considerable criticism abroad, as well as in Uganda. In a personal statement on 19 October, Professor Ali Mazrui of Makerere College, said:

'I personally know of no two people who have contributed more to the intellectual liveliness of Uganda than Rajat Neogy and Abu Mayanja.

I did not always see eye to eye with either of them. In fact, Abu Mayanja and myself have been on opposite sides in almost every debate in which he and I have taken part in the Main Hall of Makerere, and the differences between us were real. But Uganda's reputation as an open society was secure for so long as there was one Abu Mayanja free to speak out his mind, and one *Transition* leading the rest of Africa in sheer intellectual verve.

There is a sense in which intellectual freedom is indivisible. On a day like this I feel lonely and shaken.'

The government responded to these criticisms by promising to put both men on trial in open court.

However, there appear to have been other suspicions in the mind of the Government so far as Abu Mayanja is concerned.

Although he started his political life as a radical nationalist, he had in recent years moved increasingly towards leadership within the Muslim community. He became prominent in the affairs of the East African Muslim Association, which is in rivalry to the National

Association for the Advancement of Muslims with which Mr. A.A. Nekyon is involved.

There had been a clash between the rival Muslim groups in the remote Karamajong area which had led to violence and killing. Mayanja, it is alleged, had been on a trip to the Middle East in August (1968) to seek support for his Association's activities. The authorities also seem to suspect that there is a secret agreement between the East African Muslim Association – whose patron is H.H. The Aga Khan – and the *Kabaka Yekka* which is working for the restoration of the ex-Kabaka." – (Ibid., pp. 234 – 235).

The late sixties were some of the most turbulent years in Ugandan history. Not long after that, Amin seized power. It was the beginning of a new era and a downward spiral for Uganda.

Chapter Three

Amin's regime

WHEN Idi Amin overthrew Obote, Uganda entered a new era and the most violent period in its history. It was also years of lawlessness. Laws meant absolutely nothing. It was a reign of terror that lasted for eight years. Uganda has never been the same since.

Amin may have had his own reasons for overthrowing Obote. His move may have been a pre-emptive strike against Langi army officers who were going to arrest him and his supporters in the army. It was said Obote gave the order to arrest Amin because he posed a threat to his government. Amin was also accused of embezzlement involving millions of dollars.

Somehow word about his imminent arrest leaked out and he made the first move. Before he left for the

Commonwealth conference in Singapore, President Obote reportedly gave the order to have Amin arrested, prompting him to overthrow the government.

But the real players on the Ugandan political scene during that period, who are the ones who were really behind Obote's ouster, were the British and the Israelis. They are the ones who engineered and masterminded Obote's ouster. The horrendous tragedy that befell Uganda under Amin's brutal dictatorship which included massacres of hundreds of thousands of people was in a way a direct result of their involvement in Obote's downfall.

At the very least, the suffering the people of Uganda endured under Amin can be partly attributed to the British and the Israelis because they are the ones who put him in power. Had they not do so, the world would not even have heard of Idi Amin. And the history of Uganda would have taken an entirely different turn.

The British, the Israelis, and the Americans who also helped Amin, did not care about the suffering of Ugandans and continued to support him. It was only after he turned against them that they withdrew their support from him.

The rise of Amin to power was a tragedy not only for Uganda but for Africa as a whole, especially for East Africa where his reign of terror had repercussions throughout the region:

"The rise of Idi Amin to power in Uganda introduced a destabilizing factor on the East African political scene as never before. And his ouster by Tanzania eight years later also set a precedent as the first case of direct intervention by one African country in another in the post-colonial era; besides incursions by apartheid South Africa into neighbouring countries which were supporting South African freedom fighters, and the apartheid regime's almost successful takeover of Angola in the seventies, until Fidel Castro sent Cuban troops to halt the advance. South African troops penetrated deep into Angola and were headed towards the capital, Luanda, before they were pushed back by the Cubans. Tanzania's intervention in Uganda was also the first time that an African country captured the capital, and overthrew the government, of another country on the continent.

Amin came to power in a military coup on January 25, 1971, which would probably not have been launched, let alone succeeded, without external help. In announcing his seizure of power on Radio Uganda, Amin made a short speech and tried to assure his fellow countrymen in the following terms:

'Fellow countrymen and well wishers of Uganda. I address you today at a very important hour in the history of our nation.

A short while ago, men of the armed forces placed this country in my hands. I am not a politician, but a professional soldier. I am therefore a man of few words and I shall, as a result, be brief.

Throughout my professional life, I have emphasized that the military must support a civilian government that has the support of the

1

people, and I have not changed from that position.'

The contradiction is obvious. And the people who placed Uganda in Amin's hands, to paraphrase what he said, were not just the Ugandan soldiers but Israeli agents as well, with the support of the British government. The British supported the coup against President Milton Obote because of his uncompromising stand on apartheid South Africa and Rhodesia. His policies towards the apartheid regime in South Africa were diametrically opposed to those of Britain which was friendly towards the racist government and did not want to impose severe economic sanctions on the white-dominated country because of her large investments there.

African countries demanded such sanctions in order to force the apartheid regime to abandon its racist policies. In the case of Rhodesia, the British government was hostile towards President Obote because of his uncompromising stand on the white minority regime in Salisbury, demanding that Britain actively intervene in her colony with military force to end the rebellion by Prime Minister Ian Smith who had unilaterally declared independence, excluding the African majority from power.

Britain also supported the coup against Dr. Obote because he nationalized British companies in Uganda after he adopted socialist policies in pursuit of economic independence. And Western countries in general, including the United States, supported the coup against Obote as a containment strategy to neutralize 'communist penetration' of East Africa through Tanzania which was friendly towards the People's Republic of China and other Eastern-bloc nations more than any other country in the region; a false accusation, since Tanzania was not communist or communist-oriented but fiercely independent, a stance that antagonized the West as much as Uganda's under Obote who was also a close friend of President Julius Nyerere of Tanzania. Obote's Pan-African militancy and socialist policies as well as his friendship with Eastern-bloc countries, like Nyerere's, were anathema to the West and could be neutralized only by ousting him from power.

It was a grand conspiracy, further confirmed when Western countries were the first to recognize Amin's regime, and before any African country did. Britain was the first Western country to do so; an implicit admission of her involvement in Obote's ouster, or, at the very least, of her strong desire to see him ousted. But Britain's complicity and involvement in the coup was obvious; a point underscored by Western analysts as well, including the *Executive Intelligence Review*:

'General Amin came to power in Uganda, in a military coup against President Milton Obote. British sponsorship of the semi-illiterate Amin, son of a sorceress, was quickly evident; Britain was one of the first countries in the world to recognize the Amin government, long before any African country. And when relations with

78

Britain had soured after Amin expelled the Asian business community from Uganda, British intelligence operative Robert Astles remained as Amin's mentor in Uganda until the very end. Amin's tyranny, lasting until 1979, trampled Uganda's political and economic institutions, leaving the country a wreckage from which it has never recovered.'[2]

Israel's involvement in the Ugandan military coup was even more direct. The coup was masterminded by Israeli agents working in Kampala, Uganda. It could not have succeeded without them. As Dr. Milton Obote stated:

'It is doubtful that Amin, without the urging of the Israelis, would have staged a successful coup in 1971... Israel wanted a client regime in Uganda, which they could manipulate in order to prevent Sudan from sending troops to Egypt.... The coup succeeded beyond their wildest expectations.... The Israelis set up in Uganda a regime, which pivoted in every respect to Amin, who in turn was under the strictest control of the Israelis in Kampala.... The Israelis and Anya-Anya were hilarious; the regime was under their control.'[3]

The Israelis wanted to prevent Sudan from sending troops to Egypt - a frontline state in the Arab League against Israel and the most powerful in the Arab world - by tying down her troops in a war against the rebels, known as Anya-Anya, fighting for self-determination in southern Sudan against the Arab-dominated government in Khartoum in northern Sudan. Israel's support of the black rebels was motivated by self-interest more than anything else including humanitarian concern. So was the coup against President Obote.

The ouster of Dr. Milton Obote had striking similarities to the coup against President Kwame Nkrumah of Ghana five years earlier on February 24, 1966. Both leaders were ardent Pan-Africanists and strong supporters of liberation movements in Africa. Both antagonized the West because of their Pan-African militancy and the socialist policies they pursued. And both were overthrown

- with Western help including the CIA - when they were outside their countries: Nkrumah, while on his way on a peace mission to Hanoi at the invitation of Vietnamese President Ho Chin Mihn to help end the Vietnam war (and in pursuit of Nkrumah's ambition to make Africa an important player on the global scene and in major international affairs); and Obote, when he was at the Commonwealth conference in Singapore where he had gone, at the urging of President Julius Nyerere, to make a strong case against Britain because of her insistence on selling arms to apartheid South Africa and her unwillingness to take stern measures against the apartheid regime and the white minority government in Rhodesia.

Obote did not want to go to Singapore because of the internal political situation in Uganda which he felt, and rightly so, that his enemies would try to exploit in his absence. And there has been some speculation that had he not left Uganda, as urged by Nyerere, he probably would not have been overthrown. Nyerere was undoubtedly outraged by the coup against Obote who was also his friend and ideological compatriot.

But to say that he took military action against Idi Amin in order to reinstate Obote - hence make amends for his "mistakes" - because he had contributed to his downfall by urging him to go to Singapore to attend the commonwealth conference, is to distort history.

Idi Amin invaded Tanzania on October 30, 1978, and announced on November 1 that he had annexed 710 square miles of her territory in the northwest region of Kagera, triggering a counterattack by Tanzania, which eventually drove him out of Uganda. The atrocities perpetrated by Amin through the years in which hundreds of thousands of people were massacred were ignored by most African leaders and by the international community; a situation Nyerere found to be unacceptable, thus prompting him to intervene in Uganda to stop the atrocities by getting rid of Amin.

Therefore, even if President Obote had died in office and Amin or someone like him had usurped power and went on to perpetrate unspeakable horrors, as Amin did, Nyerere would still have intervened in Uganda out of humanitarian concern to stop the madness. He did not need Obote to be overthrown to do this. Obote could even have resigned, which is highly speculative, and Nyerere would still have intervened if Obote's successor - Amin or somebody else - went on to unleash terror on a scale Idi Amin did. It is in this larger context that Nyerere's outrage against the military coup by Amin should be viewed; a perspective that eludes a number of analysts or is deliberately distorted to conform to their interpretation of events at that critical juncture in Ugandan history. As Professor Ali Mazrui states in 'Nyerere and I':

'In 1971, did Julius Nyerere convince Milton Obote to leave Uganda and go to Singapore to attend the Commonwealth conference of Heads of State and government? Milton Obote had hesitated about going to Singapore because of the uncertain situation in Uganda. Did Nyerere tilt the balance and convince Obote that he was needed in Singapore to fight Prime Minister Edward Heath's policy towards apartheid South Africa? Obote's decision to go to Singapore was disastrous for himself and for Uganda. In Obote's absence, Idi Amin staged a military coup and overthrew Obote. Eight years of tyranny and terror in Uganda had begun.

I never succeeded in getting either Nyerere or Obote to confirm that it was Nyerere who convinced Obote to leave for Singapore. But we do know that Nyerere was so upset by the coup that he gave Obote unconditional and comfortable asylum in Tanzania. Nyerere also refused to talk to Amin even if the policy practically destroyed the East African Authority which was supposed to oversee the East African community. Was Nyerere feeling guilty for having made it easy for Amin to stage a coup by diverting Obote to Singapore?

I shall always remember Nyerere's speech in Tanzania upon his return from Singapore. I was in Kampala listening to him on the radio. Nyerere turned a simple question in Kiswahili into a passionate denunciation of Idi Amin. Nyerere's repeated question was 'Serikali ni kitu gani?' ('What is government?'). This simple question of political science became a powerful speech to his own people and against the new 'pretenders' in Kampala.

81

I visited Milton Obote at his home in Dar es Salaam during his first exile. Obote and I discussed Idi Amin much more often than we discussed Julius Nyerere....

In 1979, Nyerere paid his debt to Milton Obote. His army marched all the way to Kampala and overthrew the regime of Idi Amin. My former Makerere boss, Prof Yusufu Lule, succeeded Idi Amin as President of Uganda. But Nyerere was so keen on seeing Obote back in power that Nyerere helped to oust Lule. Was Nyerere trying to negate the guilt of having encouraged Obote to go to Singapore for the Commonwealth conference way back in 1971? Was that why Nyerere was so keen to see Obote back in the presidential saddle of Uganda in the 1980s?

Unfortunately, Obote's second administration was catastrophic for Uganda. He lost control of his own army, and thousands of people

4

perished under tyranny and war. Was Julius Nyerere partly to blame?'

If Nyerere was partly to blame for Obote's ouster, then he was equally guilty of the atrocities perpetrated by Idi Amin, since he "helped" pave the way for Amin's rise to power by encouraging Obote to go to Singapore to attend the Commonwealth conference; a far cry from reality, and a stretch of the imagination even Idi Amin - let alone his sponsors - would have found to be laughable. The Israelis and Western powers would still have tried and might even have succeeded, sooner or later, in overthrowing Obote with Amin's help even if he had not gone to Singapore, and even if Nyerere did not exist on the political scene to "influence" Obote one way or another.

Whatever the case, the coup which catapulted Amin into power was one of the biggest tragedies in Africa's post-colonial history and one of the most tragic cases of foreign intrigue on African soil by outside powers. And an illiterate who never went beyond standard two - what Americans call second grade - took over the leadership of one of the most prosperous countries in Africa, and ruined it.

Yet, in spite of his wicked nature and bestial character, Amin was also capable of presenting himself in an amiable way as someone who could be trusted, although he could not hide his ignorance. As Henry Kyemba, who once served as Amin's private secretary and as health minister before fleeing to Britain, said about him: 'Amin never knew anything about how a government is run. He could not write and he had problems reading. So it was very hard to work with him.'[5]

Kyemba also described Idi Amin, whom some people called the Black Hitler, as one of the friendliest people he ever met, yet had the rage of a wounded buffalo. And his government and army were dominated by illiterates who were no better than he was. As another former Amin's cabinet member, Birgadier Moses Ali who later served as Third Deputy Prime Minister under President Yoweri Museveni, also bluntly stated: 'Illiterates and sycophants were some of the people who spoilt Amin's government. They could not even read maps, they excelled in praising him, they were no better than Amin himself.'[6]

Amin's willingness to be used by external powers to overthrow Dr. Obote - one of Africa's most prominent and influential leaders - was one of the most treasonous acts in the history of post-colonial Africa. As an expression of gratitude to those who had sponsored the coup, Amin took a strong pro-Western stance immediately after he seized power and declared that Israel and Britain were his close allies.

The United States, like Britain, also supplied him with weapons. And the CIA as well as Britain's M15 intelligence service, together with Israel's intelligence agency Mossad, trained Amin's security forces; including the dreaded and notoriously brutal Public Safety Unit and the State Research Bureau, euphemisms for secret police. They also provided them with weapons and other supplies. And Israeli troops also trained the Ugandan army and air force even when Obote was president, giving them a strategic advantage when they helped Amin execute a military coup a few years later. And Amin himself once received paratrooper training in Israel.

A former CIA official publicly confirmed in March 1978 that the coup against Obote was planned by the British MI6 and the Israeli Mossad intelligence services. And it had been confirmed earlier that a British agent operating under diplomatic cover at the British High Commission in Kampala, Uganda, planned the failed assassination attempt on President Obote on December 18, 1969.

Israel's role in the execution of the coup proved to be critical when, on the advice of an Israeli colonel in Israel's army and with the help of Israeli agents in Uganda, Amin was able to secure control and command of a mechanized battalion - of paratroopers, tanks, jeeps and armored vehicles - which was able to overwhelm the majority of the soldiers and officers in the Ugandan army still loyal to President Obote. Firepower compensated for numerical disadvantage to Amin's benefit. And the ease with which the coup was carried out also confirmed Obote's suspicion that the Israelis had played a direct and critical role in his ouster.

Obote may still or may not have been overthrown had he stayed in Uganda to mobilize support among his followers against any uprising. And although he knew that the security situation in Uganda was not very stable when he left for Singapore, he agreed with Nyerere that he would be needed at the Commonwealth conference to help present strong opposition to the sale of weapons to the apartheid regime of South Africa by Britain. The strongest opponents were Nyerere and Kaunda, and Obote provided much needed support to them at the conference where other African leaders were also opposed to the sale.

At a meeting in Singapore during the conference, Nyerere, Kaunda and Obote told British Prime Minister Edward Heath that their countries would withdraw from the Commonwealth if Britain proceeded with the sale of arms to the apartheid regime. In the ensuing debate, Heath is reported to have told the three leaders: 'I wonder how many of you will be allowed to return to your own countries from this conference?'[7]

It was an ominous warning, confirmed shortly thereafter, when Obote learned in Nairobi, Kenya, on his way back to Uganda from the conference that he had been overthrown. And it directly implicated Britain in the coup. Britain's involvement in the coup was further confirmed only a few days later when the British government became the first to recognize Amin's military regime exactly one week after he seized power.

The British also rejoiced at Obote's ouster and gave Amin extensive coverage in the media, portraying him in a very positive way as Uganda's savior. According to *The Daily Express*: 'Military men are trained to act. Not for them the posturing of the Obotes and Kaundas who prefer the glory of the international platform rather than the dull but necessary tasks of running a smooth administration.'[8] And *The Daily Telegraph* bluntly stated: 'Good luck to General Amin.'[9]

The thrill in government circles was equally evident, as reported by *The Times*: 'The replacement of Dr. Obote by General Idi Amin was received with ill-concealed relief in Whitehall.'[10]

And Amin wasted no time in reciprocating these feelings.

He earned British confidence when he reversed Obote's policies in a number of areas. Unlike Obote, he supported the sale of weapons to apartheid South Africa by Britain. He also returned to private ownership British companies and other businesses nationalized by Obote. In return, Britain increased economic aid to Uganda, supplied weapons and provided further training to the Ugandan army. But the honeymoon was short-lived, and Britain as well as the United States and Israel soon learned that Amin was not the kind of leader they thought they could manipulate at will.

Amin had expansionist ambitions to conquer Tanzania and ostensibly gain access to the sea. He also toyed with the idea of annexing parts of western Kenya bordering Uganda, and even parts of Sudan, prompting Sudanese President Gaafar Nimeiri to remind Amin that he was Sudanese himself - Amin's small Kakwa tribe straddles the Ugandan-Sudanese-Congolese border, with part of Amin's lineage being on the Congolese and Sudanese side. He also threatened to destroy neighbouring Rwanda. He antagonized almost all his neighbours including Kenya whose western province, the burly dictator claimed, belonged to Uganda. But his immediate goal in this expansionist scheme was to conquer Tanzania mainly because Nyerere had offered sanctuary to Amin's nemesis, Obote. And he became incensed when Britain refused to supply him with combat jets and other sophisticated weapons to fulfill his mission.

Amin's desire to 'flatten Tanzania,' as he put it, became an obsession which made him turn to Israel to seek weapons he needed to accomplish his mission. He asked for Phantom jets and other advanced weapons. But because these weapons were manufactured in the United States and sold to Israel with permission from the American government, the Israelis could not transfer or resell them to Uganda without Washington's approval. But Israel did not even go that far.

The Israeli government refused to sell the weapons to Amin, saying that his request 'went beyond the requirements of legitimate self-defence.' The rejection of Amin's request was a prime factor in the expulsion of the Israelis from Uganda in April 1972, and in his unconditional support of the Palestinian cause and solidarity with Arab countries - and fellow Muslims - in their conflict with the Jewish state. And the failure to acquire the weapons he felt he needed, did not in any way discourage him from pursuing his expansionist ambitions to conquer Tanzania and secure a corridor to the sea.

Although he did not get the weapons he needed to inflict heavy damage on Tanzania, in his misguided belief that he would be able to conquer and occupy such a large country several times Uganda's size in terms of both area and population and which was believed to be militarily the strongest country in East Africa, Amin was provided with strategic advice and information in pursuit of this goal from an indispensable source. The advice came from a British major, working with the British intelligence service, who lived on the Tanzanian-Ugandan border on the Kagera River. He was in touch with Amin who frequently flew in a helicopter to the border for consultations with him on the planned invasion of Tanzania.

The British major had been an officer in the Seaforth Highlanders and a member of the International Commission of Observers sent to Nigeria during the 1967 - 70 civil war to investigate complaints by the Igbos and other Easterners in the secessionist territory of Biafra that they were victims of a systematic campaign of genocide by the federal military government. But he was expelled from the international observer mission because he compromised his neutral observer status when he offered his services to the Nigerian military regime as a mercenary in the war against Biafra.

However, at a hearing on his dismissal before the National Insurance Tribunal in England where he protested his expulsion from the observer mission, the major made a "startling" revelation that his real mission in Nigeria was to collect intelligence for the British government and provide strategic military advice to the Nigerian federal forces in their campaign against the Biafran secessionists and their supporters. The British government vehemently denied this, but the tribunal accepted his testimony and described him as a 'frank and honest witness.'[11]

He also proved to be an indispensable tool for Amin, as a spy, collecting vital intelligence for Amin's planned invasion of Tanzania. 'The Major took Amin's invasion plan of Tanzania seriously, undertaking spying mission to Tanzania to reconnoiter the defences and terrain in secret. He supplied Amin with a strategic and logistical plan to the best of his abilities, and although lack of hardware was an obstacle, evidence that Amin never gave up the idea came in the fact that the invasion of Uganda by Tanzanian and exiled Ugandan anti-Amin forces in late 1978 which eventually brought his rule to an end on 10 April 1979, was immediately preceded by an abortive invasion of Tanzania by Amin's army.'[12]

Full-scale war between Tanzania and Uganda began after Idi Amin announced on November 1, 1978, that his troops had captured and annexed 710 square miles of Tanzanian territory in the northwestern part of the country, Kagera Region.

Amin would not have been able to invade Tanzania and cause a lot of destruction in Kagera Region had he not been armed and kept in power by outside powers. British and Israeli involvement has received more attention than America's, but the United States' role in sustaining Amin's brutal regime cannot be underestimated.

In July 1978, Jack Anderson, a hard-hitting American columnist, revealed in one of his columns that 10 of Amin's henchmen from the notorious Public Safety Unit were trained at the International Police Academy in Georgetown, a suburb of Washington, D.C. The academy was run by the CIA, one of the three foreign intelligence agencies - together with Britain's M15 and Israel's Mossad - which helped sustain Amin in power, especially during the early years of his brutal eight-year reign. And as *The Economist* remarked, concerning the relationship between Britain and Amin's regime, 'The last government to want to be rid of Amin is the British one.[13"") – (Godfrey Mwakikagile, *Nyerere and Africa: End of an Era*, Pretoria, South Africa: New Africa Press, 2010, pp. 306 – 312. See also, cited above by G. Mwakikagile, 1.Idi Amin, on Radio Uganda, Kampala, Uganda, January 25, 1971; *Uganda Argus*, Kampala, Uganda, January 26, 1971. See also *The Nationalist*, and the *Standard*, Dar es Salaam, Tanzania, January 26, 1971; *Daily Nation*, and *The East African Standard*, Nairobi, Kenya, January 26, 1971; 2. Linda de Hoyos, "Idi Amin: London Stooge Against Sudan," in the *Executive Intelligence Review*, June 9, 1995, pp. 52 - 53. See also George Ivan Smith, *Ghosts of Kampala: The Rise and Fall of Idi Amin* (New York: HarperCollins, 1980). 3. Milton Obote, quoted in *Executive Intelligence Review*, ibid.; 4. Ali A. Mazrui, "Nyerere and I," in *Voices*, Africa Resource Center, October 1999; 5. Henry Kyemba, quoted by Wairagala Wakabi, "Idi Amin Just Won't Go Away," in *The Black World Today*, Maryland, USA, April 30, 1999. See also Henry Kyemba, *A State of Blood: The Inside Story of Idi Amin* (New York: Putnam, 1977); 6. Brigadier Moses Ali, quoted by Wairagala Wakabi, "Idi Amin Just Won't Go Away," ibid.; 7. Edward Heath's remarks to Obote, Nyerere, and Kaunda, during the Commonwealth conference in Singapore, January 1971, quoted in "The Making of Idi Amin," in *New African*, London, February 2001; 8. *The Daily Express*, London, January 1971.*The Daily Express*, London, January 1971.*The Daily Express*, London, January 1971; 9. *The Daily Telegraph*, London, January 1971; 10. *The Times*, London, January 1971; 11. Quoted in *New African*, op. Cit.; 12. Pat Hutton and Jonathan Bloch, "The Making of Idi Amin," People's News Service, 1979; *New African*, ibid. British gvernment documents, declassified at the end of the 1990s under the 30-year rule, verify earlier accounts by journalists Pat Hutton and Jonathan Bloch which said the coup by Idi

Amin against Dr. Milton Obote was engineered by outside powers - Britain, Israel, and the United States. Sky News, the London-based satellite TV channel, also quoted from one of the British documents in which the Foreign Office in London had said, "Amin was reliable."; 13. *The Economist*, August 1972. See also Ralph Uwechue, editor, *Africa Today* (London: Africa Books Ltd., 1996), pp. 1554 - 1557; Jeffrey T. Strate, *Post-Military Coup Strategy in Uganda: Amin's Early Attempts to Consolidate Political Support in Africa* (1973); Phares Mutibwa, *Uganda since Independence: A Story of Unfulfilled Hopes* (Lawrenceville, New Jersey: Africa World Press, 1992).

Amin's reign of terror was first directed against the supporters of Obote, especially the Langi and Acholi soldiers in the army. Being northerners like Obote, they supported him as a fellow northerner and had in fact tipped scales in his favour when he was in office because they were the dominant groups in the army. Now that he was out of power, they became the prime target of Obote's opponents, especially Idi Amin and his henchmen most of whom came from his home region, the West Nile District in northwestern Uganda.

Some of the biggest opponents of Obote were the Baganda. Many of them hated Obote because of what he did to them. He forcibly removed their king, Kabaka Mutesa II, from power. And he abolished all kingdoms, including Buganda.

Most Bugandans and other people in the other kingdoms were jubilant when Obote was overthrown and embraced Amin as their liberator. Some of them may even have hoped that the new military ruler would restore the kingdoms which had been abolished by Obote.

Yet it was Amin who, only a few years earlier as head of the army, invaded Kabaka Mutesa's palace and almost killed the king who was forced to flee into exile in Britain. The people of the Buganda kingdom seemed to overlook that. They were in jovial mood, celebrating Obote's downfall.

Although the new ruler was embraced by many Ugandans after he seized power, he remained a soldier and had no intention of returning the country to civilian rule. He instituted an oppressive machinery and went on to rule Uganda as if the whole country was a military garrison. Army officers and ordinary soldiers were given high positions in the government and in state-owned agencies. Even civilian government officials including cabinet members were subordinate to a military council composed of army officers who were the real government. But real power was in the hands of Amin himself.

He did not care about merit. Many soldiers who were given high government positions could not even read and write. Amin himself was virtually illiterate. He only had standard two education. He could barely sign papers. Because he couldn't read and write, he gave all orders by word of mouth. He sometimes used the radio to do that.

Military barracks became government headquarters, ministries and departments, with battalion commanders having absolute power in their areas and collectively constituting an oppressive apparatus for the whole country. They were exceeded only by Amin himself in terms of power. No one challenged them.

Amin created his own intelligence agencies, the State Research Bureau (SRB) and the Public Safety Unit (PSU), which became notorious for torturing people to death. Countless were also summarily executed through the years. Among the victims were prominent Ugandans.

Besides Benedicto Kiwanuka, who was Uganda's first prime minister not long before independence, other prominent figures who were killed by Amin included the Anglican Archbishop Janan Luwum. An Acholi, he was reportedly killed for criticising Amin's brutal dictatorship. It was said he sent Amin a note protesting against numerous killings which had taken place and which continued unabated. Amin accused him of being an agent of Obote, a fellow northerner. He was arrested on 16 February 1977, together with two cabinet members, Erinayo Wilson Oryema and Charles Oboth Ofumbi. They were all killed the following day. The government claimed they died in a "car accident." Their bodies were riddled with bullets.

However, there is another version that sheds some linght on the events which led to Archbishop Luwum's assassination. According to Professor Phares Mukasa Mutibwa in his book *Uganda Since Independence: A Story of Unfulfilled Hopes*:

"One occurrence which sent a wave of horror throughout and beyond the Christian world was the wanton murder of the Anglican Archbishop, Janani Luwum, in the company of ministers Erunayo Oryema and Charles Oboth-Ofumbi.

Why Amin killed the Archbishop has never been explained. However, it appears that at that time an attempt to stage a coup was being organised by some Acholis and Langis based in Nairobi. Archbishop Luwum was never involved, but he was informed of it by some Acholis in Uganda. When the archbishop was asked to join the group, he declined, saying that as a churchman his concern was with preaching not fighting; the plotters left him.

What led to Luwum's death was the fact that he did not tell Amin of this plot. Other people who knew of it warned Amin, and among these were a senior consultant at Mulago hospital and a senior police officer. Amin then personally accused Luwum of failing to warn him of the danger from outside the country, which meant that the Archbishop too wanted to see him overthrown.

Perhaps the killing of Oryema and Oboth-Ofumbi, who like Luwum were Luo-speakers, was for the same reason." – (Phares Mukasa Mutibwa, *Uganda Since Independence*, op.cit., p. 112).

Another victim was Frank Kalimuzo, vice chancellor of Makerere University, who was killed in October 1972. He was taken from his house. He came from Kisoro District which borders Rwanda. Amin accused him of being a spy for the Rwandan government. He also accused him of being a strong supporter of Dr. Obote:

"Frank Kalimuzo was accused by President Amin of Uganda of being a disloyal Rwandese masquerading as a Ugandan....In reality he was a Ugandan by birth and ancestry, but he came from an ethnic group in Uganda that was related to the Rwandese.

In broad daylight Kalimuzo was arrested in 1972 by Amin's soldiers from his home on campus, never to be seen again. He must have been murdered soon after his arrest. Did he die partly because his ethnic group of Ankole district was linked to Rwanda? His murder shook many intellectuals so deeply that some left Uganda for refuge in the Western world.

It was not until 1986 that the tide turned when Museveni, ethnically linked to Kalimuzo and to the people of Rwanda, captured power in Uganda. The Tutsi and the Hima of Uganda were ethnic cousins." – (Anthony Appiah and Henry Lou Gates, Jr., *Encyclopedia of Africa, Volume 1*, Fifth Edition, New York: Oxford University Press, 2010, p. 25).

The terror unleashed by Amin is well-documented. It was intended to eliminate his opponents, real and imagined, but also to instill fear in the entire population so that he would continue to rule without being challenged by anyone.

Some of the reasons he gave to explain the elimination or disappearance of some prominent figures were far-fetched even though he did not have to give any since he was the absolute ruler of the country. As Mutibwa states:

"Benedicto Kiwanuka, the Chief Justice, was arrested in his chambers and later murdered. Kiwanuka had earlier released a detained British businessman named Stewart and commented that the soldiers had no right to detain individuals arbitrarily.

It is also said that Amin killed Kiwanuka after finding out that he had agreed to work with Obote for his overthrow. This has been disputed by Grance Ibingira who says that, from what he knew of Kiwanuka, this would have been impossible.[27] However, the point is that, whether or not Kiwanuka agreed to work with Obote against him, Amin found out that the two men were in contact with each other, and this was reason enough to eliminate the Chief Justice.

The murder of Kiwanuka has also been attributed to Amin's fear of him as an alternative choice for the leadership of Uganda, due to his popularity and standing within Uganda society.[28]

Another victim of Amin at this time was Frank Kalimuzo, Vice-Chancellor of Makerere University, who was picked up from his official residence and killed later at Makindye.

Amin had on several occasions accused Kalimuzo, who was from Bufumbiro/Risoro, of being a spy for the government of Rwanda – and for Amin this suspicion was conclusive.

Basil Bataringaya, who had chaired the meetings that were planning to stop Amin's coup in January 1971, was dismembered alive outside the town of Mbarara and his severed head displayed on the end of a pole. His wife too was killed soon after, allegedly by Juma Bashir, the Governor of Western Province....

The reign of terror unleashed on the population did not spare the youth, particularly members of NUSU – the National Union of Students – at Makerere and other institutions of higher learning, of whom many fled into exile.

Others killed...included Francis Walugembe, the Mayor of Masaka, and John Kakonge, James Ochola and Shaban Nkuutu, former ministers in Obote's government. Mr (Joshua) Wakholi (former minister of public service) and Alex Ojera (former minister of information)...were captured and later murdered. Of the twenty cabinet ministers in Obote's government, eight had been killed and four were in exile within two years of the coup.

The killings were extended to the armed forces, where of the twenty-three officers of the rank of lieutenant-colonel or above at the time of the coup, only four were still in the service three years later, including Amin, the Paymaster and the Chief Medical Officer. Thirteen of these officers had been murdered.

By the beginning of 1973, Amin's true nature was emerging – what Grace Ibingira has described as 'a combination of guile, buffonery and utter ruthlessness in killing anyone even remotely suspected by him or his subordinates of being unfriendly.'" – (P.M. Mutibwa, *Uganda Since Independence*, op. cit., pp. 100 – 101. See also, cited by P. M. Mutibwa above: 27. Grace S. Ibingira, *African Upheavals Since Independence*, Boulder, Colorado, USA: Westview Press, 1980, pp. 288 – 289; 28. A prominent politician, who was a minister under Amin and who is serving the NRM – National Resistance Movement – Administration in a high office, is suspected by many Ugandans of having been involved in the death of Chief Justice Kiwanuka. This may eventually be investigated by the Ugandan Human Rights Commission sitting in Kampala at the time of writing (comment by P.M. Mutibwa). See also Richard Muscat, *A Short History of the Democratic Party, 1954 – 1984*, Kampala: Foundation for African Development, 1984, p. 88).

Yet in spite of the absolute power Amin had, including killing people at will, he failed to contain led alone end rivalries and divisions in the army and in other parts of the country. Ethnic and regional rivalries intensified during his reign. Even the people from his home region, the Kakwa and the Lugbara, turned against each other. When Obote was overthrown, they seemed to be united against a common enemy: the Langi and the Acholi who were Obote's biggest supporters. After killing the Langi and the Acholi, they started killing each other. The Kakwa and Lugbara became enemies.

Even some of Amin's fellow tribesmen in the army, the Kakwa, turned against him not long after he seized power. Kakwa army officers tried to overthrow him in April 1973 and again in March 1974. They were the last people he expected to turn against him.

Although Amin was identified as a Kakwa, only one of his parents, his father, was a Kakwa. His mother was a Lugbara. He took his father's identity because it is customary among many African ethnic groups – including mine, the Nyakyusa of southwestern Tanzania – for children to take the identity of their father.

The army mutiny against Amin in March 1974 was led by the chief of staff, Brigadier Charles Arube, a Kakwa. He was a Catholic and the first person to be appointed the army chief staff under Amin.

He was the most prominent army officer to attempt a coup against Amin. Amin accused Arube of collaborating with Lugabra army officers in a conspiracy to overthrow him.

Earlier, in 1972, Lugbara army officers also attempted to overthrow Amin. That was not long after Amin himself overthrew Obote. It was a clear signal that he had enemies even among his own people from the West Nile District on whom he depended so much to stay in power.

He also had enemies from other parts of the country within and outside the army. Ironically, the biggest threat to his regime came from the army itself, the most powerful institution in the country and of which he was in charge.

As Professor Phares Mukasa Mutibwa, a Ugandan who once taught at Makerere University in Kampala, states in his book, *Uganda Since Independence: A Story of Unfulfilled Hopes*:

"In an endeavour to tighten security the Military Police were given greater powers even than the regular army, police and prisons. A new decree (no. 19) empowered them to arrest people without a court order or an arrest warrant. They could arrest a wide range of 'criminals,' on the basis of suspicion only.

As for the armed forces, some promotions were made in May 1973 to keep them contented, but these did not stop some officers from thinking of ways of changing the leadership of the country, and the first major coup attempted by some of the most senior officers took place in March 1974. It was an event that had a lasting effect on Amin and influenced subsequent events.

However, this coup attempt was not the first against Amin since the September 1972 invasion (launched by Ugandan exiles from neighbouring Tanzania); there had been one led by Colonel Wilson Toko, commander of the Air Force, in April 1973. It was Toko who had read the citation for the decoration of Amin after the expulsion of the Asians!

Up to that time, the threats to Amin had come from outside Uganda, particularly from Tanzania; this was the first major coup attempt mounted from within. The 1974 coup was organised and led by Brigadier Charles Arube who, with Elly (Colonel Elly Aseni) and a few others (including Justice Mathew Opu), had just returned from attending a course in Moscow. It was spearheaded by the Malire Reconnaisance Regiment whose commander, Major Juma, did not particpate.

Arube's coup almost succeeded; all the important installations – Malire, Makindye and Kampala – were captured, and all that remained was to announce the overthrow of the government on Radio Uganda. In fact, the coup started so well that in the early hours of Sunday, 25 March 1974, Arube started celebrating its success with a dancing party at his house, but he was then arrested by soldiers loyal to Amin and shot and killed there and then.

It would seem that one of the major causes for Arube's coup attempt was dissatisfaction at Amin's appointment of non-Ugandans to key posts in the army and government agencies. For instance, he had elevated Malera, a Sudanese, to the high post of Army Chief of Staff, and he later relied heavily on Brigadier Taban, Lt.-Col. Gole, Lt.-Col. Sule (all Sudanese) and Brigadier Issac Maliyamungu (a Zairean). Other influential Sudanese nationals in Amin's regime at that time were Farouk Minaawa, Chief of the State Research Bureau, and Ali Towelli of the Public Safety Unit.

According to some sources, the aim of the coup organisers was to arrest Amin, Brigadier Malera and the other notorious killers from southern Sudan and place them on public trial at the Clock Tower in Kampala, where the guerrillas were executed in February 1973.

Amin was shaken by the attempted coup, which had been organised and led by Kakwa officers, his fellow-tribesmen. He felt betrayed and abandoned, but because there were very few officers whom he could appoint, he decided not to eliminate his betrayers. Instead, officers such as Lt.-Col. Elly were sent abroad as ambassadors.

Throughout 1974 Amin continued to feel threatened from all sides. On top of the abortive coup of March 1974, reports of guerrilla invasions from Tanzania in August and Sudan in November alarmed him further, and caused him to live in constant fear of being toppled by Obote.

He also believed there was an international conspiracy to unseat him, engineered by international media such as BBC and British and Kenyan newspapers. That was partly why, early in June 1974, his government banned all 'imperialist' newspapers in Uganda 'for, among other points, their perpetual stand against the Ugandan government.'

It was in these circumstances that so many innocent Ugandans died or disappeared, all suspected of working against him.

It is impossible to fathom the extent to which Amin really believed in these stories of invasions, but those who were in Uganda at that time cannot forget the tension that existed between Tanzania and Uganda, which put the country on a war footing.

Because of the increasingly serious security problems from the time the Economic War was declared, particularly in view of Toko's attempted coup in June 1973 and Arube's in March 1974, Amin took measures to strengthen his position in the army. After Arube's attempt, Amin was never the same again, a point to which those who served in his cabinet at the time have testified.

However, the reorganisation of the army to bring it directly under his control began well before March 1974, although it was speeded up thereafter. Thus in November 1974 Uganda was divided into five military commands. At the same time, civilians and non-West Nilers were removed from cabinet posts and (other) key positions." – (Phares Mukasa Mutibwa, *Uganda Since Independence: A Story of Unfulfilled Hopes*, London, England: C. Hurst & Co. (Publishers) Ltd.; Trenton, New Jersey, USA: Africa World Press, Inc., 1992, pp. 106 – 108).

It was also clear that without ethnic and regional loyalty from his people in the West Nile District in the northwest, Amin would not have been able to exterminate the Langi and the Acholi in the army most of whom remained loyal to Obote, even though there were also divisions among them, with the Langi, his fellow tribesmen, being the most loyal to him.

After the other northwesterners abandoned or turned against Amin, the only people Amin could depend on were

99

the Nubians and former rebels from southern Sudan, the Anya Anya, who had settled in Uganda especially in the West Nile District, his home region.

Ethnoregional loyalties in the military and the police played a prominent role in determining the balance of power between the northerners and the rest of Ugandans after independence, tipping scales in favour of the north especially when coercive power of the state had to be employed. As Donald L. Horowitz, professor of law and political science at Duke University in the United States, states in his book, *Ethnic Groups in Conflict*:

"Obote placed a loyal Northerner in the position of Inspector General of Police. The overwhelming majority of the police had long consisted of Northerners. A Lango himself, Obote packed the army with Langi and Acholi officers and men, and expanded its budget rapidly in the early years of independence.[28] Conservative estimates gave the Acholi, less than 5 percent of the population, at least one-third of the army.[29] Northern N.C.O.s were frequently commissioned, particularly after the East African army pay strikes of 1964 and the repatriation of British officers that followed. The paramilitary General Service Unit, composed heavily of Langi, was strengthened.

Like the army, the GSU was distinctly hostile to the Baganda and clashed with them from time to time.[30] Both the army and the GSU got their chance when Obote's forces attacked the palace of the Kabaka of Buganda in 1966, driving him into exile. At that point, many of the remaining Baganda officers fled the army.

When Obote further suppressed the Baganda and banned all opposition parties after an unsuccessful attempt on his life in 1969,[31] there were no further southern threats, electoral or military, to his control. The equilibrium had been destroyed.

Instead, the locus of conflict moved to the North." –

(Donald L. Horowitz, *Ethnic Groups in Conflict*, Berkeley, Los Angeles, London: University of California Press, 1985, p. 487 – 488. See also, cited by D.L. Horowitz in the preceding quotation: 28. A special correspondent, "The Uganda Army: Nexus of Power," *Africa Report*, December 1966, p. 39; cf. Michael Lofchie, "The Uganda Coup: Class Action by the Military," *Journal of Modern African Studies* 10 (1972): pp. 19 – 25, and 21 – 23; 29. Ali A. Mazrui, *Soldiers and Kinsmen in Uganda*, Beverly Hills: Sage, 1975, p. 113; David Martin, *General Amin*, London: Faber & Faber, 1974, p. 105, says the Acholi share (in the army) may have been closer to three-fifths. Later, Martin claimed the army was only about half Langi and Acholi. *Boston Globe*, 15 August 1976; 30. A special correspondent, "The Uganda Army: Nexus of Power," *Africa Report*, December 1966, p. 38; 31. After the shooting, twenty-six people were arrested, twenty-one of them Baganda. The total number of people detained, according to an official list, was sixty-six. Of these, fifty-one were Baganda, fifteen other Southerners. No Northerners were on the list. These were signs of the extent to which conflict had polarized along North-South lines. *Africa Report*, March 1970, pp. 6 – 8).

Professor Horowitz goes on to state:

"The Northerners who supported Obote were far from homogenous, and there is evidence that in the end he trusted only Langi, preferably relatives. He placed his cousin at the head of the GSU (General Service Unit) and the secret service[32]....

A Northerner, Amin was neither an Acholi nor a Lango, but a Kakwa.[34] In the army, he seemed to command the special loyalty of members of the Kakwa, Lugbara, and Alur ethnic groups from his own West Nile district and of the Madi next door.

Amin was also in contact with Southern Sudanese

rebel groups, and it is said that he supplied them with arms to be used against the Khartoum government.[35] The Kakwa straddle the Uganda-Sudan-Zaire border.

Himself a former N.C.O., Amin maintained contact with N.C.O.s after losing favor with Obote.[36] In the months preceding the coup, Amin also manipulated the ethnic composition of certain army units. He relied particularly on West Nilers and 'Nubians,' the latter an elastic category that includes descendants of Muslim Sudanese brought to Uganda as soldiers in the nineteenth century, certain groups of West Nile Muslims, and apparently even some recent converts to Islam.[37] Amin packed one unit with Nubians, only to have Obote break it up in late 1970.[38] By then, however, Amin had transferred some twenty-two Nubian and West Nile officers to another unit, the Malire Mechanized Battalion.

By the time of the coup in 1971, thirty-two of the Malire unit's forty-three officers were Nubian, Kakwa, or Lugbara; only five were Acholi, and three were Langi.[39] When the coup came, the loyalty of this unit to Amin was a key factor. When Obote threatened to move against Amin in January 1971, troops from Malire surprised Obote's forces and seized power.[40]" – (D.L. Horowitz, *Ethnic Groups in Conflict*, ibid., pp. 488 – 489. See also, cited above by Horowitz: 32. Another cousin (of Obote) headed one of two Muslim organizations, the one friendly to the regime. A younger brother (of Obote) served in the Ministry of Home Affairs. Other Langi headed the Public Service Commission, with its important power over appointment and promotion, and the Immigration Department; 34. David Martin, *General Amin*, op. cit., p. 14, says Amin's father was a Kakwa who lived many years in Southern Sudan. According to Martin, Amin's mother was a Lugbara; 35. Ibid., pp. 138 – 139; Henry Kyemba, *A State of Blood: The Inside Story of Idi Amin*, New York: Ace Books, 1977, p. 28; 36. A correspondent, "Uganda After the Coup," *Swiss Review of World Affairs 20*, March

1971, pp. 9 – 10; 37. Nelson Kasfir, *The Shrinking Political Arena: Participation and Ethnicity in African Politics*, Berkeley and Los Angeles: University of California Press, 1976, p. 220; 38. David Martin, *General Amin*, p. 89; 39. Ibid., p 59; 40. Ibid., pp. 25 – 61).

The ethnicization of the military by both Obote and Amin deeply divided the armed forces as well as other security organs including the police and entrenched ethno-regional loyalties across the spectrum. Amin exploited those sentiments when he launched a military coup against Obote. He divided the country even more when he targeted the Langi and the Acholi for elimination because they were supporters of Obote. He also fuelled regional hostilities when he favoured his fellow tribesmen and their allies from the West Nile District by recruiting them into the army in large numbers to replace the Langi and the Acholi:

"Amin's coup depended on ethnic loyalties. Its perpetrators were principally West Nilers and Nubians, as well as some Southern Sudanese recently recruited into the Uganda army.[41] The results were visible soon after the coup.

The General Service Unit was abolished, and Acholi and Langi soldiers were massacred to the point where virtually no officers from either group were left in the army.[42] (Most of Obote's guerrillas who later invaded Uganda from Tanzania were Acholi and Langi who had fled the army in 1971). Much of the killing was done by the Malire unit. Punitive expeditions were launched into the Lango district, where AWOL soldiers were hunted down, there to be killed with their families.[43]

West Nile men were promoted to take the places of the Acholi and Langi officers and soldiers. The army was expanded. Many of the new recruits were also West Nilers. Of the twenty-four top military posts in 1973, only three were not held by West Nilers; some of the new commanders had formerly been N.C.O.s.[44] Among West Nile groups, the Lugbara in particular assumed a new prominence in the army.

If 'Northerner' is not a homogeneous category, neither is 'West Niler.' With the Acholi and Langi decimated, fissures developed among their military successors. Madi and Alur officers were rather quickly purged; they were gone by 1973. The Lugbara proved more persistent.

Beginning in May 1972, and extending over the next two years, Lugbara officers planned a series of at least seven coup plots, assassination attempts, and confrontations with Amin, all of which miscarried.[45]

Amin had begun to rely increasingly on Muslim officers, particularly Kakwa. In 1972, for example, the armories were placed securely in Muslim hands. Whether these steps provoked disquiet among Lugbara in the army or resulted from it, the reliance on Muslims and the Lugbara unrest were certainly related. No longer certain of their loyalty, Amin transferred a number of prominent Lugbara officers. Finally, in March 1974, Lugbara troops, from a unit whose Lugbara commander had been replaced by a Kakwa, staged an unsuccessful revolt.[46] No senior Lugbara officer remained in the army thereafter." – (D.L. Horowitz, *Ethnic Groups in Conflict*, ibid., pp. 489 – 490. See also, cited above by Horowitz: 41. David Martin, *General Amin*, op.cit., pp. 59 – 61; 42. Amin said later that he had moved against Obote only after Obote had ordered Acholi and Langi troops to disarm the rest of the army and kill Amin. Whether intended as such or not, this statement proved to be a signal to Amin's own supporters to take violent action against Acholi and Langi soldiers. A final purge and slaughter of all remaining Acholi and Langi soldiers was reported six years later. *The Washington Post*, 3 March 1977; 43. David Martin, *General Amin*, ibid., 137; 44. Ibid., p. 240. Of the twenty-three top officers in army service at the time of the coup, only four were still on duty three years later; at least thirteen of them had been murdered. Ibid., p. 154. See also Holger Bernt Hansen, *Ethnicity and Military Rule in Uganda*, Uppsala: Scandinavian Institute of African Studies, 1977, p. 108; 45. See David Martin, *General Amin*, pp. 182, 230, 238 – 239; Colin Legum, ed., *Africa Contemporary Record*, *1973 – 1974*, p. B310. Compare Henry Kyemba, *A State of Blood*, op. cit., pp. 134 – 136).

The ethnic cleansing by Amin did not stop there. Other groups were targeted as well.

The intention was to achieve hegemonic control of the entire country by his people, the Kakwa, and the few allies they had from his home region, the West Nile District.

In the southern part of the country, the biggest victims of Amin's purges were the Baganda. It was also time for the Asians to go, about whom we will learn more later:

"While this sorting out was taking place among West Nile groups, the very few remaining Southern sources of power were also being eliminated. Prominent civil servants, among them many Baganda, were dismissed or murdered in 1972 – 73. West Nilers, and especially Muslims, succeeded to many of these positions, as they also did to many of the businesses left by the Asians Amin expelled from Uganda at about the same time.[47]

Then, in 1974 and again in 1977, there were attempts by air force officers to kill Amin. There were still some Baganda officers in the air force – as might be expected, given the difficulty of replacing highly trained personnel in a short time. These plots 'had a definite 'Buganda flavor,' '[48] and they led to more bloody purges of Baganda in the armed forces and civil service.

In the four years following the anti-Obote coup in 1971, all of the most sensitive positions – including defense minister, armed forces chief of staff, and air force squadron commander – came to be occupied by Muslim

Kakwa, Nubians, and certain increasingly prominent groups of foreigners.

The various secret police and terror units were commanded and staffed by Nubians. There was an increase of Southern Sudanese, some of them ex-Anyanya rebels, in the army, as well as some ex-Simba rebels from Zaire. The military police was commanded by a Southern Sudanese. Most of the young cadets and officers sent abroad for military training were Kakwa, Nubians, Sudanese, or Zaireans. The presidential bodyguard was composed of some 400 Palestinians.[49]

At each stage of this narrowing process, ethnic rivals were eliminated, and then the previous successful alliance disintegrated. First the North-South conflict was resolved on terms unequivocally favorable to the Northerners, who were left in control of the government and the army; then the Northern groups supporting Obote, the Langi and Acholi, were eliminated by the West Nile groups; and then the Alur, Madi, and Lugbara were eliminated by the Kakwa and Nubians....

Ultimately, Amin ended up ruling with the active support of ethnic groups comprising well under 10 percent of Uganda's population[50]." – (D.L. Horowitz, *Ethnic Groups in Conflict*, ibid., pp. 490 – 492. See also, cited above by Horowitz: 47. David Martin, *General Amin*, op.cit., pp. 168, 213, 234 – 235; Colin Legum, ed., *Africa contemporary Record, 1973 – 1974*, op. cit., pp. B294 – 295; 48. C. Legum, ed., *Africa Contemporary Record*, 1974 – 1975, p. B311; 49. Ibid., p. B309. On the various terror units and their commanders, see Henry Kyemba, *A State of Blood*, op.cit., pp. 111 – 114; 50. Some estimates put the Kakwa at less than 1 percent of the Uganda population. See Kasfir, *The Shrinking Political Arena*, op. cit., p. 110. Muslims, all told, are probably 10 percent or less of the population. See also C. Legum, ed., *Africa Contemporary Record, 1973 – 1974*, pp. B294 – 297).

In fact, Amin's regime was more divided than Obote's ruling Uganda People's Congress Party was.

Amin divided the country even further when he decided to expand the army. He recruited soldiers mainly from the north, especially from his home region in the northwest, unlike Obote who recruited soldiers from all parts of the country although even during his presidency, the army was dominated by northerners, especially the Acholi and the Langi, an imbalance inherited from colonial rule when the British depended on the north to recruit soldiers.

To remain in power, Amin also spent lavishly on the army. Such lavish expenditure proved to be a big financial burden on the country and almost drained the treasury. He also promoted many soldiers to make them happy even though they were illiterate.

He also severed relations with Israel and expelled all Israelis from Uganda in order to forge and strengthen ties with Arab countries, especially Libya. He accused the Israelis of plotting against his government.

Establishment of strong ties with Arab countries was an expression of solidarity with the Arabs in their struggle against Israel for the rights of Palestinians although it also had financial benefits. Amin also identified with the Arabs as fellow Muslims since the majority of them are Muslim.

After expelling the Israelis, he seized all property owned by Israelis in Uganda:

"Before the Asian expulsion, President Amin turned his attention to another group of people, the Israelis. Early in 1972, he left to visit West Germany, and on his way back visited Libya, Chad and Ethiopia. In Libya, President Amin and Col. Gaddafi signed a communique affirming their support for the Arab people in their struggle against Zionism and imperialism, and for the right of the Palestinian people to return to their land and homes.

Until this time, relations between Uganda and Israel

had been close and cordial. Some Israeli companies were carrying out large building contracts in Uganda for the Government, and Israel had a close link with the Uganda Army which dated from 1964, when Israel supplied material and assistance to form a Uganda Air Force.

Now, however, President Amin alleged that Israel was planning subversion against Uganda, and ordered first the Israeli military training personnel, and then all Israelis, out of Uganda. Uganda broke diplomatic relations with Israel on March 30, 1972, and something like 700 Israelis were expelled. President Amin has since stated that he took this action because Israel was insisting on being paid for work done in Uganda, and for material supplied to that country, and he has said that this is the reason he expelled them." – (Charles Harrison, "Uganda: The Expulsion of the Asians," in Willem Adriaan Veenhoven, Vinifred Crum Ewing, Stichting Plurate Samenlevingen, *Case Studies on Human Rights and Fundamental Freedoms: A World Survey, Volume 1*, eds., Martinus Nijhoff, The Hague, Netherlands, 1976, p. 304. See also David P. Forsythe, ed., *Encyclopedia of Human Rights: Volume 1*, New York: Oxford University Press, 2009, p. 58;).

After Amin expelled the Israelis and established strong relations with Libya, Libyan military ruler Muammar Gaddafi responded by providing Amin with financial and military assistance.

Amin also strengthened ties with Saudi Arabia in order to secure financial aid.

A substantial amount of all that money was spent on the army. Soldiers were happy. In return, Amin secured protection from them although some of them did not like him and even tried to kill him. Even a lot of the property he seized from the Asians whom he expelled from the country was given to soldiers.

But it was his decision to expel the Asians, including those who were Ugandan citizens, which had far-reaching consequences politically and economically. The decision thrilled black Ugandans. It made him extremely popular across the country. He told them it was the ordinary people including the poor who would be the biggest beneficiaries of the economic war against the Asians..

However, the biggest beneficiaries turned out to be those who were closest to him, mostly soldiers. They seized property owned by the expelled Asians, including shops, houses and cars. Many other black Ugandans, especially those with ties to the government, also shared the loot.

Amin said he expelled the Asians after God told him in a dream that he should kick them out. The decision amounted to a declaration of war on the Asians. It was an economic war waged in the name of black African nationalism to Africanise the economy and everything else in Uganda, a country which belonged only to black Ugandans, according to this rationale.

He gave the Asians 90 days to leave the country.

An event which set the stage for their expulsion was a speech Amin delivered to the leaders of the Asian community on 6 December 1971. He called the meeting to express a number of grievances against the Asians which he said caused disharmony in the country between the indigenous people and the Asians. The speech was an ominous warning to the members of the Asian community. But no one thought it would lead to their expulsion from Uganda.

It was a prepared speech. Amin did not write it himself. It was written for him. But it reflected his thoughts and was perhaps dictated by him. Everything in the speech was what he had in mind. It was probably all his ideas, although he did not have the intellectual sophistication to express and elaborate them the way they were in the speech.

And he did get some help from his subordinates to polish the language in order to present it in good English.

He did not have any formal education – only up to standard two – and did not want to deliver his speech in broken English which he normally spoke. This is what he said:

"This particular Conference has been convened as a follow-up of the many public statements and letters in the press complaining against the Asian community in this country.

At this Conference you as representatives of Asian groups throughout Uganda can brief the Government about the different aspects which have made Africans in this country complain against the Asians.

My aim is to ensure that like a father in a family, understanding and unity between the different communities in this country is established on a permanent basis.

I am sure that, having received your views as expressed through this Conference, and the memoranda which you produced to the Chairman, Hon. A.C.K. Oboth-Ofumbi, the Minister of Defence, whom I directed to chair your Conference, and having listened to what I am going to tell you this afternoon, I hope the wide gap between the Asians and the Africans in the different economic and social fields will narrow down, if not disappear altogether, so that all of us, whether citizens or non-citizens, African or non-African, can live a happier life in the Republic of Uganda.

No one doubts the various positive contributions which you Asians have made since the arrival of your forefathers in East Africa as railway builders. Some of the Ugandan Asians even received Government assistance to undertake different types of courses, including post-graduate training in medicine, engineering, law and other professional fields. Whereas some of these people after completing their training joined the Government, and have done a good job, I regret to point out to you that many of them have shown total disloyalty to the same Government which financed their training and enabled them to use other training facilities.

For instance, between 1962 and 1968, the Government of Uganda sponsored as many as 417 Asians for training as engineers. Today, however, only 20 of the 417 Asians work for the Government. Within the same period, the Government sponsored 217 Asians to train as doctors, but to date not more than 15 doctors of these are working for the Government.

Finally within the same period, the Government sponsored 96 Asians to undertake law courses, but of these only 18 are now serving in the Government.

You can ask yourselves the question as to where the majority of the Asians trained by the Uganda Government have disappeared. My information is that many of them either took up private practice immediately after their training or joined the Government but resigned to go into private practice. In view of the fact that it is extremely expensive to sponsor a student to undertake a professional course at graduate level, I consider that these Asians who deliberately refused to return to serve the Government, or who did so briefly and then left, have cheated this nation.

I am further informed that some of these Asians who were sponsored to take courses abroad refused to return to Uganda after they qualified, which means that they have contributed absolutely nothing in return for the training benefits which they received from this Government. Moreover, I am told that some of them who resigned from Government service did so on very selfish grounds, such as working in the Government on the condition that they would not be transferred away from either Entebbe, Kampala, Mbale or Jinja to up-country stations.

Although some of them gave the excuse that they would not agree to be transferred up-country because of lack of schools, housing, appropriate medical facilities etc., yet we know fully well that in most cases their refusal

111

was due to the fact that a good number of them have side businesses outside the Civil Service, such as shops, garages, transport businesses etc., from which they get extra huge sums of money, and which therefore they dislike to leave behind while they go on up-country transfer.

My government deplores this attitude and I wish to direct all the Ministries in which Asians are employed at any level to report to me from now on any Asian who refuses to go on up-country transfer for any reason at all.

I am particularly disturbed in this matter because according to reports which the Minister of Health has given me, some of the Asians who refused to be transferred to hospitals such as Gulu, Apach, Aturtur, Iganga, Soroti and even Butabika Mental Hospital, and who in some cases resigned in protest against those transfers include some consultants on whom the Government obviously heavily relies for the improvement of the medical services to residents of Uganda at large. This is but one of the many disturbing aspects of your community.

Having made the above point on the general disloyalty of some members of your community to the Government, I now wish to turn to probably the most painful matter around which public statements and correspondence in the press have centred. That is the question of your refusal to integrate with the Africans in this country.

It is particularly painful in that about 70 years have elapsed since the first Asians came to Uganda, but despite that length of time the Asian community has continued to live in a world of its own; for example, African males have hardly been able to marry Asian girls. For example, a casual count of African males who are married to Asian females reveals that there are only six. And even then, all the six married these women when they were abroad, and not here in Uganda.

In the cases where there have been moves by Asian

112

girls to love Africans, it has been done in absolute secrecy. I as well as you yourselves certainly know that these girls are under their parents' strict instructions never to fall in love with Africans.

On the other hand, it is interesting to note that many Asian men in this country are loving and living with African girls without favourable pressure from the parents of those girls. This is the sort of attitude which I would welcome because it points the way to integration between Africans and Asians. Asian parents should leave their sons and daughters free to integrate with Africans, instead of imposing against them social restrictions that are completely out of date.

Although I am aware that this lack of integration between the Africans and the Asians is due to the extension of the Asian caste system and ways of life generally, the Government of the Republic of Uganda is of the firm view that if there is goodwill on the part of the Asian communities it is possible for you to reach an understanding whereby integration among all the people in this country would be easy. I am therefore appealing to you here as the representatives of all the Asian communities in Uganda to consider this point seriously in the interest of integration between you and the Africans at all levels. I am saying this because I know that if we do not integrate in this country the situation which would be build up could easily lead to serious racial disharmony.

I am aware that one of the causes of the continuing distant social relations between the Asians and the Africans in this country was the policy of the colonial Government which ensured that the Africans, Asians and Europeans had entirely separate schools, hospitals, residential quarters, social and sports clubs and even public toilets – with the facilities to serve the Africans being of the poorest quality and hopelessly inadequate. We have, of course, now changed all this, but there are Asians who still live in the past and consider, like the former colonialist Government, that the Africans are below them. This living in the past cannot help Asians in any way, nor can it foster the desired harmony and unity.

One sector which greatly disturbs my Government are the numerous malpractices which many of your community members are engaged in. We are, for instance, aware of the fact that some Asians are the most notorious people in the abuse of our exchange control regulations. Some of you are known to export goods and not to bring the foreign exchange back into Uganda. On the other hand some of you are known to undervalue exports and overvalue imports in order to keep the difference in values in your overseas accounts. Another malpractice for which many of you are notorious is that of smuggling commodities like sugar, maize, hoes etc. from Uganda to the neighbouring territories.

This has on many occasions created an artificial shortage of those commodities within Uganda, with the result that whatever was left here at home was finally sold at unduly high prices.

You are all aware of the recent importation of sugar from India. In this particular case, the Government was told that the shortage of sugar within the country was due to the drought which had hit sugar production at Kakira and Lugazi. What we know, however, is that the sugar shortage which we suffered was mainly due to the fact that a number of Asian businessmen and smuggled sugar into the neighbouring countries.

Another bad practice which many Asian businessmen practise in the hoarding of goods in order to create an artificial shortage, again resulting in higher prices for these goods. A typical example is the recent court case in which Hussein Shariff Velji Mawji was convicted for hoarding oil and selling it at black market above the Government-controlled price.

These malpractices show clearly that some members of your community have no interest in this country beyond

114

the aim of making as much profit as possible and at all costs. As I have already said on other occasions, my Government will not tolerate those malpractices and will take all necessary measures to stamp them out. If any businessman is found smuggling or hoarding goods in this country, such businessman should not expect any mercy and he will permanently lose his trading licence whether he is a citizen of this country or not.

My government also feels strongly about the practice of some of your traders in deliberately sabotaging government policy by, for instance, renting to African traders only the front room in the shops in controlled areas, while retaining the back rooms, toilet and the cooking facilities.

Your community made use of the policy of establishing their own commercial and trading organisations which played a big part in the economic life of this nation. Here I am thinking of thousands of shops which the Asians built all over Uganda to deal in a wide variety of goods. I am further thinking of big industrial concerns and farming activities which, for example, have all along been spreaheaded by such outstanding families as the Madhavanis, Mehtas, etc. All these activities have assisted employment opportunities without which some people might have been forced to take up criminal activities.

Besides your contribution to the commercial and industrial life, I must also mention the part some of you have played in the expansion of educational and medical facilities in Uganda.

I should also like here to pay tribute to some of your members who have served and are serving in the different fields in the Government. There is no doubt, therefore, that the work of some of your people as judges of the High Court, magistrates, doctors, engineers, teachers, accountants, etc., has been vital in the development of the country.

But, and this is a big but, there are several disturbing

matters which I now want to point out to you frankly as, indeed, this is the purpose of this Conference. Firstly, I want to say that it is a well-known fact that the Uganda Government has made available facilities for the training of Ugandans as well as non-Ugandan Asians in the local and overseas educational institutions.

Some Asians have deliberately locked up their premises in areas which have been declared restricted areas, and have refused to rent them to African businessmen. It is also common knowledge that some of you who decided to rent their premises to the African traders did so at inflated rates.

I must remind you that any Government worth its name cannot sit back and allow a minority group of any kind deliberately to work against the policies of that Government, which are aimed at the overall national development of that country. I therefore intend to instruct the Ministry of Commerce, Industry and Tourism to double its efforts in tracking down such offending Asian traders in order to completely wipe out these malpractices that are aimed at defeating government policy.

Another malpractice I may mention is that of under-cutting African traders, and unfair competition. It is well-known that you are generally importers, wholesalers, and retailers at the same time. Many of you have taken advantage of this position to frustrate aspiring African businessmen in every possible way. Again, many of practise price discrimination against African traders, in that you supply your fellow Asians with goods at lower prices than those at which you supply your African traders. In this respect, it is up to you Asian businessmen to do everything possible to see that the competition between you and the African businessmen is conducted fairly, with the aim of balanced commercial and economic development of this country, otherwise here again Government will be forced to take action.

While still on the subject of malpractices in trade, I

should like to mention the tendency of Asians to keep all their business within their family circles.

When Government insisted that you should absorb as many Africans as possible into your businesses, some of you started to employ some outstanding Africans in the posts, for instance, managing directors, personnel managers, sales managers etc. What we know, however, is that all these appointments were mere window-dressing, and that those Africans whom you have employed, although they earn fat salaries, know next to nothing as far as the secrets of your enterprises are concerned.

Apart from this, I also regret to note that you have been most reluctant to trust Africans in your different trades. Thus you find that even the Africans you employ at your counters in your shops have to consult you practically every time a customer approaches them, to ask the price of whatever you will sell. This shows that, apart from your giving them the jobs in your shops, you have not given them the necessary authority and trust to finalize even simple deals with customers.

It is also disturbing to note that some of your members have carried out practices which are meant to evade the payment of income tax. They do this, for example, by keeping two sets of books. One set is specially for inspection by the Income Tax Department, whilst another, which shows the true and correct accounts of the business, is kept for your own use.

Of course, one of the advantages which you derived from the Colonial Government in this case is that you were also permitted to keep your accounts books in your Gujarati writing which cannot be read by your African directors and the officials of the Income Tax Department. It is not my intention to direct the Minister of Education to introduce Gujarati in our schools yet, but I urge you to refrain from such practices which made the reading of accounts by the authorized officers impossible.

It is also very well-known that many Asians in this

country believe that they cannot get any services rendered to them by any Government department or para-State organisation without their extending favours to the officers who are dealing with their problems. There appears to be a belief that unless one corrupts somebody one might not get such things as licences, passports, tenders, applications for citizenship, medical treatment, a plot in the town, or eating-house licence approved at all, or approved quickly enough.

This malpractice has unfortunately been generally accepted by some of the public officers in this country, because of the constant pressure they receive from the members of your community who practise corruption. This practice of corruption by some Asians has, therefore, interfered with some of the officers' decisions which should otherwise be based on truth, equality, nationality and justice.

As I appealed to the taxi-drivers to report any cases of policemen who asked them for bribes, I appeal to report any case where any public officer asks you for a bribe. Equally, I expect all of you to stop tempting public officers with bribes.

I turn to the question of citizenship. As already stated on many occasions in the past, my Government is committed to upholding all the legal obligations inherited from the previous Government. This means, in short, that in the matter of citizenship my Government will respect all citizenship certificates which were properly issued before the 25th January 1971. However, with respect to such certificates as were illegally obtained, these will not be respected and will be cancelled in accordance with the provisions of the law.

Concerning old applications for citizenship which were outstanding as on the 25th January 1971, my Government does not consider itself in any way bound to process such applications and regards them as having been automatically cancelled by lapse of time. Some of them had been outstanding for as many as seven or eight years.

For the future, all those who are interested in obtaining Ugandan citizenship will have to make fresh applications, and these will be processed in accordance with new qualifications which my Government is in the process of formulating and which will be announced in due course. In this respect, information and particulars which Government will obtain from the recent census of Asians, when finally worked out, will be relevant and of much use.

However, my Government is disturbed because it is clear that many of you have not shown sufficient faith in Ugandan citizenship. This is indicated by the fact that the vast majority of you refused to apply for citizenship which was offered after independence.

Another point is the practice whereby one family is composed of individuals all of whom are citizens of different nationalities. For example, whereas a head of the family may be a British passport holder, his wife may turn out to be an Indian or Pakistani citizen, whilst their children might be citizens of either Kenya, Uganda or Tanzania. Sometimes two brothers are registered as different citizens. This shows clearly that many of you have no confidence at all in Uganda or any of the other countries, for that matter. I will not hesitate to say that you are gambling with one of the matters which my Government takes most seriously, and that is citizenship.

Therefore I will remind you that, if there is any blame which you might later on wish to bring against my Government about your citizenship, the persons responsible for any confusion were yourselves.

Having drawn your attention to the above points, I now strongly wish to appeal to you to come together as a single community and discuss these points and present to Government a memorandum showing clearly what you are going to do in order to eliminate the complaints I have made against your community. My Government is going to take steps to see where the malpractices stated above are a breach of the laws of this country or exploitation of loopholes.

Those laws will then either be amended so that they work more tightly, or their enforcement will be strengthened. What I do not want to convey to the group whom you represent here this afternoon is the impression that Government considers your community an abandoned child. It is yo yourselves, through your refusal to integrate with the Africans in this country, who have created this feeling towards you by the Africans. But as far as my Government I concerned, and until the issue of the Asians who hold British passports is cleared, I consider you as one of a family of this nation.

Therefore, when you discuss what to do in order to eliminate the misunderstanding which has been created between you and the Africans in this country, you should remember that the solutions you are looking for are for the improvement of the relations within this family – Uganda. Furthermore, I wish to reassure those of you who might be panicking because I called this Conference, that this Conference, like the Uganda Development Master Plan Conference, the Baganda Elders' Conference, the Muslim Leaders' Conference, the Church of Uganda Leaders' Conference, and the Agricultural Officers' Conference, is meant to fulfill the aspirations of this Government, which is to improve the unity, understanding, love and racial integration among all the people of this country.

In other words, this is not an isolated Conference which is aimed at attacking your community because of the malpractices which I have outlined above. What I want of you is self-examination and the correction of any weaknesses which affect your community and which have made the Africans speak and write against you. I am doing this because I believe in God in Being Frank. That is why I did not discuss the public allegations against you secretly with my Cabinet or the Defence Council, but I decided to put it to you as prominent leaders of the Asian community in this country.

I, therefore, hope that you will take my address to you this afternoon and probably the whole night counting nthe various malpractices which are common among the Asian community, particularly in commerce and industry, but as it is not my intention to accuse, but rather to remedy an unsatisfactory situation, I consider that the examples I have given are sufficient to illustrate the concern of the public and of my Government over the activities of your community in this country." – (Charles Harrison, "Uganda: The Expulsion of the Asians," in Willem Adriaan Veenhoven, Vinifred Crum Ewing, Stichting Plurate Samenlevingen, *Case Studies on Human Rights and Fundamental Freedoms: A World Survey, Volume 1*, op.cit., pp. 296 – 303; Jean-Marie Henckaerts, "A Catalogue of Grievances: Speech of President Amin to a Meeting of Leaders of the Asian community in Uganda, December 6, 1971," *Mass Expulsion in Modern International Law and Practice*, The Hague, The Netherlands: Martinus Nijhoff Publishers, 1995, pp. 210 – 215).

The speech was published in the *Uganda Gazette 1972*, Government Printer, Entebbe, Uganda.

Amin used mild yet very strong language in his speech to the leaders of the Asian community. And it was clear he intended to warn them strongly of what was to come, although he was not specific. But there was no question Asians were no longer welcome in Uganda as long as he was president.

Still, many of them did not think he would take the extreme or drastic measure he did by confiscating their property, including money in the bank, and by kicking them out of the country.

There were those who left even before he gave that speech. They believed he was hostile towards them. But the majority stayed. They never thought he would expel them or simply hoped for the best.

I remember their expulsion well. It was during the same period that I left my home country, Tanzania, for the United States for the first time aboard East African Airways (EAA).

I left Dar es Salaam on 4 November 1972. After a stop in Nairobi, Kenya, the plane flew to Entebbe, Uganda. Almost all the people who boarded the plane at Entebbe were Asians, expelled by Amin, on their way to Britain and elsewhere.

I did not get off the plane. Relations between Uganda my country were very bad during that period and I did not want to take chances with my life by getting off the plane even for just a few minutes.

When the expelled Asians boarded the plane, an elderly man, who was one of those expelled, came to sit next to me. I knew he was one of the victims. He asked me where I was going. I told him I was going to school in the United States. He wished me the best and remained quiet during most of the flight, probably pondering his future after being expelled from Uganda. As I state in one of my books:

"I remember the expulsion well. I was on the same flight, East African Airways (EAA), with some of the expelled Asians in November 1972 on my way to Britain, and got the chance to talk with an elderly Indian sitting next to me. He was one of those kicked out of Uganda by the burly dictator and talked about this forced exodus, about which I had known when I was a reporter at the *Daily News* in Dar es Salaam, Tanzania.

The flight originated from Dar es Salaam, Tanzania's capital, where I caught the plane on my way to the United States for the first time as a student. Our first stop was Nairobi, Kenya; next, Entebbe, Uganda, where the expelled Asians boarded the plane on their way to Britain and whatever other countries would take them in.

122

Stripped of their possessions including financial assets, they landed in Britain, and in other countries such as Canada and the United States, destitute. Most of them ended up in Britain, Uganda's former colonial ruler. Almost all the passengers on the flight I was on from Uganda were Asians expelled by Idi Amin, as were those on subsequent flights, booked full.

President Julius Nyerere of Tanzania publicly condemned Idi Amin for expelling the Asians and called him a racist. Two other African leaders, President Kenneth Kaunda of Zambia and President Samora Machel of Mozambique, also criticized Amin for his brutalities and eccentric behaviour in general.

But it was Nyerere who was most explicit in his condemnation of Amin, and strongly criticized other African leaders for their silence and tolerance - and even admiration - of the Ugandan despot and for practising tyranny in their own countries.

He reminded them that had Idi Amin been white, and had the apartheid regime of South Africa gone on a genocidal rampage, slaughtering blacks across the country, these same leaders would have been furious. There would have been an outcry across the continent, calling for severe sanctions and even military action against the white murderers. But because Amin was black, other African leaders simply looked the other way, as they did when other atrocities were being committed across the continent by fellow Africans. Black leadership had become a license to kill fellow blacks." – (Godfrey Mwakikagile, *Nyerere and Africa: End of an Era*, op. cit., pp. 65).

Amin claimed he wanted to put the economy in the hands of Africans, a term synonymous with blacks. But the expulsion of Asians proved to be disastrous. The economy, once robust but then in tatters because of mismanagement under his leadership, virtually collapsed.

He had accused the Asians, mostly of Indian and

Pakistani origin but mostly Indian, of economic sabotage. Yet it was he who ended up destroying the economy by expelling them and by appointing people who were not qualified to help him govern the country.

Many stereotypes against the Indians – a collective term of ethnic identity since the vast majority of the Asians who were expelled were of Indian origin – were used to justify the expulsion. The term "Indians" also denotes a broad or an elastic category comprising all the people of the Indian subcontinent and their descendants – originally from India, Pakistan and Bangladesh.

They were labelled as exploiters whose only objective was self-enrichment at the expense of the indigenous people.

They were accused of hoarding wealth. They were accused of milking the economy. They were accused of overcharging Africans and discriminating against them.

Everything that went wrong with the economy was blamed on them. Africans were poor because Indians were exploiting them. The economy was not growing because of the Indians. They were guilty of economic strangulation. They were also guilty of impeding progress across the spectrum because they controlled the economy. It was time to declare war on them. But in the long run, the war proved to be too costly for Uganda in more than one way:

"Some of the Asians had been born in Uganda and were Ugandan citizens, whereas many others held foreign passports. For Amin, this did not matter – they were foreigners and spies in his country and needed to be expelled.

The Asians held many civil service jobs and essentially formed the middle class. With their expulsion, Amin established the foundation for the destruction of the Ugandan economy. He seized the pillaged Asian assets and properties for himself and his cronies. Some estimates suggest that this amounted to more than five thousand firms, factories, ranches, and agricultural estates and about $400 million in personal possessions.

In January 1973 Amin decided to nationalize all British-owned businesses in Uganda – without compensation. This naturally strained ties between Great Britain and Uganda, and the situation came to a head when Amin embraced Libya and the former Soviet Union over Britain and Israel, Uganda's traditional allies.

The United States closed its embassy in Uganda in 1973, and Britain followed suit, shuttering the doors of its high commission in 1976....

Amin's economic war was initially met with jubilation from many Ugandans, who believed that Asians were foreigners who had profited off the backs of Ugandans. Little did they know at the time that Amin's pillaging would not stop with the Asians' property and assets.

The impact of Amin's economic war on the Ugandan economy was not felt immediately, because the nation's main export, coffee, continued to do well on the international market. But by 1977 the Ugandan economy was in shambles, with inflation averaging 1,000 percent. The Ugandan infrastructure was also in bad shape, with an inept civil service. Soon the economy collapsed. Peasants refused to grow coffee, as often they were not paid for months, if at all." – (David P. Forsythe, editor, *Encyclopedia Human Rights, volume 1*, New York: Oxford University Press, 2009, p. 58).

Forty years after the Asians were expelled from Uganda, one Asian, Nina Lakhani, recalled that tragic event in her article, "After the Exodus: 40 years on From Amin's Terror Offensive Against Asians in Uganda," in *The Independent*, London, 24 June 2012:

"A dozen or so children are gathered outside 2 Nile Gardens in Jinja, Uganda, playing and preparing mogo (cassava), as we pull up outside the detached, corner bungalow around lunchtime. They all stop, momentarily shy of strangers, but relax as my mum explains in Swahili that this was her home 40 years ago – and she has just come back to remember the old days.

The children are excited to hear her stories, following her around the house as she points out the old bedrooms, a coal-room, the store-room for sacks of rice and flour, and the tiniest room, which once served as a mini-temple in which my grandmother would pray.

The wide-eyed kids can hardly believe her tales, as 40 years later, this once-comfortable bungalow is now in a dilapidated state: many windows are broken and there is no running water or electricity. Once home to my prosperous, extended family, these days it houses 10 extremely poor Ugandan families, one to each cramped room.

The best-preserved part of the house is the shady veranda out front, where every afternoon the women would once have gossiped while chopping vegetables and the toddlers played. Back then, the older children could usually be found outside on the oblong grassy gardens, around which 20 Asian families lived for decades.

It was from this very veranda that my mum got her one and only glimpse of General Idi Amin Dada, not long after he overthrew the elected government in a military coup in January 1971. 'He was standing on the corner of the neighbour's house talking politics, and we secretly watched him from here. He was so big, tall and fat, with big, red eyes. We were all scared of him because he was a military man and they used to say he drank human blood.'

Then, Ansuya Lakhani was a 27-year-old mother of one, and little did she know that this scary man, fanciful rumours aside, would go on to become one of the world's most brutal dictators. In eight short years, Idi Amin, the self-professed 'Last King of Scotland,' slayed hundreds of thousands of his countrymen suspected of harbouring loyalties to the previous government, and oversaw devastating economic and social ruin.

In 1972, Amin expelled more than 70,000 Asians, including my family, as part of his incoherent, sadistic plans that he claimed would make Uganda thrive. This decisive intervention led 29,000 Asians to come to Britain over a three-month period – one of the largest diasporas since the Second World War – uprooting my family from the only country they had ever called home and, in doing so, determining the course of my life before I was born.

In 2012, the year that marks the 40th anniversary of the Asian exodus, I have come to Uganda for the first time, to the place that would have been home.

I grew up with romantic stories about the old life, in the country known as the Pearl of Africa, so fertile that a few chilli seeds carelessly thrown out of the kitchen window would bestow a new plant.

My dad and his seven siblings were born in Jinja, where the majestic River Nile begins its journey across Africa. Ironically, Uganda's second city has, since 1963, been twinned with Finchley, a north London suburb where more than a handful of Ugandan-Asians ended up.

My mum, now 67, laments the pitiful state of her former marital home, which is the most ramshackle on the square. 'It makes me want to cry to see what it has become. We lived a good life here. We worked hard, but it was a relaxed life, it was our home.'

Nile Gardens was, back then, part of Asian Town, exclusively home to the city's 10,000 or so Asians, with every shop on Main Street owned by and largely catering for their needs. British-imposed segregation, broadly accepted by the 1.2 million Asians then living in Africa, had meant that before Ugandan independence in 1962, it was rare for the three racial groups to mix in school, work or play.

The sprawling Rock View School in Tororo, my mum's home-town near the Kenyan border, is now attended by almost 3,000 primary-aged schoolchildren, many travelling far from surrounding villages for a chance to learn. But it opened in 1942 as the fee-paying Indian public school, with only Asian teachers teaching only Asian girls, no more than 20 per class.

'It wasn't until we went to Britain that we really understood that what we had been doing was so bad. We never hated the Africans, and we never once treated them badly, but we never played together, or lived together. We wouldn't even use the same plates,' admits my mum.

'They lived in their areas, we lived in ours and the British lived in Europe Town, that's just the way it was and I didn't question it. When I saw how some of the British people treated us [when we arrived], I understood, and felt so bad about how we had lived our lives in Africa.'

It was in Tororo that Amin announced on 4 August 1972 his decision to rid the country of the 'bloodsucking' Asians who he declared were sabotaging the country's economy and taking African jobs. His intention to rid the country of what he called the 'British Asians' sent shockwaves around the world, nowhere more than here.

Three-quarters of East African Asians had opted for a British passport at independence, though most were still subject to strict immigration controls. But worsening race relations and dwindling job opportunities meant more and more Asians wanted to emigrate, from Kenya in particular. MPs such as Enoch Powell warned of an impending race-relations crisis, so in 1968 the Labour government stemmed the flow of immigrants (legally British citizens) by introducing an annual quota system.

Yet, in August 1972, Edward Heath's Tory government was suddenly faced with having to honour promises made to colonial subjects a decade earlier.

At first nobody believed Amin, but within days it became clear that this was no joke – and my family was among tens of thousands of Asians forced to flee. Further absurd decrees from Amin, together with violence and looting by his undisciplined army, spread fear across the country. The mood was exacerbated by the British government's initial refusal to accept responsibility for its citizens.

Officials first tried to negotiate with the General, whom they believed to be a man Britain could work with, and then tried to offload as many evacuees as possible to other Commonwealth countries. Government documents reveal attempts to find an island on which to house (some might say dump) the Asians, amid fears that the public wouldn't tolerate such a huge influx of coloured migrants.

My mum remembers those dark days well: 'Everyone was frightened for their lives. We would hear stories of dead bodies floating in the Nile, dumped from trucks by Amin's men; we were too scared to go outside.'

The expulsion came at a time when my family had been prospering. Several aunts and uncles were working or studying in the UK, my dad was progressing at Standard Bank and the family's transport business was expanding fast; they were on track to becoming millionaires when the carpet was pulled from under their feet. But, at the same time, many families were almost destitute – banned from jobs under Africanisation policies – and so cheered when Amin forced the British to accept them as citizens.

My mother and grandmother, who arrived in Uganda in 1934 from India aged 13 after marrying my grandfather, always described Tororo as an idyllic place where everybody knew everybody else, and children played with bottle tops, filling their bellies from fruit-laden mango and papaya trees.

This magical place turns out to be a twee two-street affair with a roundabout and an impressive, imposing rock overlooking the town as its most notable landmarks. My grandfather's shop, which had sat on the main street selling bicycles, hardware and textiles, is now a lawyer's office and mobile-phone shop.

Next door, the tailor, Owino William, who owns the

shop where he once worked, immediately recognises my mum: 'Matoto ya matoto,' he exclaims, jumping up to embrace her. 'The little girl of the little boy' – the latter being how my grandfather was known from the time he arrived from Gujarat at the age of 13 to the day he reluctantly left his beloved Africa 48 years later. Like the vast majority of Asians in East Africa, he had come voluntarily in hope of a better life, encouraged by the colonial masters to help develop the economy and provide goods and services for the coolies brought over to build the railways.

The long, narrow, very simple one-storey house behind the shop is almost unchanged. Local land disputes are now resolved from the old lounge which once doubled as a bedroom for my mum and her sisters. Behind that, the rest of the house is office and home to the lawyer Opino Walter Simali, who couldn't be more welcoming.

His father had moved in not long after my grandparents left, but Mr Simali only bought the place from my family after – in the late 1980s – Uganda's current president, Yoweri Museveni, allowed Asians to claim back properties in the hope they might return to help rebuild the economy.

By happy coincidence, my mum bumps into an old neighbour, Ramesh Pathani, who she hasn't seen for more than 40 years. He lives in London, too, but has been in Tororo for 10 months, embroiled in legal shenanigans to reclaim the house and soap factory his family left behind.

Their factory, like all Asian businesses, had been handed over to favoured Ugandans by Amin as part of his great economic war. The move was a populist one – but had catastrophic consequences, as most new owners had no business experience, which, together with trade embargos and blocked credit, quickly led to desperate shortages.

In Jinja, we meet shop owner and landlord Hitesh Dahia, whose family was permanently split by the troubles. His grandmother went back to India; he, his mother and sister were allowed into Britain; but his father and grandfather, Ugandan citizens, were not, so they, along with several hundred others, stayed put and tried to carry on. The pair were personally guaranteed protection by Amin, but in 1976, the grandfather was shot dead in his shop by military looters. It was a sign that Amin was losing his grip.

Dahia, like most Asians who have returned to Uganda, divides his time between this country and Britain, with economic and emotional ties to both.

As does Alibhai Kara, 69, who in 1972 left his textiles shop in the safe hands of an African childhood friend. In 1987 he left his family in Bolton, to return to a city that he found was in dire straits. 'The roads were ruined; so many people had been killed, it was a mess. But I was born here, it is my home, and anyway, who would give someone my age a job in the UK?'

These shopkeepers stand out in Jinja's high street amid the new generation of immigrants from India, thousands of whom have come on work permits from one rural region of Gujarat over the past 10 to 15 years. They own many of the country's mini-supermarkets and predominantly employ only Indians because, they tell us, local people cannot be trusted to work hard or to be left with money.

The blatant and insidious racism dished out by some of this new and expanding population is fuelling tensions, which are never far from the surface. In 2007, two Indian men were killed after protests triggered by a controversial government plan to sell part of a protected forest to an Asian sugar-cane mogul turned into full-blown race riots.

'These new Indians treat the local people as if they are doing them a favour by selling them something,' says Dahia, 'so I don't blame them for being so upset. We had a meeting in the town hall recently, and the local government told the Indians to behave better or get out.'

In Iganga, a small town between Jinja and Tororo, we

get into an argument with some shop owners. 'Haven't you people learnt anything from what happened to us?' asks my mum. 'You are in someone else's country and you can't even treat people properly with a little respect; you are all asking for the same trouble.'

A few minutes later we get chatting to three Ugandan market stallholders while buying some sugar. 'Thank you, mama, for teaching your children good manners,' says one woman to my mum. 'The Indians here don't even reply when we say 'Jambo' [Hello] – we want you people to come back.'

My mum looks heartbroken. She never wanted to leave, but nor can she imagine going back after so long.

My parents holidayed in Britain in 1971, when my dad's younger brother, Himat Lakhani (who ran away from Uganda in 1962 for a better education) tried to convince them to buy a house in Golders Green, going cheap for £5,000. 'I told him not to be stupid,' says my dad. 'Uganda was our home and when we got old, we had ideas of retiring in India, never Britain.'

So when Amin's explusion took effect a year later, my mum and dad, aged 28 and 33, seriously considered a life in India. Not that they had ever been, but for them, it somehow seemed less alien, less of a risk than coming to the UK, because neither had an education to fall back on (my mum left school at 12, my dad at 18). 'But we knew it would be better for our children if we came to the UK, as they would get a good education,' explains my mum.

My family was temporarily split during those mad three months. One aunt left quickly with three of her four children because they had a coveted unrestricted passport, foiling the looters by "smuggling" out the family's gold jewellery among the children's bags.

Most people queued for hours in the heat to get the correct paperwork from the somewhat unsympathetic British High Commission, and then outside the Bank of Uganda to buy plane tickets and exchange 1,000 shillings for £50 – the total foreign currency each person was allowed to leave with.

Daily reports of brutality in Uganda, allied with Amin's declaration of allegiance with Hitler and government assurances that the Asians were middle-class, educated people who would easily assimilate into British life, meant that by the time the first chartered plane landed at a wet and dreary Stansted Airport on 18 September, the British public was largely persuaded that these were worthy victims.

My parents, brother Deven, two, and cousin Avni, three, were among the last to leave, at the end of October 1972. The family left behind five trucks, two cars, a lifetime of belongings and most of their money – split between their staff. For some reason they shipped blankets, pots and pans, and huge cooking utensils with hollow handles stuffed with pound notes, which miraculously arrived in London, box by box, over the coming months. Those saucepans are still used: 'They came this far, how can I throw them away,' we're always told.

My family was lucky: they were quickly reunited, while many, including thousands of Ugandan passport-holders declared stateless, spent months apart in different countries, waiting for refuge. Most of my family started out in a rented house in Sudbury, north-west London, where the kids got their first glimpse of a TV. But my dad went to Stradishall, a former RAF station in Suffolk, one of 17 refugee camps set up by the government's Ugandan Resettlement Board. More than 20,000 people spent time on these disued barracks in far-flung places such as Yeovil, Greenham Common and Tywyn in north-west Wales, which were criticised for being cold, cramped, unfit for purpose, isolated.

Despite protests from the National Front and strikes by Smithfield meat porters (presumably worried about their jobs), hundreds of volunteers rallied with a war-like spirit to help out, with church groups, the WRVS and Citizens Advice on hand with warm clothes and welfare counsel.

My dad stayed in Stradishall for almost two months, filling out job applications, trying to acclimatise himself to his new country. He was offered a junior post by both the Midland and Standard banks, with a clerk's starting salary of £1,400 per year.

But then along came Peter Black, a Jewish man who had escaped the Nazis by hiding in a truck, and now wanted to help someone in a similar plight. 'He offered me a job in the accounts department of his factory in Yorkshire for £1,500 a year, but also free accommodation for a year,' explains my dad. 'We had never heard of Yorkshire, and of course I personally would have preferred a bank job, but I needed a house for your mum and brother, so we said yes and took the train to Keighley.'

They spent nine years in West Yorkshire, where they had two more children – my brother Mehul and me – improved their English and bought their first house. 'It was so cold, it snowed and snowed, but I felt so embarrassed to wear trousers because I thought everyone was laughing at me,' says my mum. 'But we didn't have too many problems – sometimes people would call us 'Paki' or say, 'Go back home,' but we just ignored them. We made friends, but we were lonely as we had never lived without the rest of the family.'

Mum got her first ever job in Peter Black's factory, but became depressed and lonely– so when my dad got the chance to start his own business with a friend in London, a toy shop near West Ham's stadium, they headed south.

My dad, now 72, was perhaps too trusting to be truly successful in business, and after trying his hand at a succession of small ventures, settled at a friend's post office, where he still works. My mum "retired" in 1997 to care for my grandmother – for it was the elderly who found the exodus most difficult, arriving in the UK too old to learn the language or find a job; too cold to venture outside much; and never again really feeling free. This trip made me realise just how much families like mine gave up – not just their homes and jobs, but their identities, relationships, often hopes and dreams. Though we hear about how successful these immigrants became, this truth is anecdotal rather than being based on any real evidence about what became of their lives.

Being witness to some hateful racism dished out by those Indians who have more recently made the move to Uganda has made me think not that Amin was justified or right, but why he might have thought it would be a popular decision. The long-standing mutually beneficial relationship between the Asian businessmen and President Museveni cannot last forever. What happens to the Asians then... well, anything is possible.

Naturally, I've often wondered what my life might have been like had Amin not been a deranged despot. It's odd but I felt something I can't quite explain when I was in Uganda – though not the powerful connection I had visiting India for the first time. And I now can't stop thinking about how different I might have been. My mum's take on these musings: 'Don't think too much, everything happens for a reason.' Spoken like a true survivor."

The expulsion of the Asians from Uganda by Amin was only one aspect of his brutal dictatorship. His reign of terror covered every aspect of Ugandan life. It was synonymous with destruction. He left his imprint everywhere, in every part of Uganda, and on the life of every Ugandan. Even after he was long gone, evidence of his destruction was clearly visible. No part of Uganda was left untouched.

Farmers, on whom the country depended so much, resorted to smuggling since they were not being paid enough for their products. Many simply stopped growing cash crops, such as coffee and cotton, or produced very

135

little. It was a major blow to the country. Agriculture was the backbone of its economy. Without it, it was doomed.

Most of the smuggled goods went to Kenya. Amin gave orders to shoot smugglers on sight. His adviser, Bob Astel, a British, was given the responsibility to take whatever measures he considered appropriate to address the problem. But that did not save the economy from collapsing.

He did not even have the people to help rejuvenate or revive the economy. The infrastructure and institutions such as the civil service had also collapsed. Technocrats and other skilled people were either dead or had fled the country.

Uganda suffered a tremendous loss of its highly trained manpower during the seventies. That was when about a third of its highly skilled people and professionals were killed or fled into exile. Newly trained ones overseas refused to return home.

All sectors of the economy became paralysed. Even the vibrant manufacturing sector, which functioned well under Obote, came to a grinding halt. The treasury was almost empty and the people who were put in charge of the economy did not not know what they were doing.

Amin made a complete mockery of merit.

Even the army, on which he depended so much, was not spared. He appointed many civilians as army officers and promoted them rapidly. Most of them were illiterate or barely literate. They were mostly members of his tribe, the Kakwa, or of other tribes from his home region, the West Nile District, in northwestern Uganda. One of his most bizarre appointments was when he chose a former telephone operator to be the head of the air force.

The West Nile District was one of the most neglected. Under Amin, it was the most favoured. When he doubled the size of the army by 1977, most of the soldiers who were recruited during that period came from the West Nile District.

He also recruited into the army many people from neighbouring countries – Sudan, Zaire and Rwanda – whom he believed would be loyal to him by doing them such as a favour. But such a policy had unintended consequences. A very large number of soldiers in the army were not only foreigners; they could not communicate well because they spoke different languages. Not all of them understood or spoke Kiswahili, or Swahili, a language that is commonly used in the armed forces.

There were also disciplinary problems. Some army officers and their units were out of control and virtually established independent fiefdoms, terrorising local civilians, without the slightest fear of punishment from the central government because it had no control over them and didn't even care to discipline them. Thus, while Amin was the overall military ruler of Uganda, a number of army officers were also absolute rulers in their own areas. And they ruled with impunity.

The security forces Amin established, especially the State Research Bureau (SRB) and the the Public Safety Unit (PSU), grew rapidly and had about 15,000 people by 1979. They were some of the most brutal and most efficient agents of state-sponsored terror, probably the worst in post-colonial Africa up to that time, rivalled only by President Masie Nguema's regime in Equatorial Guinea where an entire third of the country's population was either wiped out or was forced to flee into exile.

Amin's terror squads which collectively constituted his security forces started to undermine themselves. They competed and fought against each other along tribal lines. The Kakwa, Amin's fellow tribesmen, were the most influential. They had the highest and most powerful posts in the State Research Bureau, the Public Safety Unit, the army, the air force and the police. Members of other tribes and ethnic groups including foreigners such as Sudanese in the army resented that.

The Lugabara fought the Kakwa, although they were

allies and fellow northwesterners. The Sudanese also tried to undermine the Kakwa. Other groups in the army were also involved in violent conflicts, further weakening the army.

The economy also continued to deteriorate. And during the same time, Amin was faced with another major problem: attempts by Obote and his supporters to overthrow him.

The first attempt took place in September 1972 when a small and ill-equipped invasion force entered Uganda from northwestern Tanzania in order to capture a military post at Masaka and spark an uprising against Amin. They failed to capture the military post. And no uprising against Amin took place. The invaders were routed and fled back to Tanzania. Some of them were killed. But Obote did not give up. He was determined to return to Uganda and lead the country again.

The invasion by Ugandan exiles living in Tanzania scared Amin and his supporters. His security forces became even more brutal. They spread fear throughout the country, arresting, torturing and killing suspected opponents of Amin. Countless were killed. Most of them were innocent civilians who were not involved in any plot to overthrow Amin.

To instill even more fear in the population, Amin used a very effective scare tactic by having his subordinates announce on the radio the names of some of the people who were about to "disappear." Lives of his fellow countrymen, even some who were very close to him, meant absolutely nothing to him.

As terror intensified, even some of the people who were closest to him fled. Some were killed. Amin himself was under siege.

The beginning of the end came when troops of the Malire Mechanised Regiment mutinied. Ironically, it was the same regiment which played the most decisive role in the January 1971 military coup and helped Amin to seize power. In October 1978, Amin sent loyal troops to quell the rebellion. The mutineers fled to Tanzania. Even some of the troops loyal to Amin crossed the border and joined his opponents in Tanzania.

Amin blamed Nyerere for all that. He accused him of trying to overthrow him. In order to divert attention from domestic discontent with his brutal dictatorship, he tried to mobilise his fellow countrymen against an external enemy, Nyerere, and invaded Tanzania.

On 1 November 1978, Amin ordered the Suicide Battalion in Masaka and the Simba Battalion in Mbarara to invade Tanzania and annex part of its territory. His soldiers occupied about 700 square miles of Tanzanian territory in Kagera Region in the northwest and claimed it as Ugandan territory.

Tanzania fought back and drove Amin's troops back into Uganda. The Tanzanian army, known as the Tanzania People's defence Forces (TPDF), was joined by an army of Ugandan exiles, the Uganda National Liberation Army (UNLA), who were trained in Tanzania and began the long march to Kampala to oust Amin. His friend Gaddafi sent 3,000 troops to help save him. But they were no match for Tanzanian soldiers and were easily routed. Many of them were captured or simply surrendered.

Kampala fell on 10 April 1979 and Amin fled to Libya. He lived in Libya until 1989 when he fell out with Gaddafi and sought exile in Saudi Arabia where he spent the rest of his life. He died on 16 August 2003.

He was at least in his seventies when he died. Most biographers claim he was born in 1925. Other sources say he was born in 1923; yet others claim in 1928. He probably was born in the mid-1920s.

Chapter Four

Obote returns to power

AFTER Amin was ousted, Obote started to make plans to regain power. But before he could do that, there were other Ugandans who led the country.

It was a period of uncertainty. And the person who was really in charge of Uganda during that period was President Julius Nyerere of Tanzania. His admirers and detractors alike concede that Nyerere was the real president of Uganda during that time. Nothing was done in Kampala without his permission. He was effectively president of two countries at the same time: Tanzania and Uganda.

The first person to lead Uganda after Amin was overthrown was Yusuf Lule. He became president on 13 April 1979. It was Nyerere who put him in power. Lule was replaced by Godfrey Binaisa on 20 June 1979, also with Nyerere's support and approval. As John Kato stated in an article, "Julius Nyerere, the Godfather of Uganda's Political Set-up," in *New Vision*, Kampala, Uganda, 4 April 2012:

"In June 2011, prayers were held at Namugongo Martyr's Shrine for Nyerere, in which President Museveni made one of the brightest eulogies about him: 'I am happy when I speak of Nyerere because I am his supporter. He was the greatest black man that ever lived. There are other black men such as Nelson Mandela and Kwame Nkrumah, but Nyerere was the greatest...,' Museveni said.

Between 1979 and 1980, Tanzanian leader Julius Nyerere was the 'defacto' president of Uganda. Nothing was done without consulting him and anything attempted without consulting him was quashed.

'Even if you wanted to sneeze or move your leg, you had to first inform Julius Nyerere about it,' mused late President Godfrey Binaisa, in his testimonials, *Binaisa ne Yuganda*. That was the depth of Nyerere's influence in Uganda. It is easy to understand why Nyerere is attracting all these praises. At the peak of the anti-Amin struggle, many Ugandan exiles – politicians, academicians and otherwise, sought refuge in Tanzania, and were directly aided by Nyerere.

Among them were Milton Obote, Yoweri Museveni, Oyite Ojok, Tito Okello and Bazilio Olara Okello. When time came to organising and hosting the Moshi Conference in 1979 to determine Uganda's future, Nyerere was at the forefront. Most anti-Amin fighters were in Dar-es-Salaam with their families, all funded by Nyerere.

'The good people in Mwalimu's office assisted us to get an apartment in another neighbourhood called Upanga,' Janet Museveni, who too was in Tanzania with her husband, Museveni, recalls. 'Milton Obote was living in the presidential guest house in Musasani, supported by

Mwalimu's government,' Janet wrote in her book *My Life's Story*. It was also clear that on Obote's behalf, Nyerere was willing to fight Amin.

'On return to Dar-es-Salaam, Nyerere told me the Tanzanian army had suggested that if I could find a pilot, some of my men could be flown to Entebbe on the night of the invasion. The plan was for the government of Tanzania to commandeer an East African Airways aircraft from a Tanzanian airport,' Obote wrote.

He adds:

'From 1973 to 1978, I requested President Nyerere to allow me to arrange for the infiltration of the men to Uganda, but the president who was always very kind to me, who he used to come to my residence, sometimes twice a week, for conversation and would invite me to functions at his house, rejected every request.'

Obote also wrote that when Idi Amin's forces invaded Tanzania via Mutukula on the Ugandan southern border President Nyerere briefed him and concluded: 'This is the opportunity we have been waiting for.' This culminated into the struggle led by the Tanzanian army and the Ugandan exiles that ended the bloody rule of Idi Amin in 1979.

Apparently, Nyerere had learnt that sections of Ugandans did not want Obote to return as president. This is why he accommodated other fighters like Yusuf Lule, who later became president after the toppling of Amin, and Godfrey Binaisa. Earlier, while Obote had advised Nyerere against bringing a young man called Yoweri Museveni closer, Nyerere embraced Museveni. You can as well argue that other than Idi Amin and Sir Edward Mutesa, all the other Ugandan presidents, seven out of the nine, had Nyerere's blessing."

Binaisa was ousted on 12 May 1980, again with

Nyerere's approval, and was replaced by Paulo Muwanga, Obote's close associate who paved the way for Obote's return to power. Muwanga served as president of Uganda from 12 – 22 May 1980 when was chairman of the ruling Military Commission. He was replaced by the Presidential Commission whose members were Saulo Musoke, Polycarp Nyamuchoncho, and Joel Hunter Wacha-Olwol. Muwanga also served as prime minister of Uganda from 1 August – 25 August 1980.

The Presidential Commission led Uganda from 22 May – 15 December 1980.

General elections were held on 10 December 1980 and Obote was declared the winner. Muwanga was the chairman of the Electoral Commission. But there was a bitter dispute over the elections.

Obote's opponents, including Yoweri Museveni, claimed the elections were rigged. Muwanga was blamed for rigging the elections in favour of Obote. Museveni launched a rebellion to overthrow Obote. But it took years before he finally succeeded in doing so.

Yet it was those elections which set the stage for Museveni's rise to power years later. They galvanised the opposition and helped plunge the country into a civil which came to be known as the Bush War.

The Commonwealth election observers conceded there some irregularities but concluded that the elections were fair; a conclusion that was not accepted by Obote's opponents.

Obote's ally, Paulo Muwanga who was chairman of the Electoral Commission, had full control of the electoral process and even disqualified Obote's opponents, especially members of the Democratic Party (DP) led by Paul Ssemogerere, from the ballot although there was evidence showing that some of them had defeated the candidates of Obote's Uganda People's Congress (UPC).

It was also alleged that many ballot boxes of the Democratic Party (DP) were simply seized on orders from

Muwanga and given to the Uganda People's Congress to give Obote's party more votes. Empty ballot boxes were also allegedly stuffed for the same purpose, enabling the Uganda People's Congress to get even more votes.

It was easy to seize the ballot boxes of the Democratic Party, UPC's main challenger, because there was no secret ballot. Muwanga had decreed that each candidate should have his own ballot box, making the electoral process even less democratic but securing an easy victory for Obote. And as Professor Frederick K. Byaruhanga, a Ugandan, states in his book, *Student Power in Africa's Higher Education: A Case of Makerere University*:

"President Binaisa was removed from power after serving just a few months and was placed under house arrest, to be replaced by Paulo Muwanga, who was appointed not as president, but as Chairman of the Military Commission.

The appointment of Paulo Muwanga, a UPC enthusiast, was seen by many as a clear pathway for the return of former President Obote. Muwanga quickly lifted the ban on political parties and began preparations for multiparty general elections, which took place December 10, 1980.

Former president Obote and his UPC party won the elections, which were widely considered rigged and fraudulent. As a result, many of Obote's opponents, including the current president Yoweri Museveni, took up arms to wage guerrilla warfare against the government." – (Frederick Kamuhanda Byaruhanga, *Student Power in Africa's Higher Education: A Case of Makerere University*, New York: Routledge, Taylor & Francis Group, 2006, p. 11).

Even if Obote could still have won the election because his party was better organised across the country and was better financed, although he probably would have won with a smaller electoral mandate if he were to win at all, the fact that his party employed coercive tactics because it controlled the electoral process means the legitimacy of his victory was seriously in doubt even among some of his supporters although it was at the same time validated by international observers who concluded that he did, indeed, win, although there were some violations during the electoral contest.

On the other hand, the Democratic Party claimed victory at the polls. And some analysts believed the party did indeed win the election. Others said the Democratic Party did not win but would have won if the election was free and fair.

The opposition capitalised on all that and did everything it could to discredit Obote and the Uganda People's Congress because of what Muwanga and his subordinates had done to help the UPC secure many votes it was not entitled to.

Therefore the UPC discredited its own victory, thus legitimising claims by Museveni other opponents of Obote that Obote did not win the election.

Had the election not been manipulated by Muwanga and other UPC supporters who controlled the Electoral Commission, Obote's opponents would have had a hard time building a case against him. And they would not have been able to mobilise forces against him across the country on the scale they did – except in northern Uganda, Obote's traditional stronghold with the exception of the West Nile District in the northwest which was Amin's home region.

The 1980 elections were also held during a period when Tanzania exerted a lot of influence on Uganda because of the role she played in ousting Amin. And it was taken for granted that whoever was to be elected the next president of Uganda had to have the approval and blessings of Tanzania's president, Julius Nyerere, who on 14 November 1978 ordered the Tanzania People's Defence Forces – popularly known as TPDF – to launch a counteroffensive against Amin's forces which had annexed the Kagera Salient in northwestern Tanzania:

"The forces which overthrew Amin contained a variety of groups with different ideologies and aspirations, whose only common goal had been to remove Amin.

The Tanzanians remained powerful behind the scenes, retaining a sizeable military force in the country....

Throughout, the Tanzanians appeared determined to re-establish Obote in power....

Acholi and Langi soldiers in the Uganda National liberation Army (UNLA) proceeded to revenge the massacres of Amin. Indiscriminate killings in West Nile, Idi Amin's home area, destroyed most of the town of Arua. According to the UN High Commission for Refugees, over a quarter of a million refugees from West Nile fled to neighbouring countries like Sudan and Zaire (Karugire, 1980).

The general election which followed Binaisa's overthrow was contested by the traditional political parties – the Protestant anti-Baganda Uganda People's Congress (UPC) led by Obote, and the Catholic and Buganda Democratic Party (DP) – as well as the new Uganda Patriotic Movement (UPM), led by Yoweri Museveni.

The election was rigged, however. Although it appears clear that the DP won the majority of votes, the Military Commission declared Obote the winner." – (Jeni Klugman, Bilin Neyapti and Frances Stewart, *Conflict and Growth in Africa, Vol. 2: Kenya, Tanzania and Uganda*, Paris: Development Centre Studies, OECD Publications Service, 1999, p. 24).

The reaction by opponents of Obote to what was widely perceived to have been a rigged election varied. The biggest challenger, the Democratic Party, decided to operate within the system by assuming the role of official opposition in parliament. Museveni, who had been vice-chairman of the Military Commission under Paul Muwanga which ruled the country before the election, stayed out and chose to go to war against Obote's government.

And although the Democratic Party did not win the election according to official results, it still managed to win a significant number of seats even under those circumstances. As George Lugalambi, a lecturer and head of the mass communication department at Makerere university, states in his work, *An Assessment of Democratic Deliberation in Uganda*:

"Four parties contested the elections: UPC fielded Obote as its candidate; DP fielded Paul Ssemogerere; Uganda Patriotic Movement (UPM) fielded Museveni; and the Conservative Party (CP) fielded Jehoash Mayanja-Nkangi.

UPC won 73 of the 126 parliamentary seats and returned Obote to power. DP won 52 seats, UPM one, and CP none.

Obote's controversial return to power marked what became known in public parlance as the Obote II regime.

There is wide agreement that the 1980 general elections were marred by extensive irregularities and fixed in favor of UPC. Whereas all losing parties disputed the results, DP opted to join parliament as the opposition party. Museveni, on the other hand, opted to mount an armed rebellion against Obote's UPC regime." – (George W. Lugalambi, *An Assessment of Democratic Deliberation in Uganda: A Case Study of The Framing of Key Issues in The Press* (A Thesis in Mass Communication submitted in partial fulfillment of the requirements for the degree of Doctor of Philosophy, Pennsylvania State University, December 2006) UMI Microform, Ann Arbor, Michigan, 2009, p. 39).

The general consensus that the 1980 general elections

were rigged has been validated by different analysts. They articulate the same position. As Professor Kefa Otiso, a Ugandan, states in his book, *Culture and Customs of Uganda*:

"In December 1980, a general election monitored by a Commonwealth team saw Obote regain the presidency, even though his Uganda People's Congress (UPC) was accused of electoral fraud." – (Kefa M. Otiso, *Culture and Customs of Uganda*, Westport, Connecticut, USA: Greenwood Press, 2006, p. 18).

According to Edward Khiddu-Makubuya, a renowned Ugandan lawyer, in his work, "Violence and Conflict Resolution in Uganda," in *The Culture of Violence*:

"In December 1980, Uganda held its first general elections since independence. The campaigns leading up to the elections were partially characterized by violence and intimidation; some candidates were violently prevented from even processing or presenting their nomination papers.
A few shooting incidents were reported and, and one candidate was abducted and murdered shortly before the elections (Bwengye, 1985; commonwealth Secretariat, 1980).
In the end, the Uganda People's Congress (UPC) was declared the winner; it formed a new government headed by President Obote. The election was immediately denounced as a fraud by several influential groups within and outside Uganda." – (Edward Khiddu-Makubuya, "Violence and Conflict Resolution in Uganda," in Kumar Rupesinghe and Marcial C. Rubio, eds., *The Culture of Violence, Vol. 81*, Tokyo: United Nations University Press, 1994, p. 152).

The election also intensified rivalries between the

people of northern Uganda, especially the Langi and the Acholi who strongly supported Obote, and those of the southern regions; a division which historically has also been viewed as a competition between the Nilotic people of the north and the Bantus of the south.

Many Ugandans were also not satisfied with the results because they believed that the electoral process was manipulated by Tanzanians, even if by remote control, because they wanted Obote to return to power. And as Professor Devra C. Moehler of the University of Pennsylvania states in her book, *Distrusting Democrats: Outcomes of Participatory Constitution Making*:

"In 1980, Uganda held its postindependence general election. Four parties contested the election: the UPC, led by Obote, the DP, headed by Paul Ssemogerere; the Uganda Patriotic Movement, recently formed by Museveni; and the Conservative Party of Baganda tradionalists.

The UPC was declared the winner, but international observers and opposition candidates argued that gross malpractise had occurred (Kasozi 1999, 136 – 43).

The period that followed the contentious 1980 election is dubbed Obote II, and many observers consider it the most brutal time since independence (Human Rights Watch 1999, 34 – 35; Kasozi 1999, 145). Rebel groups became active throughout the country, and government troops responded with massive abuse and killing.

Museveni's Popular Resistance Army, which later became the National Resistance Army, was among the guerrilla movements that formed in opposition to the Obote government (Kasozi, 1999, 165). The movement was militarily most active in the central Buganda region known as the Luwero triangle.

Many of the Baganda who aided the NRM (National Resistance Movement) in their struggle did so in the hope that removing Obote would allow for the restoration of

their former kingdom and federal status (Mulondo 2001).
– (Devra C. Moehler, *Distrusting Democrats: Outcomes of Participatory Constitution Making*, Ann Arbor, Michigan, USA: The University of Michigan Press, 2008, p. 46).

When Obote became president for the second time on 17 December 1980, Uganda was in shambles. But there was also a lot optimism, considering what the country had gone through during eight years of terror and destruction under Amin. Obote also did achieve early success during the first years after he returned to power:

"Just like his predecessor, Idi Amin, President Obote's initial moments were accompanied by much hope and enthusiasm on the part of the population. Amin fatigue, as well as the obvious substandard performance exhibited by the successive interim governments, provided a positive political environment for the new government.

President Obote's immediate approach was to jump-start the economy and to re-establish relations with his neighbours. He made an immediate move to attract foreign investment, especially by encouraging and facilitating the return of Asians, his long time allies, whom Idi Amin had expelled in 1972. In addition, the president was able to obtain financial support from bilateral and multilateral funding organizations, such as the World Bank, IMF and (the) European Economic Community, which identified prospects for economic growth.

Evidently, the country's economy began to show positive signs – up to 5% growth by 1982 and 1983, leading to the first recorded balance of payments surplus in 1984 (Furley, 1987).

But the economic gains were eclipsed by reports of gross human rights violations. The army, which was President Obote's most formidable power base, used its military power and privilege to suppress any kind of opposition – often with massive brutality, resulting in killings and disappearances, as well as a colossal outflow of asylum seekers, reminiscent of Idi Amin's dictatorship." – (F.K. Byaruhanga, *Student Power in Africa's Higher Education: A Case of Makerere University*, op.cit., p. 11).

Obote did not even have the chance to do much because of the instability in the country. Therefore his successes and failures during his second presidency have to be measured against that background.

But his government was also at war with its own people. Suppression of dissent led not only to large-scale abuse of human rights; it also led to more instability across the country, providing fertile ground for rebellion against his rule.

Obote did not have the electoral mandate to rule. This democratic deficiency compromised his ability to lead the country and win acceptance from his fellow countrymen besides his supporters. As Professor Joshua B. Rubongoya, a Ugandan teaching in the United States, states in his book, *Regime Hegemony in Museveni's Uganda: Pax Musevenica*:

"Following the fall of Idi Amin in 1979, a series of leaders from Lule to Binaisa and, then, finally to Milton Obote tried their luck at rebuilding the state without much success. The main proposition is that at the root of the failure in state reconstruction was the continuing deficiency in democratic legitimacy....

Obote rose to power in 1980 by way of a botched election. This very fact, which was itself a consequence of failure to muster broad popular support, seems to have forecast the character of Obote's government between 1980 and 1984. The illegitimacy of the 1980 election and, therefore, of Obote's power was soon thereafter exposed by the emergence of a strong guerrilla opposition mounted by what would become the NRA/M (National Resistance

Amry/Movement).

Thus, not unlike his first term, Obote's second term presented unique challenges to democratic governance. In his analysis of the illegitimate government of Obote, Khadiagala argues that

> Obote had again to resort to segments within the military to subdue a growing opposition. As before, despotic power used without infrastructural power confirmed the vulnerability of state managers and, at most, emboldened opposition factions. (1995: 38).

Right from the start, Obote had to wrestle with an economy that had one leg in the grave and the other in intensive care. The state was hobbling along under the weight of the *magendo* economy and its accompanying moral and ethical malaise. Social cleavages between town and country, between Christians and Muslims, and between haves and have-nots left very limited room for national unity.

The chasm between northerners and southerners represented another political fault line.

All told, the political culture was too distorted to support a democratic civil society, but equally important was the fact that the policies of Obote II restricted the emergence of an effective civil society.

To add to this mix, the political parties of old were reintroduced to contest the 1980 elections, thus, creating new political and social fault lines.

There were several credible reports confirming claims of election fraud and rigging carried out with the express intention of ensuring victory for Obote's UPC party. Indeed, it was in response to the contested nature of the 1980 elections that Obote's Minister of Defense Yoweri Museveni abandoned the government to launch a rebel opposition that would lead to the ouster of Obote in 1986.

What, then, could any post-Amin government do, to restore the rule of law, democratic legitimacy, accountability, and economic productivity? Success in these three (sic) areas would at least restore the instrumentalist prerequisite of legitimacy, namely, state effectiveness." – (Joshua B. Rubongoya, *Regime Hegemony in Museveni's Uganda: Pax Musevenica*, New York: Palgrave Macmillan, 2007, p. 53).

It was therefore a combination of problems Obote faced during his second presidency. He inherited the post-Amin state that was in shambles. It was not his fault. It was Amin who destroyed the country during his eight-year reign of terror. But Obote also created his own problems for the country and exacerbated the situation when he went into office without full mandate from the electorate. He also alienated many people who could have joined him to rebuild the country when he resorted to draconian measures to achieve his goals by suppressing dissent. And as Professor Rubongoya goes on to state:

"First, with respect to the economy, Obote's 1981 budget speech announced the following policies in order to correct state-imposed economic distortions and to end the black market:

The shilling was allowed to float in order to wipe out arbitrary profits.

Administered profits were removed from all consumer goods except petrol, to permit prices of state-owned commodities to rise to their market value.

Prices paid to growers for export commodities were raised and border patrols were reinforced to reduce coffee smuggling and to encourage production of other export crops, and in 1982, a 'second window' for purchasing – by auction – foreign exchange for business purposes was opened, this was an effort to break the black market in currency that had survived the float.

These policies helped stem the intensity of coffee smuggling and the foreign exchange black market known locally as *kibanda*. However, state prices for cash crops remained fairly low relative to what farmers were paid by the *mafuta mingi*. Furthermore, the state apparatus was still unable to protect the peasant from the violence of the *mafuta mingi* that, as Kasfir argued, could still seize agricultural produce with impunity, thus, creating an opportunity for primitive accumulation outside and independent of the state (1983: 97). It is quite possible, also, that *mafuta mingi* funds ended up supporting UPC campaigns, thus, compromising the ability of the government to act as honest broker between state and society." – (Ibid., p. 54).

Whatever achievements Obote's government made in the economic realm were also compromised by corruption which was a major problem during his second presidency.

In an interview with Ugandan journalist Andrew Mwenda of the *The Monitor* in April 2005 in Lusaka, Zambia, where he lived after being offered asylum by President Kenneth Kaunda soon after he was overthrown, Dr. Obote maintained that he was not corrupt. He also said his ministers were not corrupt and that subsequent investigations even by Museveni, his nemesis, produced no reports which showed investigators had found or uncovered evidence of corruption.

But even if Obote himself and his cabinet members were not corrupt, which is questionable, it is hard to believe that his entire government was not corrupt.

There was corruption in his government during his second presidency, probably even more so than in the first. But many corrupt officials and state agents as well as UPC functionaries were not exposed or arrested because of the culture of secrecy to protect each other and during a time when opponents of the government were muzzled, suppression of dissent was institutionalised, and when the primary focus of the government was on fighting the rebels who were trying to overthrow Obote. As Rubongoya states:

"As Obote's second tenure wore on, the above-mentioned policy achievements were weakened by rampant corruption, mostly among agents of the state entrusted to realize financial commitments to the war against rebel insurgencies. By 1985, inflation was out of control, unemployment high, and foreign investment was declining. As the economy worsened and the Museveni-led rebel attacks intensified, Obote's attempts to restore the institutional logic of the state began to wane and so did the chances of reconstituting viable sources of legitimacy.....

Obote had the difficult task of winning popular support ...because of perceptions of electoral fraud....The bungled elections further weakened his claims to legitimacy and forced him to concentrate power in a few trusted supporters. Secondly, it became increasingly difficult to separate the UPC regime from the state. Yet, the post-Amin UPC party was a weakened party, in fact, a shadow of its old self. It was not only split along several political and ethnic factions, but it was also facing a stronger and resurgent Democratic Party (DP) and a highly politicized military with representatives in the Parliament.

UPC MPs were beholden to the members of the executive branch, specifically to President Obote personally. The president had control over the party, the executive branch, and a very politicized military. The UPC was too weak internally to perform the functions of mass mobilization, interest aggregation, and provider of viable policy alternatives. Under these circumstances state-society relations were so constrained as to block the emergence of a governance realm.

Values of trust, reciprocity, accountability, and authority were all linked to party loyalty or to personal relations with the president and other high-ranking party/government political elites. Limitations on political space precluded the expected activities of opposition parties, civil society, and particularly the media.

The peasantry once again exited the formal economy, resorting instead to smuggling, trading in local foodstuff, or simply subsistence agriculture. As the prospects for establishing a governance realm dwindled, the ensuing legitimacy deficit was only reinforced by the emergence of a fortified statist regime type and a neopatrimonial state.

Obote could not extricate himself from the forces that had been central to his political resurrection, namely, the Uganda National Liberation Front and its military wing, the Uganda National Liberation Army (UNLA). He used them in his futile attempts to restore law and order. Not only did influential elements in these bodies pave the way for Obote's political fortunes, bu they also threw their support behind the political parties, particularly the UPC. In this process, two crucial developments emerged: the militarization of politics on the one hand and the politicization of the military, on the other. The result of this syndrome was that interests peculiar to the military would be taken care of by military representatives, and military representation would also enable the army to participate in the decision-making processes in top civilian organs.

The military, therefore, became increasingly central not only in maintaining law and order, as had been the case in Obote's first government, but also in administration. The reinstitutionalization of the General Service Unit and other intelligence organs perfected the structure of coercion without which Obote could not maintain control. The military, together with the political elites, formed a strong alliance that used the state as a conduit for the delivery of patronage to select groups of clients. This form of patrimonial legitimacy sealed any hopes of a transition to democracy in Uganda.

Ironically, Obote allowed the ethnic factor – a policy

responsible for his downfall in his first term – to undermine the coherence of the military and its capacity to keep the peace and defend the nation. This is because he once again sought to purge the army of the Acholi elements while elevating his fellow Langis – a sign that even in the military, support for him was narrow and, in fact, tenuous. In the spirit of this policy, Obote's commanders disproportionately deployed the Acholis to the frontline to face a strengthened guerrilla force in the name of the National Resistance Army (NRA).

So, while Obote relied on the army to maintain order by rounding up, torturing, detaining, and terrorizing suspected citizens in several urban centers, his policy of ethnic cleansing within the military seemed to undermine the very institution he needed to gain legitimacy, if not control. It was, indeed, the victims of this ethnic cleansing, the Acholi army officers, who led a coup that toppled Obote for the second time." – (Ibid., pp. 54 – 55).

Obote made a fatal mistake not only by alienating the Acholi in the army who eventually overthrew him; he failed or was unwilling to reach out to other groups who did not support him or vote for him in the 1980 general elections, especially when he knew that he did not have the mandate of a substantial segment of the population to rule. There was widespread belief in Uganda and among other observers and analysts that he did not have majority support to lead the country.

He could have formed an inclusive government which reflected a broad consensus across the spectrum not only to sustain himself in power but also as a concession to his opponents and as a compromise to appease the people whose fundamental democratic rights were violated when the 1980 elections were rigged by his supporters led by Paulo Muwanga.

And just for the sake of peace and stability, he should have agreed to hold another election, to avoid civil conflict, especially for a country that was in such political turmoil after eight years of terror under Amin. It had barely emerged from its dark past.

If Obote knew or really believed that he won the first election, he also should have believed he was going to win the second one. He should have had nothing to fear to legitimise his victory for the second time by holding another election, as demanded by his opponents, just to save his country, instead of allowing the situation to degenerate into chaos and civil war.

The legitimacy of the state under Obote was further eroded and compromised as time went on and by the continued use of coercive tactics including violence to achieve his goals.

The erosion of this legitimacy was compounded by the effects of the war against the rebels whose ability to destabilise the country demonstrated that Obote's government was not in full control of the situation.

But in spite of all those problems, there were some achievements during Obote's second presidency especially in the economic arena although they were not longterm. They were also compromised by corruption.

Obote implemented austerity measures demanded by the IMF to rejuvenate the economy under structural adjustment programmes (SAPs) as a condition for aid. He had undergone an ideological conversion and renounced his past policies which he implemented during his first presidency to achieve socialist transformation of his country. Those polices were enunciated in *The Common Man's Charter* in 1969. In an interview with Andrew Mwenda of the Ugandan newspaper, *The Monitor*, in April 2005, Obote conceded that his first government made a mistake when it pursued socialism and nationalisation. As he put it:

"I also regret the move to the left. With hindsight, I think we should not have attempted socialist or nationalisation policies." – (Obote, in an interview with Andrew Mwenda, *The Monitor*, April 2005).

After Uganda adopted free-market policies under Obote, the economy improved although the people also suffered because benefits did not trickle down to the grassroots as as the neoliberal advocates of economic liberalisation claimed they would.

Still, there were some economic gains in a number of areas during Obote's second tenure, even for some people on the lowest rung of the economic ladder, just as there were some during his first in the sixties when he achieved even more economic success. But they were negated by the cost of the war against the insurgents during his second term and could not be sustained in a chronic state of uncertainty and instability as the conflict with the insurgents went on.

Adoption of IMF-mandated policies also won Obote some credibility from donor nations as a responsible leader who also had the experience to rebuild his country. Also, Obote's assumption of power during his second presidency coincided with the recommendation of structural adjustment programmes by the IMF to Third World countries as a solution to their economic plight. As Dr. Frederick Golooba-Mutebi, a senior research fellow at the Institute of Social Research, Makerere University, Kampala, Uganda, states in his work, "Economic Liberalization and Politics in Uganda," in *Economic Liberalization and Political Violence: Utopia or Dystopia?*:

"The second Obote administration – Obote II – inherited a virtually collapsed economy, a political environment that was already poisoned by accusations of electoral rigging, and a realistic threat of renewed civil war by losers unwilling to accept the election results. Rather than devote its energies and resources to repairing

160

the country's torn political fabric and rebuilding the economy, the new regime found itself caught up in an insurgency that further poisoned the political environment and polarized the country's political elites.

The new administration made an effort to implement, with the support of the World Bank and the IMF, economic reforms and even scored some successes. However, their sustainability was undermined by the civil war and the damage it inflicted on the productive sectors and, consequently, the country's revenue-earning capacity.

The accession to power by the Obote II government coincided with the beginning of pressure by Bretton Woods institutions on African governments for economic reform. In Uganda it was therefore the Obote II government which was the first to implement the IMF's earliest economic restructuring programs in Africa....

(But) the 1980 elections which were held after nearly a decade of dictatorship, were not the outcome of the pressure donors were exerting on African governments to adopt multi-party politics alongside economic liberalization. Instead, they were the outcome of acrimonious debate among local political elites about the form of government best suited to the country's circumstances following years of despotism and political turmoil.

Rather than usher in a period of peace and stability as would have been expected by war-wary Ugandans and foreign observers, the elections sparked a five-year civil war responsible for the limited success of the IMF-backed economic reform program and which eventually led to the collapse of Obote's second administration." – (Frederick Golooba-Mutebi, "Economic Liberalization and Politics in Uganda," in Francisco Gutiérrez, Gerd Schönwälder , eds., *Economic Liberalization and Political Violence: Utopia or Dystopia?*, New York: Pluto Press, 2010, pp. 94 – 95).

Had the 1980 elections been free and fair, the

economic recovery programme would probably have been implemented on long-term basis regardless of who was in power, even if it was Obote himself who was reviled so much by his opponents for rigging the electoral contest, had he won fairly. And there probably would have been no civil war to wreak havoc across the country, at least not on the scale it did during Obote's second tenure.

Golooba-Mutebi goes on to state:

"By 1980, the economic devastation wrought by the Amin regime rendered efforts at economic reconstruction an absolute necessity. As with other countries undergoing economic reform, in Uganda the central objective was to reduce the need for external financial support.

In 1981, under the guidance of the IMF, the government embarked on programs of economic stabilization. In what has been characterized as 'the first experiments in structural adjustment programs for Third World countries,' the donor community insisted on 'liberalizing (or floating) the Uganda shilling and a considerable reduction in state expenditure as the price of financial assistance' (Hansen and Twaddle, 1998, p. 2). They sought to 'halt the deterioration of the economy, revive production, restore confidence in the Uganda shilling, eliminate price distortions, improve fiscal and monetary discipline, and lay a firm foundation for sustained recovery' (Ochieng, 1991, p. 44).

The economy responded positively, leading to the transformation of GDP growth rates from negatives to positives during 1981 – 83. In 1982 and 1983, all the sectors experienced positive growth. Only electricity (1982) and agricultural primary processing (1983) did not.

However, the economy had negative growth rates during 1983 and 1984. Although in agriculture the area planted and production of all food crops increased between 1980 and 1983, both declined between 1983 and 1985. While for cash crops there was no change in the area planted, production increased between 1980 and 1983, only to decline and register negative growth rates from 1984.

The industrial sector also showed signs of revival in capacity utilization, but only temporarily. Only soft drink and cigarette production maintained the revival momentum and were operating at 40 percent and 75 percent capacity respectively by 1985, while other industries operated at less than 20 percent capacity utilization (Ochieng, 1991, p. 46)." – (Ibid., pp. 95 – 96).

Therefore, in spite of the problems the country faced, there is evidence to show that it was able to achieve economic growth in some sectors even if for only a short period. But economic recovery was also a daunting task because of the war and corruption; a point underscored by Golooba-Mutebi:

"Under Obote, the adjustment program had therefore managed to attain only short-term success in reviving the economy.

The major cause of the government's failure to sustain its reform success was the damage inflicted by the civil war on the productive sectors and its drain on the government's meager resources.

There were, however, other factors not related to the war. According to Hansen and Twaddle (1998, p. 2), the reforms begot a great deal of corruption among ministers and officials seeking to benefit from the black market sale of foreign currency, which discredited Obote's government and increased support for the insurgents.

In July 1985, the embattled Obote government fell to a military coup led by the army commander, General Tito Olara Okello. Behind the coup were ethnic divisions that had severely factionalized the military, and its inability to contain the insurgents.

The putsch ushered in a short-lived government which,

following failure to negotiate peace with the insurgents, was toppled in 1986 by the Museveni-led National Resistance Movement (NRM), the largest and best-organized of the several armed group that had declared war on the Obote II regime following the 1980 elections.

The failure by the Obote government to sustain the initial successes of its economic reform efforts and to carry out a successful economic reconstruction program was the outcome of the civil war into which it was plunged after the elections.

The civil war itself was the consequence of two related phenomena. First was the failure by the country's political elites to reach a consensus about how to move the country forward following the collapse of the Amin regime. Second was the systematic and arrogant manipulation of the pre-election political process and the elections themselves by Obote's allies in the transitional Military Commission government. Also, after the war broke out, the government steadfastly refused to engage the insurgents in talks to try and resolve their differences peacefully, and instead sought to defeat them militarily.

Further, as the civil war grew in intensity, the Obote government and its allies took to harassing and eliminating members and supporters of opposition parties – activities that served only to isolate it from major sections of the general public." – (Ibid., pp. 96 – 97).

Another major problem during Obote's second tenure was widespread lack of discipline which led to chaos and even amounted to anarchy in some areas, facilitated by the security forces themselves which had no respect for the law. Security agents constituted terror squads. Soldiers fighting insurgents brutalized civilians with impunity and even in areas where there was no fighting.

There was no-one to discipline them. They were above the law. The government had lost control over its own forces of law and order.

All that had unintended consequences. The security forces and the military, hence the government itself, became one of the best recruiting agents for the insurgents. State-sponsored terror became a blessing for the rebels. It fuelled the rebellion:

"Furthermore, the government failed to impose discipline on and create cohesion within the military and the security agencies. Widespread indiscipline culminated in the military and security agencies committing atrocities against civilian populations, especially in areas where the insurgents were active, thereby forcing many civilians to join the armed rebellion.

Conflicts within the military, especially between the dominant Acholi and Langi factions, undermined its effectiveness as a fighting force, leading to a failure to defeat the insurgents and eventually to the Acholi-led coup d'état of 1985.

Such were the demands on the government's energies, resources, and organizational capacities that made failure in the twin arenas of economic reform and post-war reconstruction inevitable. Indeed, it was in the midst of trying to respond to the exigencies of the civil war and its effects, against the advice of the IMF, that the latter withdrew its support.

It is clear, therefore, that the main factor behind the failure of reform under the Obote II regime was political instability and its underlying sources: elite polarization and the consequent zero-sum politics underlain by the desire on the part of competing political factions, once they acquired power, to monopolize it and hold on to it for as long as possible." – (Ibid., p. 97).

The failure of Obote's second presidency was a direct result of the rigged 1980 general elections. His economic recovery programme was not fully implemented because of the devastating impact of the civil war, itself a product of the rigged elections.

Obote's opponents went to war against him because of the rigged elections.

And he could not govern effectively because he did not have the electoral mandate to lead the country except from his supporters – who were outnumbered by his opponents who did not have the opportunity to express their wish because the 1980 elections were rigged in his favour. Had the elections not been rigged, the country would not have been plunged into civil war. And the economic recovery would probably have been successful.

In less than three months after Obote assumed power for the second time, he faced rebellion. Museveni, one of the leading political figures in the country, announced in February 1981 that he and his supporters had formed the National Resistance Army to fight Obote. There was a lot of resentment against the government which suppressed the opposition and because of the unfair elections which had taken place in December, rigged by Paulo Muwanga who was now serving as vice president and minister of defence under Obote.

Museveni said Obote's opponents were going to overthrow the government by launching a popular rebellion, drawing support from ordinary people, especially peasants who constituted the bulk of the population. That was the beginning of what came to be known as the Bush War. It was, up to that time, the most successful grassroots insurgency against an established government in post-colonial Africa.

Museveni's group was the best-organised. There were others which tried to undermine Obote's government. But they were disrupted and defeated by the security forces including the army.

Museveni mobilised forces in the former kingdoms of Buganda, Bunyoro, Toro and Ankole where Obote was not very popular because he had abolished the kingdoms; his government waged a bitter campaign against his opponents in those areas; and he was a northerner and a Nilotic who was accused of favouring his fellow northerners against southern Bantus.

Most of Museveni's support during the campaign against Obote came from the rural areas. But his operational stronghold was in the central part of the former Buganda kingdom not far from the capital Kampala.

And there were enough complaints against the government to justify a sustained campaign of popular opposition. Although Museveni came from Ankole in the southwestern part of the country, he also had enough support in the other western kingdoms – Bunyoro and Toro – and in Buganda in the central part of the country – to be able to wage a prolonged military campaign which eventually toppled Obote. And as Moehler states:

"Museveni claims that he 'went to the bush' to wage guerrilla war in response to the rigged election, government corruption, political manipulation of sectarian interests, and gross human rights abuses (Human Rights Watch 1994, 34; Mukholi 1995, 24; Museveni 1997, 123).

The NRM's political philosophy was enshrined in the 'Ten-Point Programme,' the first point of which was the restoration of democracy. This democratic rhetoric was accompanied by generally democratic behavior during the insurgency (Kasfir, 2005).

Museveni maintained strict control over the use of violence by his soldiers against civilians. In areas 'liberated' by the NRM, the Resistance Council (RC) system of elected local officials was established (Kasfir 2005; Okoth 1996, 58). – (D.C. Moehler, *Distrusting Democrats: Outcomes of Participatory Constitution Making,* op.cit., p. 46.)

Obote spent four years to try to crush his opponents. The toughest was Museveni's National Resistance Movement. In an attempt to do so, the army wreaked havoc in many parts of the country, especially in central Buganda which came to be known as the Luweero Triangle during the war and which is where Museveni launched his guerrilla campaign.

Launched in 1983 and known as Operation Bonanza, the government military offensive against the rebels earned Obote even more enemies.

It also drove many civilians into the rebel camp. They joined the insurgency or supported the rebels by various means.

The military campaign also divided the country even further, between north and south, because most of the government soldiers waging the war against the insurgents and brutalising civilians were northerners, Langis and Acholis, Obote's traditional supporters and fellow northerners. The perception among the victims, most of whom were southerners especially the Baganda in the former Buganda kingdom, was that this was a war between the north and the south; it was also a war between the Nilotic tribes of northern Uganda and the Bantu tribes in the south.

At least 100,000 people died in the conflict. Some sources give higher figures, as high as 500,000, equal to or more than the number of victims who perished under Amin. Others say more people were killed under Obote. Estimates of those who were killed under Amin range from 300,000 to 800,000.

Even Obote himself conceded that he lost control over his army which caused a lot of misery and destruction including many deaths during the war against the rebels, especially in the Luweero Triangle in the central part of the former Buganda kingdom. But he blamed Museveni and his rebels for most of the deaths, implying those caused by his army was mere collateral damage, a byproduct of the justified military campaign against the insurgents.

It is difficult to imagine how Museveni and his

insurgents would have deliberately killed so many people in the Luweero Triangle, only to alienate their supporters in an area where he launched the rebellion and among the people on whom he still depended so much to carry on his campaign against Obote.

It is much easier to see how the national army, composed mostly of northerners, the Acholi and the Langi, would have gone on the rampage killing the Baganda in the Luweero Triangle since they had no love for southerners and saw them as their enemies simply because they were not fellow northerners.

It is also hard to believe that Obote had many supporters among the Baganda in the kingdom he abolished in the sixties, let alone in the Luweero Triangle which was the operational base of the military campaign against him only a few miles north of the national capital Kampala.

In an interview with Ugandan journalist Andrew Mwenda in Lusaka, Zambia, where he and his wife lived in exile, Obote admitted that failure to control his army was his biggest mistake during his second presidency. As he put it:

"I regret that my second administration was unable to stop the killings and massacres of innocent civilians in Luweero by Museveni and his insurgent army." – (Obote, in an interview with Andrew Mwenda, "Liberation from Colonialism Was My Greatest Contribution," *The Monitor*, Kampala, Uganda, 16 April 2005).

The conflict also assumed ethnic and regional dimensions. Many Langis and Acholis – Obote's traditional supporters – who had joined the Uganda National Liberation Army to overthrow Amin went on to attack the people of the southern tribes, just as Amin did, who were opposed to Obote. Many of them were not even in the army. But they still had weapons and military uniforms they wore during the war against Amin. And there were those who remained in the army which toppled Amin and which became the national army known as the Uganda National Liberation Army (UNLA).

The destruction they unleashed was not limited to the southern part of the country. They also fanned out into the northwest, Amin's home region, exacting retribution for the atrocities committed against them by Kakwas, Lugbaras and other northwesterners during Amin's eight years of terror.

They did not identify with southerners who were Bantu. They also did not identify with the people of the northwest in the West Nile District, although they were fellow northerners and fellow Nilotics, because of what the kinsman of those northwesterners, Idi Amin, did to them. They also came from a different part of northern Uganda. The Langi and the Acholi homeland is in the central north.

After Amin seized power, he exterminated the Acholi and the Langi in the army and even sent killer squads to the north to hunt down Acholi and Langi soldiers who had left the army and fled there for security. Those who were found hiding among their tribal kinsmen were killed by Amin's soldiers – who were mostly Kakwa, Lugbra and Nubian – together with their families and others. The Acholi and the Langi never forgot that. It was now time for vengeance. And the northwest became another killing field.

As Museveni's rebellion intensified, the government decided in 1983 to remove hundreds of thousands of people in the Luweero Triangle in order to deprive the rebels of an operational base and civilian support. It was a massive relocation involving about 750,000 people and resulted in massive violations of human rights and countless deaths.

The people were forcibly relocated in internment camps, similar to what happened to the Hutu in Rwanda and Burundi during the civil wars in those countries under Tutsi-dominated armies, and led to many abuses without any intervention by the government to stop the violations including rape and looting. Any civilians who lived outside the camps were automatically considered to be rebels or rebel sympathisers, targeted for elimination.

Amidst all this, Obote still tried to rebuild the economy and even got foreign aid to do so. His government also worked with the International Monetary Fund and followed austerity measures recommended by the IMF. He was also concerned about his country's international image and tried to curb excesses unlike Amin who had no use for diplomacy or any respect for international law.

Obote was one of the leading African statesmen and had won international respect as one of the founding fathers of modern Africa and as a staunch supporter of the liberation movements in southern Africa together with leaders such as Kwame Nkrumah, Julius Nyerere and Kenneth Kaunda all of whom were also his friends. He was also a strong advocate of African unity and greatly admired fellow Pan-Africanists such as Nkrumah, Nyerere, Kaunda and Ahmed Sekou Toure. He stood tall and as an equal among them as an embodiment of Pan-Africanism.

He also had experience running a country which he acquired during his first presidency. Many donors felt, because of all that, he would be able to restore stability and rebuild the economy. But he failed on both counts.

The rebellion led by Museveni continued to gain momentum. The Ugandan national army could not neutralise the insurgents and it became notorious for human rights abuses. Torture and murder became common. It is estimated that between 1981 and 1985 when Obote was ousted, about 300,000 Ugandans lost their lives, according to Amnesty International.

The CIA said the death toll was more than 100,000, implying it did not reach let alone exceed 300,000.

171

The highest death toll was in the Luweero Triangle, the site of the bloodiest conflicts between the army and the rebels.

The Red Cross estimated that in the Luweero Triangle alone, hundreds of thousands were killed. According to Human Rights/Watch Africa in its work, *The Scars of Death: Children Abducted by the Lord's Resistance Army in Uganda*:

"According to Kasozi and Omara-Otunno, Obote's return to power also restored the Acholi and Langi dominance within Uganda's military, and heralded the beginning of another period of widespread violence. Yoweri Museveni's guerrilla National Resistance Army – dominated by southerners and westerners – sought to topple Obote by force, and the International Committee of the Red Cross ultimately estimated that fighting in Uganda's Luwero triangle region left several hundred thousand dead. The bulk of the dead were civilians." – (Human Rights Watch/Africa, *The Scars of Death: Children Abducted by the Lord's Resistance Army in Uganda*, New York, Washington, London, Brussels: Human Rights Watch, September 1997, p. 63).

Obote's government sought assistance from North Korea which sent military advisers to help the army fight the insurgents in what was supposed to be the final offensive against the rebels. The war was already draining the nation's resources, making economic recovery impossible. It was time to take decisive military action to end the conflict and start rebuilding the country. Obote's government was determined to win the war at any cost. Victory became its priority to the exclusion of everything else.

But such victory against the National Resistance Army (NRA) proved to be impossible because of its stamina, organisational skills and ability to wage a sustained guerrilla campaign. As Robert Barlas states in his book, *Uganda: Cultures of the World*:

"In the government that succeeded Idi Amin, Museveni served briefly as Minister of Defence. After Obote rigged the general election in 1980, Museveni opposed the tyranny of the Obote regime.

During the struggle, Museveni's troops achieved a very high level of leadership and managerial skills, as well as clear political and military policies. They also established excellent working relations with the civilian population in areas where they operated.

After a five-year guerrilla war against the regimes of Obote and his successor Tito Okello, Museveni became president of Uganda on January 26, 1986. He formed a broad-based government in which formerly hostile factions were brought under the unifying influence of the National Resistance Movement (NRM).

His reading of liberal Western thinkers such as American economist John Kenneth Galbraith shaped his intellectual and political outlook." – (Robert Barlas, *Uganda: Cultures of the World*, Times Books International, 2002, p. 35).

The guerrilla fighters frustrated the army which was soon beset by combat fatigue. It also suffered another major blow when the army chief of staff, Major-General Oyite Ojok, died in a helicopter crash on 2 December 1983. He was 43.

Ojok was a highly respected soldier with great combat skills and even won admiration from his enemies as a great soldier.

When he was army chief of staff, he planned and carried out effective military campaigns against the National Resistance Movement (NRM), and the Uganda Freedom Movement (UFM), led by Dr. Andrew Kayiira, which also had guerrilla fighters trying to overthrow the government. The UFM was based in the capital Kampala, unlike the NRM which operated from the rural areas of the Luweero Triangle.

Major-General Ojok distinguished himself as a great strategist and successfully neutralised the guerrillas in a number of battles. But the campaigns by the army were so brutal that civilian populations suffered immensely. In addition to those who were killed in the Luweero Triangle, many people in Kampala also became victims of violence at the hands of soldiers. They were rounded up and taken to army barracks where they were tortured and killed.

The fighting in Kampala intensified when the Uganda Freedom Movement (UFM), waging urban guerrilla warfare, attacked government buildings and other institutions which had to do with the government. The army fought back and easily neutralised the rebels by cordoning off areas where they launched search-and-destroy missions to hunt down the rebels. Civilians in those areas were tortured until they were forced to tell the soldiers where the rebels were hiding. Within two years, the UFM was defeated, earning Ojok credit for leading a successful military campaign against the guerrillas.

It was an entirely different story fighting the NRM rebels. They used typical guerrilla tactics, operating from the bush, and ambushing army patrols and convoys, then melting into the general population. They used hit-and-run tactics effectively.

After defeating the UFM rebels, Ojok turned his attention to the NRM rebels who proved to be much tougher.

He did achieve some success and would have consolidated his gains as time went on had he not suddenly died in a helicopter accident. His death was such a blow to the army, which was already demoralised, that it began to fall apart from sustained attacks by the NRM rebels since it no longer had a leader of his calibre to carry on a successful military campaign against the insurgents.

There was much speculation about Ojok's death. Some sources, including Obote's government, said it was just an accident. Others said it was shot down by NRA fighters; it probably was. As Professor A.B. K. Kasozi, states in his book, *The Social Origins of Violence in Uganda 1964 - 1985*:

"His (Ojok's) success in storming the UMF camps gave him the hope that the NRA would be as easy to crack. In June 1982 Oyite Ojok commanded the five-battalion offensive termed 'Operation Bonanza' against the NRA, but the Resistance Army was victorious.

UNLA soldiers vented their wrath on civilians, whose skulls still litter the Luwero Triangle. Further offensives against the NRA between 1983 and 1984 proved equally futile as the Resistance Army grew from strength to strength.

Having built a fighting force that could engage Obote's army effectively, the NRA turned from guerrilla to conventional warfare and successfully attacked Masindi, Hoima, Gombe, and other areas formerly not considered part of the fighting zone.

Obote's decline in the period 1983 – 84 was partly brought about by a change in international attitude towards his regime. As evidence of his brutality leaked to the outside world, he began to lose credibility. His stay in power was financed, in large measure, by foreign sources. When these backers began to shuffle their feet, his problems increased. The Canadian and Australian members of the Commonwealth Military Team were withdrawn in this period.

There was an erroneous assumption that Obote's problem was the lack of a well-trained army, so trainers were sent in to help him. Their trainees were, however, no match for the NRA.

Outsiders did not want to recognize that Uganda's problem was mainly political; that unless the political problem was resolved nothing could be accomplished.

The NRA sent videos overseas exposing the atrocities of the UNLA and the Obote regime against civilians. The IMF and World Bank began to reassess their involvement in Obote's Uganda. Although he had done almost everything they had asked him to do, Obote's misrule frustrated their hopes that Uganda would become a 'model' of economic structural adjustment.

Decreasing financial resources and intensification of armed struggle led to thousands of casualties in Obote's camp, among whom was Oyite Ojok, the chief of staff, whose helicopter was shot down by the NRA – though the government claimed it was an accident. Soldiers began to resist having to face the NRA 'gorillas,' as they called them; in 1983 many soldiers mutinied rather than fight.

As usual in Uganda, sectarian cleavages began to emerge. The Acholi complained that their deaths were disproportionately high and that only Langis were being promoted. They were confirmed in their belief when Obote, bypassing senior officers, chose a Langi, Smith Opon Acak, as his new chief of staff. The cabinet was divided." – (A.B. K. Kasozi, *The Social Origins of Violence in Uganda 1964 - 1985*, Montreal, Canada: McGill-Queen's University Press, 1994, p. 172).

As the fighting went on, the army began to fracture along ethnic and regional lines. The national army under Obote was still dominated by the Acholi and the Langi as much as it was during his first presidency and even during the colonial era when the British recruited northerners into the army in disproportionately high numbers. But it now began to fall apart.

After Ojok died, Tito Okello became the head of the army. Like Obote, Ojok was a Langi; Okello, an Acholi. The conflict in the army pitted the Langi against the Acholi. Most of the foot soldiers were Acholi. They suffered the highest casualties during the war against the rebels and wanted to end the fighting by negotiating with the insurgents. In remarkable contrast, elite troops and most of the army officers who were very close to President Obote were his fellow tribesmen, the Langi. They did not want to negotiate with the rebels. The split between the two northern groups in the army became final when Ojok died and Okello took over as the army chief of staff.

But the rivalry between the Langi and Acholi was not a surprise. Although the two groups were allies and worked together as fellow northerners since colonial times, they did not constitute a monolithic whole. They had their own differences and interests as distinct and separate ethnic groups even though they had a common identity as Nilotics and as northerners who were different from southern Bantus.

The conflict between the two northern tribes and former allies was another major blow to Obote and his government. It provided impetus to the insurgents who now sensed victory.

Obote himself further alienated the Acholi when another Langi, Smith Apon-Achak (Opon-Acak), a junior army officer, was chosen to be the new chief of staff after Ojok died, instead of an Acholi.

Obote said he did not appoint Apon-Achak to be the army chief of staff; he said he did not even know him. He said it was the military commission which chose Apon-Acak to be the new chief of staff after Ojok was killed in a helicopter crash which Obote blamed on Museveni. He said he believed it was Museveni's fighters who shot down the helicopter in Luweero.

Yet there was a perception that it was Obote himself who, as president, was responsible for Apon-Achak's promotion to be the new army chief of staff. Or, at the very least, he should have vetoed the decision in order to refute claims that Apon-Achak got the position because he was a fellow tribesman, especially after the death of Ojok who also was a Langi and whom Apon-Achak replaced.

177

As Obote stated in an interview with Andrew Mwenda:

"Sometime in 1983, I was in India on a state visit and Paulo Muwanga rang me to say he was giving me sad news.

He said, 'We have lost Oyite Ojok in Luweero, it is a helicopter crash.' Then he explained the details. I stopped him.

I said, 'Paul, stop there, go back to the beginning.' So he started again from the beginning. He explained, I understood.

Then he said, 'I am sending you a cable,' which he did. That same day I informed Indira Ghandi, the prime minister of India and a close personal friend and political ally that we could not continue with the state visit and she graciously accepted the state visit to stop and we returned to Uganda the same day.

I still think it was Museveni's guns that shot the aircraft, but other people think it was an accident. Even in government there were two views; there were people who thought it was Museveni's guns, there were people who thought it was an accident. Peter Otai knows the details better than me.

Then the Ministry of Defence did not immediately produce a replacement. I was not running the Ministry of Defence; the suggestions should have come from the Ministry of Defence for a replacement.

I used to write to them asking them to propose a name. Paulo Muwanga used to reply only informally, 'You know I have only two names and I can not propose one.'

There was only Smith Opon and Bazillio Okello both of whom were brigadiers. Muwanga used to say that he could not propose Bazillio Okello because he had been promoted above his level of education and training and Smith Opon was good on paper qualifications but weak in administration and command.

Later, after one and a half years, the two names were

brought to the Defence Council, which I chaired, and included Otai, Samwiri Mugwisa, Tito Okello and Muwanga. In the middle of the vetting of the candidates, Muwanga and Okello asked to be excused to go out and consult.

They returned to the meeting and proposed that we drop Bazillio Okello and consider only Smith Opon Acak which we all accepted.

Some people then began to claim that I appointed Acak because he was a fellow Langi.

My only contribution to his appointment was ceremonial i.e. that I chaired the Defence Council, and that it is the commander in chief who was the appointing authority.

I personally did not know Acak. At least I knew Oyite Ojok and he was a personal friend. I did not appoint Oyite Ojok as army chief of staff. I found him in that job just like I found Tito Okello army commander.

Tito Okello was an ignorant person, he should not have remained army commander. I accept that to have been a mistake, actually a fatal one, we made." – (Obote, in an interview with Andrew Mwenda, "Museveni is Responsible for Most of the Killings in Luweero," *The Monitor*, 15 April 2005, Kampala, Uganda. See full interview in appendix II: Obote Speaks).

Many Acholi army officers expected Bazilio Olara-Okello to be the new chief of staff. He was a senior army officer who was also one of the commanders of the Uganda National Liberation Army (NLA) which together with the Tanzania People's Defence Forces (TPDF) ousted Amin. Instead, it was alleged that Obote chose a fellow tribesman to lead the army.

Whoever made the decision to appoint Acak (Achak) as the new chief of staff, it was a choice which helped pave the way for Obote's ouster by Acholi army officers and soldiers about two years later on 27 July 1985.

Obote was already beset by accusations that he rigged the 1980 elections and had even lost some cabinet members who decided to join the opposition demanding new elections. As Jacob J. Akol states in his book, *Burden of Nationality: Memoirs of an African Aid Worker/Journalist 1970s – 1990s*:

"Accusations that Obote had rigged the 1980 elections persisted. Some of his own ministers deserted and joined the opposition to demand fresh and fair elections. Obote took offence and declared war on any opposition; he began to rely more and more on the military personnel who had toppled Amin in 1979 and paved the way for his return to power.

But the military itself was now more divided than ever and was riddled with corruption and tribal rivalry between the Langi, his tribe, and the Acholi. Obote's own reversion to tribalism became apparent when, in August 1984, he tactlessly insisted on appointing his fellow tribesman Lt. Col. – later Brig. – Smith Opon Acak as his chief of Staff while more senior officers from the Acholi tribe were overlooked." – (Jacob J. Akol, *Burden of Nationality: Memoirs of an African Aidworker/Journalist 1970s – 1990s*, Nairobi, Kenya: Paulines Publications Africa, 2006, p. 249).

The military coup against Obote was led by General Tito Okello and Brigadier Olara-Okello. The two Okellos were not related but shared a common Acholi name.

Olara-Okello commanded a brigade composed mostly of Acholi soldiers which executed the coup. It was also said that, not long before the coup, Obote gave orders to have Olara-Okello arrested by the Special Force Units which were dominated by Langis.

After overthrowing the government, Olara-Okello served for only a few days as chairman of the powerful military council, hence as Uganda's head of state. He was replaced by General Tito Okello, a fellow Acholi, who became president. Olara-Okello was promoted and became a lieutenant-general and head of the army.

The split between the Langi and the Acholi in the army could have been avoided if Obote did not favour his fellow tribesmen at the expense of the Acholi. The Acholi also complained that they did not even get the rewards they were entitled to for serving in the army and for fighting the rebels. The split also made it impossible for the army to wage an effective military campaign against the rebels of the National Resistance Army (NRA).

It was a rivalry which not only facilitated Obote's downfall but also Museveni's victory and rise to power. As Professor Byaruhanga states:

"One of President Obote's major challenges was the multiple rebel forces, most portentous of which was the National Resistance Movement led by Yoweri Museveni. This aura of uncertainty was further exacerbated by the growing rift between Obote's trusted factions in the army – the Langi, his own tribe, and the Acholis, their neighbour.

The Acholis accused the president of sectarianism – favouring his own tribe (the Langi) by awarding them with frequent promotions, and intentionally putting Acholis and other tribes in harm's way during the incessant combat engagements with the rebels.

It was against this background of power struggle within the army, that President Obote was overthrown, July 27 1985 by Acholi army officers led by Tito Okello, who became President.

But the Okello military government lasted only a few months, a period that was characterized by violence and political uncertainty. Meanwhile, as the Nairobi-based peace negotiations with Yoweri Museveni's National Resistance Movement failed to reach fruition, Museveni and his National Resistance Army (NRA) overran the capital of Kampala and took over power January 25, 1986.

Yoweri Museveni then became president and has been at the helm of power to date." – (F.K. Byaruhanga, *Power in Africa's Higher Education*, op.cit., pp. 11 – 12).

There has also been an undercurrent of suspicion between the Acholi and the Langi for tribal reasons since colonial times, although they have been allies through the years and have always been collectively identified as "northerners" in contrast with southerners. The suspicion and even tensions between them have also been exacerbated by the disparity in the number of soldiers from the two groups. The Acholi have always outnumbered the Langi and other groups in the army. There was a time when an entire half of the army was Acholi.

It was during Obote's leadership when the Langi made quantum leaps in terms of promotion and recruitment into the army, although they were already there in substantial numbers since colonial times, surpassing members of other tribes but not the Acholi. It was also during his presidency that tensions and rivalries between the two northern tribes degenerated into violence and destroyed the bonds which existed between them as close allies against southerners because the Langi were favoured by Obote. Without unity between the two in the army, it was impossible for Obote to survive in office. As Professor Moehler states:

"Obote's reliance on the military to maintain power eventually led to his downfall. As rebel activity against the government intensified, ethnic cleavages deepened between the Langi and the Acholi, two ethnic groups from the north that dominated the military.

In July 1985, Obote, a Langi, was once again removed from power in a military coup, this time led by Brigadier Bazilio Okello and General Tito Okello, two Acholi officers (Kasozi 1999, 171 – 74). Museveni's NRM made great progress in its guerrilla war and continued to fight the Okello government until the NRM captured Kampala and the Ugandan government on January 26, 1986 (Human Rights Watch 1999, 35 – 36; Mukholi 1995, 24)." – (D.C. Moehler, *Distrusting Democrats: Outcomes of Participatory Constitution Making*, op. cit., pp. 46 – 47).

Obote's second presidency was dominated by tensions, instability, and by civil war almost from the beginning. The first priority was to win the war and bring peace without which nothing else could be done, especially to rebuild the country after years of destruction by Idi Amin.

But Obote himself ruled that out when he excluded his opponents from meaningful participation in the political process when he had the election rigged in his favour. The result was war which eventually drove him out of office.

He may also have underestimated Museveni who eventually emerged as the winner. Besides all the resentment and plots against him by Acholi soldiers, Museveni was the person to watch.

Since his student days at the University of Dar es Salaam in Tanzania, he had shown great interest in revolutionary changes and even worked with FRELIMO guerrillas in Mozambique when they were fighting against the Portuguese colonial rulers.

He also fought against Idi Amin and was one of the prominent leaders in the anti-Amin coalition which was formed in Tanzania. As Akol states:

"Museveni was still studying (at the University of Dar es Salaam in Tanzania) when Obote was overthrown by Amin in 1971. He remained in exile in Tanzania till 1979, when he returned to Uganda as a leading member of the Uganda National Liberation Front (UNLF), which had kicked out Amin.

He later formed the Uganda Patriotic Movement (UPM) to fight the 1980 elections. His party won only one seat in the elections, which, supposedly democratic, brought Obote back to power. He was so upset by his defeat and so disgusted by the way the elections had been rigged that he took to the bush and formed the National Resistance Army/Movement (NRA/M).

When Obote heard that Yoweri Museveni had formed the NRA in order to remove him by force, he derisively referred to him: 'A *Mnyarwanda!* What can he do?' meaning a foreigner from Rwanda could not succeed in removing him.

But Obote should have known better. As a student in the University of Dar es Salaam, Museveni's idea of a worthwhile holiday was reportedly to join the Mozambique nationalist fighters, FRELIMO, to fight against Portuguese colonialism there.

As time went by and the NRA/M gained more ground militarily and politically, the hallmark of the movement became 'discipline.' This fact, more than anything else, won the movement more and more supporters and respect all over the country.

Even Obote's own Vice President, Paulo Muwanga and Prime Minister Otema Alimadi, were said to be secretly in league with the NRA/M long before Obote lost power for the second time through a military coup. The two Acholi generals who later spearheaded the coup in 1985 were said to be in contact with the NRA, though the NRA has consistently denied this." – (Jacob J. Akol, *Burden of Nationality*, op. cit., pp. 249 – 250).

The rivalry and violence that erupted between the Langi and the Acholi in the army also signalled the beginning of the end of Obote's second presidency. He could not depend only on his fellow tribesmen, the Langi, to keep him in power in an army that had more Acholis than Langis.

It also meant that the ethnic and regional solidarity Obote had depended on so much to stay in power since the sixties had come to an end. It was the alliance between the two northern groups in the army, the Langi and the Acholi, which tipped scales in his favour against his rivals, including Kabaka Mutesa II who was ousted by military means – mostly by Langi and Acholi soldiers and security forces – in May 1966 under the leadership of another northerner, Idi Amin, although a member of the Kakwa tribe from the northwest. As Akol goes on to state:

"Following NRA's gains in the west of the country, a dispute between the two main Nilotic tribes, who dominated the army, began to surface.

The Acholi troops had long complained that the new Langi Chief of Staff, Opon Acak, expected them to do the brunt of the fighting with the NRA. The Acholi soldiers rebelled against the Langi 'Special Force' soldiers who were sent by Acak to take them from Jinja to the front in early June (1985). They would rather fight the Langi forces than face the guerrillas of Museveni.

The Jinja rebellion was followed by a more serious confrontation between the two tribes early in July at Mbuya barracks near Kampala. The dispute over the ownership of a large cache of weapons left 30 dead. The Langi overwhelmed the Acholi troops, took them to Makindye barracks and murdered them.

Army Commander Tito Okello, together with many Acholi soldiers and their weapons, hurried north to the Acholi capital of Gulu, where they joined Basilio Okello, who was already there as Commander of the Northern Brigade.

The Acholi troops, led by the two Okellos, attacked Acak's forces at Karuma Falls on the River Nile. Soon afterwards, the Lango capital, Lira, was taken without resistance.

In the end, it took less than a day for the Acholi-led troops to sweep down to Kampala through Soroti and Jinja in the east and Bombo in the west. Obote and Acak fled to neighbouring Kenya in a helicopter with only minutes to spare.

The mid-day coup was successful and the victorious tribal-led army announced on Radio Uganda:

> The tribalist government of Milton Apolo Obote has been overthrown. We appeal to our brothers in the bush and honourable Yoweri Museveni to join us.

There was no immediate response from Museveni.

The two Okellos then set up 'an interim government' in Kampala and promised a general election within a year.

However, reports of atrocities being committed by the soldiers were coming in daily and it seemed that, apart from Obote's absence, nothing much had changed. In contrast, the areas controlled by the NRA in the west were reportedly peaceful.

It was now clear to the NRA that the new military government in Kampala was nothing but old wine in, well, old bottles really, since the generals had been part and parcel of the Obote regime.

Peace talks, and even an agreement, between General Okello's government and Museveni's NRA/M took place in Nairobi under the Chairmanship of the Kenyan President Daniel arap Moi. But all that came to nothing, as Museveni soon adopted a winner-take-all attitude.

On January 25, 1986, Museveni's NRA took the capital, Kampala, from the generals.

But Lt. Gen. Basilio Okello and former Defence Minister, Col. Wilson Toko, had retreated to their home town, Gulu, and tried to convince the people that the NRA was coming to loot, rape and savage them.

For the first two weeks, thousands of Acholis and their Nilotic cousins, who had been warring among themselves, now buried the hatchet and congregated daily at Gulu army barracks to be given weapons. The seeds of the present opposition to the government of Museveni were thus sown." – (Ibid., pp. 250 – 251).

Although northern leaders – Obote and later the two Okellos – were swept out of power, northern opposition to southern leadership of the country, whose most prominent symbol was Museveni, did not stop. Museveni was the first leader from the south to lead Uganda since independence. And northerners were determined not to make it easy for him if they could not overthrow him.

He also faced strong opposition from fellow southerners, including his former allies during the struggle against Obote and the Okello regimes. Others were his own people who had left the National Resistance Movement to oppose him:

"Museveni's honeymoon in Kampala was over only six months into power. By the end of 1986, a full-blown war between the NRA and the northern rebels was already underway.

In a Christmas Eve attack on the NRA near the town of Kitgum, the rebels claimed having killed more than 100 NRA soldiers and taking 50 prisoners. The NRA claimed they killed 115 rebels while they lost 'only 23 men, due to some mistake' on their part.

The significance of that attack was that a new chapter in the unending cycle of killings in Uganda had been ushered in. The players had merely switched places, with the former rebels now the government while the former rulers were now the rebels.

As if the opposition in the north were not enough, opposition within the government had become apparent. By January 1987, some former allies of Museveni, the leader of the Uganda Freedom Movement (UFM), Dr Andrew Kayiira, and the leader of the Federal Democratic Movement (FEDEMO), David Livingstone Lwanga, were already in jail, charged with treason. Also, 18 top-ranking army officers were arrested and charged with plotting a coup against the government.

Dr Kayiira was murdered in a BBC correspondent's home shortly after his release from five months' detention. The correspondent, himself a Ugandan, went underground and later turned up in Kenya, claiming that Dr Kayiira's killers were NRA soldiers. His movement, Uganda Freedom Army (UFA), announced their return to the bush in the south to fight Museveni.

But UFA would be just one of the multitude of armed anti-NRA/M movements which have since been formed.

In spite of the wide publicity given to the so-called 'Holy Spirit Movement,' which was led by Alice Lakwena, that organisation was never a real threat to the government of Museveni. The 'Holy Spirit' followers were massacred each time they mounted their suicidal attacks against the NRA. The real problem came from the 'Uganda People's Democratic Army' (UPDA"). – (Ibid. p. 251).

Dr. Andrew Kayiira, who once was a cabinet minister under President Yoweri Museveni, was killed on 9 March 1987 only about a year after Museveni seized power. He was was born on 30 January 1945 and was 42 when he was killed.

His death was an assassination.

Kayiira's assassination raises some questions about Museveni's leadership and the National Resistance Movement (NRM) among many Ugandans including some NRM supporters because of the alleged involvement by the National Resistance Army (NRA) in that brutal murder. As Ugandan journalist David Kibirige stated in his article, "Who Killed Kayiira?" in *The Monitor*, Kampala, Uganda, 6 March 2004:

"For 17 years now, mystery still surrounds the gruesome murder of former minister and guerrilla leader Dr Andrew Lutakome Kayiira.

Kayiira was the Uganda Freedom Movement (UFM)

military leader with lawyer Francis Bwengye as head of its political wing.

On March 7, 1987 Kayiira was shot dead at the home of a friend, then BBC correspondent Henry Gombya, at Konge, Makindye on the outskirts of Kampala.

Mr Gombya, who was around the house at the time of the murder, later fled to exile in Britain.

Because of its high profile, President Yoweri Museveni ordered that the famous Scotland Yard investigate the murder.

Scotland Yard did come and investigate but several years later, nothing is known about the report, or who killed Kayira.

Not surprisingly, Kayiira's death has dogged the country and at every presidential election, his ghost returns to haunt President Yoweri Museveni.

In 1996 when Paul Kawanga Ssemogerere stood against Museveni, Kayiira's death became a hot issue.

Fingers were pointed at Museveni saying it was he who did not want the Kayiira report made public.

Ironically Mr Ssemogerere was the minister of Internal Affairs at the time of Kayiira's death.

The police, which carried out initial investigations, fall under the Internal Affairs ministry.

Ssemogerere resigned his ministerial post in 1995 to contest for the presidency.

So the question is why has Ssemogerere kept quite all this long?

Contacted by *Sunday Monitor* on Wednesday Ssemogerere said he could not discuss the Kayiira issue on the phone. He said he was going to attend a funeral. Again *Sunday Monitor* tried to speak to him on Thursday in vain.

Kayiira was a Democratic Party (DP) firebrand politician who as early as 1986 had started calling on Ssemogerere to relinquish party leadership.

Again in the March 2001 presidential elections, Kayiira's death cropped up.

Museveni's closest challenger, Dr Kizza Besigye, challenged the president to tell Ugandans who had killed Kayiira.

Again ironically, Besigye was time minister (sic) of State for Internal Affairs, at Kayiira's death.

In his book *The Price of Freedom* which he wrote after Kayiira's death, Mr Bwengye blamed government for the murder. Informed sources told *Sunday Monitor* that government bought off all copies. Even Bwengye does not have one.

Highly placed sources told *Sunday Monitor* that after writing the book, government sent then national political commissar, Col. Kizza Besigye and Lt. Gen Salim Saleh off all copies in addition to 'oiling Bwengye's hand' which persuaded him to come back home.

Bwengye conceded that it was Saleh and Besigye who negotiated his return but denies ever receiving money.

'The book was published abroad and I had no contact with government, so how could I have negotiated for a buy off,' Bwengye told *Sunday Monitor* on March 4.

Asked if *Sunday Monitor* could borrow his copy since as the author he might have one, Bwengye said; 'My copies were borrowed and never returned.'

Again asked why there is no reprint, Bwengye said; 'I am not a publisher. So I do not know.'

He however said that at one time he requested *The Monitor's* then managing editor, Charles Onyango Obbo, to publish the book but that he received no reply.

Last month during Monitor FM's popular Andrew Mwenda live programme, Bwengye gave his reasons why he suspects elements in government eliminated Kayiira.

'I and Kayiira were acquitted of treason charges because there was no evidence. Peter Kabatsi [then solicitor general] said we were free. Two days later, President Museveni while addressing the Law Society said although people like Kayiira were released, they were guilty. Two days later Kayiira was killed,' Bwengye said.

Pressed if he thought it was Museveni who killed Kayiira, Bwengye said: 'soldiers did it.'

When asked if he thinks Museveni can assassinate someone, he said: 'I do not think Museveni is an assassinator (sic) but a man who has been fighting wars can not shoot into trees.'

Advised to drag the government to court for killing Kayiira, Bwengye said; 'When Lule was removed, some people went to court and court ruled that he had been removed illegally but nothing happened. There have been many court rulings but this does not change the system.'

Museveni-Kayira background

Immediately after the December 10, 1980 general elections, Kayiira was of the view that a guerrilla war was inevitable.

On the other hand Ssemogerere as party leader said they should form the opposition in parliament.

So Kayiira formed the Uganda Freedom Movement (UFM). In fact it was Kayiira who went to the bush first; to be followed by other guerrilla groups including that of Yoweri Museveni.

Kayiira felt that by telling the youths not to join the bush fighters, Ssemogerere denied him a block of Baganda fighting force.

In fact when Museveni appointed Kayiira minister after the fall of the Gen. Tito Okello Lutwa's junta, he (Kayiira) felt that it was not because of his DP leanings but because he had a fighting force.

As early as 1986 Kayiira had shown 'signs of being problematic.'

For instance even before the whole of Uganda had been 'liberated' by the NRA, he was telling Museveni to come clean on issues like multiparty politics and federalism.

Some of his commanders were arrested and killed by

the NRA. This was on suspicion that elements within UFM were planning to overthrow Museveni's government.

At the end of 1986, Capt. Abbey Kalega Sserwada, one of the UFM commanders was arrested and detained at Lubiri. Up to now no one knows his fate but *Sunday Monitor* has learnt he was probably tortured by senior NRA officers and had his ears cut off before he was killed.

On October 7, 1986 Kayiira, then minister of Energy, was arrested for allegedly planning to overthrow Museveni's government. He was arrested with two cabinet colleagues; Evaristo Nyanzi and Dr David Lwanga.

Baganda army officers had apparently spied on them.

During court proceedings senior Baganda officers came out and testified that the politicians had approached them. They had recorded proceedings which the court dismissed on technicalities.

The Baganda officers who featured prominently in the treason case included Col. Fred Bogere and Col Drago Nyanzi (RIP).

Later some people tried to kill Bogere by showering his car with bullets.

Court acquitted Kayiira for lack of evidence.

A few days after his acquittal in the wee hours of March 7, 1987, armed people stormed Gombya's place and showered Kayiira with bullets.

Uganda police makes arrests

After the death, police arrested five men who it alleged had killed Kayira. Government said two had escaped from Luzira. They were Robert Magezi and Sylvester Wada. Those paraded in court were John Katabazi, Peter Kiwanuka alias Backfire and Musisi Kizito.

In the trial that followed, Justice C.M Kato of the High Court acquitted them but they were re-arrested by security operatives outside court and to date, their whereabouts remain unknown.

Scotland Yard comes in

When there was a general outcry that government was covering up investigations, Museveni suggested that the famous Scotland Yard should carry out independent investigations.

British officers came, carried out investigations and compiled a report, which is a top government secret up to now.

Sniffer dogs that were used had moved from Kayiira's house and had reportedly led investigators to the Lubiri barracks. That is when the matter became tricky.

Though government might not have been involved, some elements within the army may have had a hand in the high profile murder.

Because of these developments, the matter took a very dramatic turn.

Top security sources told *Sunday Monitor* that police did not have access to the report but it was with State House.

Criminal Investigations Department (CID) boss Elizabeth Kuteesa was cagey when contacted March 4.

Asked whether as the boss of CID she had the report, she said; 'That is not a priority matter now, as there are many files. I will check and see if that report is here.'

Asked how soon she could avail the report to *Sunday Monitor* she said, 'I do not know; I do not work according to your deadlines.'

She could not delve more into the matter.

The president's legal assistant and acting principal private secretary, Fox Odoi, said the report was not given to State House.

'The report was given to the Attorney General for legal advice since he is the chief legal advisor of government and, then Directorate of Public Prosecution was directly under him,' said Odoi.

Justice Joseph Mulenga who was the attorney general then says he does not remember receiving the Scotland Yard report.

'I do not recall receiving the Scotland Yard report. That is not something one can easily forget. I recall the trial but I do not recall ever getting that report,' Mulenga told Sunday Monitor on March 5.

More and more mystery

Days after the murder of Kayiira, Capt. Sajjad Sooria alias Sajjabi, a Pakistani fled the country. He was a UFM mercenary and Kayiira had employed him in 1981.

Just days after the murder, Gombya also fled to exile where he has lived up to now.

Gombya had apparently managed to divide Shs 40 million into two – under the hail of bullets – after they had been attacked and reportedly threw at the attackers to buy his escape.

This was the official version Gombya gave to the press then and even in the 1990s he maintained his explanation in articles he used to write for *The Monitor*. And with his weight, Gombya apparently managed to jump from a fifteen feet high wall and fled.

In April 1987, Bwengye during a press conference in London attended by Sajaad announced that the UFM was returning to the bush to fight Museveni's government. Bwengye insisted government had killed Kayiira.

Who was Kayiira?

He was born in Mawokota, Mpigi district. He went to St. Peter's Nsambya Primary School in Kampala before proceeding to Namilyango College.

After secondary school he joined the Prison Service as a cadet officer. He left for Britain for further studies.

On his return he was promoted to the rank of assistant

superintendent of prisons.

In 1968 he went to the USA to study at the University of New Haven where he did a degree course in criminology and mathematics. He did a master's degree in criminology, themed on criminal justice.

In 1975 he returned to complete his research paper on kondoism – armed robbery – for his PhD. He spent much of his time at Makerere Institute of Social Research when he was writing the paper.

He married Betty Mutema after which he returned to the USA. He joined groups which were fighting Amin. He formed the Uganda Freedom Union with other people like former president Godfrey Lukongwa Binaisa and Olara Otunu, a former Foreign minister and now based at the United Nations.

After Binaisa, the firebrand Kayiira became UFU leader.

He represented UFU at the Moshi Conference, which charted the way forward after Idi Amin's government. He was elected a member the National Consultative Council (NCC).

He was a deputy minister of commerce in the short-lived Yusuf Kironde Lule's government, which replaced that of Amin.

He later became minister of Internal Affairs.

After the removal of Lule he formed the Uganda Freedom Movement with the mission of fighting to restore the professor.

Kayiira's deadly missions

On June 10, 1976 Kayiira participated in an assassination attempt on President Idi Amin Dada during a passout parade at Nsambya Police barracks. Three grenades were hurled at the presidential jeep.

Idi Amin's driver was killed prompting Amin to drive the jeep up to Mulago.

Panic-stricken soldiers opened fire into the crowd killing more than 50 people.

On February 23, 1981 Kayiira's Uganda Freedom Movement (UFM) attacked Lubiri army barracks and the battle lasted eight-hours.

UFM was one of the groups, which was fighting Apollo Milton Obote's government after the December 10, 1980 elections, which were allegedly rigged in favour of UPC.

UFM lost 67 fighters while government claimed it lost 5 soldiers.

UFM claimed that Museveni had assured them that his National Resistance Army (NRA) would reinforce the attacking but betrayed them at the last moment.

Lt. Col. Sonko of UFM delivered a truckload of guns, which Kayiira had captured, to Museveni.

He later defected to NRA.

This caused bad blood between Museveni and Kayiira.

After the unsuccessful attack on Lubiri, Kayiira left for the USA to secure funds for his group.

While he was away there were differences within his group leading to the formation of the Federal Democratic Movement of Uganda (Fedemu).

Before he could reorganise his group, Tito Okello Lutwa and Bazillio Okello overthrew Obote's government.

He joined the Military Council with Lutwa as head of state.

He constantly warned the military council not to underrate the NRA.

By the time the NRA captured power, Kayiira was in charge of parts of Kampala. He was in charge of areas like Ggaba, Konge, Muyenga and parts of Makindye.

Kayiira's six children and wife live in the USA."

Kayiira's assassination sheds some light on the National Resistance Movement – and its army, the RNA) – as an organisation whose leaders will not hesitate to use any means including extra-judicial killings to silence its opponents and as a warning to others in spite of its reputation as a "disciplined" movement which respects the rights of all Ugandans.

Ugandan journalist, Rodney Muhumuza, talked to one of the NRA soldiers sent to kill Kayiira. As he stated in his article, quoting the killer, entitled, "I Took Part in Kayiira Murder," published in *The Monitor*, Kampala, Uganda, 13 January 2007:

"In a voluntary confession that is likely to send shock waves across the nation, a former National Resistance Army (NRA, now UPDF) child soldier (kadogo), Corporal Eddie Sande, has come forward to say he was part of a platoon of 33 government soldiers that murdered former Energy Minister Dr Andrew Lutaakome Kayiira in March 1987.

Dr Kayiira, the leader of the former rebel group, the Uganda Freedom Movement, was murdered shortly after being acquitted of treason. Less than a week before his murder, President Yoweri Museveni told the BBC World Service Radio that even though the High Court had acquitted Kayiira, Museveni was sure he was guilty of treason, based on the intelligence reports available to him.

Cpl. Sande says he was a member of the NRA's Lubiri-based Central Brigade, which the Democratic Party (DP) has said is implicated in the murder by a still secret investigative report into the murder by Britain's Metropolitan Police of New Scotland Yard.

On the late evening of Saturday, October 14, 2006, Cpl. Sande took this reporter by surprise when he walked into the *Daily Monitor* offices in Kampala and volunteered to tell the story of Dr Kayiira's assassination at the home of his friend, BBC journalist Henry Gombya.

The short and slender Sande, who claims he participated in other 'liquidations,' wanted to see a journalist who would help him write the story of his life.

He initially asked for *Daily Monitor's* Political Editor, Mr Andrew Mwenda, who is away in the United States.

He then asked for our former Editor in Chief, Wafula Oguttu, who was unavailable, following which he told this reporter a shocking story.

Cpl. Sande gave his army number as RA 34452, which records from the Chieftaincy of Military Intelligence have since showed to be valid.

The records, confirmed on Thursday by army spokesman Maj. Felix Kulayigye, show that Cpl. Sande is currently attached to State House, and has been involved in a number of 'special intelligence assignments' on behalf of the state. Although there are some inconsistencies in the dates Sande gives in his story, the army records tally with most of his claims. Maj. Kulayigye said it was possible the corporal had deserted the army and gone underground.

In a series of interviews, initially clouded by some doubts from this reporter, Cpl. Sande recalled the events of an evening in 1987 when soldiers from the 19th battalion of the Central Brigade were allegedly briefed about a mission to eliminate an 'adui' [Swahili word for an enemy] that turned out to be Dr Kayiira.

'Before going to Libya [for training], in 1987, I was in the 19th battalion [Central Brigade] under [now Brigadier] Peter Kerim. When we were called in the evening, I was at the headquarters in Lubiri. We were called for assembly at night [and told] that we were going for an operation,' he said. 'That was after people who were supposed to go for patrol had already left. We were all from the Brigade headquarters, not from companies.

'By then, the OC (Officer-in-Charge) of Headquarters was one Otto, sometimes called John Byuma Otto. I understand he is now in Lira.' (*Sunday Monitor* has confirmed the existence of this officer but has been unable to locate him and has not been able to obtain his confirmation or denial, and we urgently want to hear his side of the story – Editor).

Although the call to get ready for the operation was made by Kerim, Sande recalled, it was the brigade's Intelligence Officer, (now Lt. Col.) David Kaboyo, who briefed the platoon of some 33 soldiers before heading to Makindye, the Kampala suburb in which Kayiira was sharing a house with Mr Gombya, who mysteriously survived the attack and fled into exile.

'Peter Kerim, the 19th battalion commander, told us that we were going for an operation. For that operation, he told us, there was someone who would brief us. And then we left the barracks and went to the brigade headquarters. When we reached there, we met the brigade intelligence officer. He was called Kaboyo.'

Sunday Monitor has since independently confirmed that 19th Battalion was under the 163rd Central Brigade and that Lt. Col. Kaboyo was indeed Intelligence Officer at the time. We have also confirmed Brig. Kerim was at the time Commander of the 19th Battalion.

Brig. Kerim is now the army's Director of Training, operating under the office of the Deputy Chief of Defence Forces. Lt. Col. Kaboyo is still in the army as a zonal commander of land forces in the Lake Albert (Bunyoro) region.

'Kaboyo talked to us and there was another officer present called Peter Nkola. Kaboyo told us we were going for a crucial mission 'right now'. We asked him what the mission was. He said: 'No, jeshi apana wuliza maswali [soldiers do not ask why]."

Contacted for comment, Lt. Col. Kaboyo turned down several requests from *Sunday Monitor* to say anything about Cpl. Sande's claims or the murder of Dr Kayiira. He would neither confirm nor deny anything on record, saying 'the government which I serve does not allow me to comment on that issue.'

Sunday Monitor has since been told by intelligence sources that the Chieftaincy of Military Intelligence became aware of this newspaper's intention to publish this story a few days ago and that all soldiers named by Sande had been ordered to make no comment.

Other security sources have since told *Sunday Monitor* that Kaboyo's role was to 'secure the scene of crime' of Kayiira's murder but they declined to clarify whether this took place before or after the crime and this newspaper is still keen to obtain Col. Kaboyo's comment.

Cpl. Sande claims on that fateful March 6 1987 night, his platoon of soldiers took a truck ride to the house in which 'the enemy' [Dr Kayiira] was said to be residing, and although they were there by 8.30 p.m., it would be a long wait before the mission was executed. He said that although they travelled under the command of Otto, the NRA's deputy army commander, the late Maj Gen Fred Rwigyema (a Rwandan Tutsi and founder and leader of the Rwandan Patriotic Front – RPF – together with the current Rwandan President Paul Kagame), later joined them. Sande says the Isuzu truck on which they travelled was driven by one 'Godie,' whom he has since lost contact with. He insists the truck belonged to the 163rd Central Brigade.

'When we reached there, we were asked to get out of the vehicle. Then Rwigyema came and found us. He was in a jeep. But for us, we had gone with Otto, who is now retired. We got out of the vehicle, and we were told to line up and take positions. There were some selected people who advanced. We were told that if we heard gunshots we should advance up to the scene, and be ready.'

Cpl. Sande says he and other soldiers present were told to shoot any suspicious person moving in their direction and to preserve their concealment, although some of his senior colleagues were frequently radioed.

But it would be hours before they heard the gunshots, he recalled. 'It was late in the night when soldiers entered the house. So when we heard a gunshot we advanced as we were told,' he said, explaining that they soon stumbled upon a man lying in a pool of blood – the victim of gun-wielding assassins who were still hovering over the corpse when Sande arrived.

Sande's account, however, does not tell who actually pulled the trigger. He told *Sunday Monitor* he did not know the identity of the actual killers because he arrived after the murder. 'When we reached the scene we saw a tall, big man lying in a pool of blood. Then (the late) Major Dr Peter Baingana (a former NRA Director of Medical Services) told Rwigyema (the two later led the Rwandan liberation war but were killed in its first month) that 'mission imeisha' [mission is complete] after checking [the body].'

Cpl. Sande claims that after Dr Kayiira's killing, Maj. Gen. Rwigyema – travelling in a jeep, and followed by some soldiers among whom was Cpl. Sande – travelled to the Kololo home of the then Central Brigade Commander, Gen David Tinyefuza, to convey the good news.

'We followed Rwigyema up to Kololo, where we found the afande. He was up (awake). 'Tumerudi [we are back],' Rwigyema allegedly told Tinyefuza, to which Tinyefuza allegedly replied, 'pole kurudi [welcome back].'

This part of the account attracted much sceptical questioning from this reporter because Tinyefuza was a subordinate to Rwigyema and whether he would therefore report back to him after a mission appeared highly unlikely. It also appeared unlikely that the Deputy Army Commander would take part in such an operation. Cpl. Sande said he also found it strange.

But he suggested that, judging by the brevity and nature of their discussion, Rwigyema's reporting to Tinyefuza could have been more in the spirit of comradeship than hierarchy. Tinyefuza has vigorously denied any involvement in the murder of Dr Kayiira, whom he says was killed by his former comrades in UFM and its breakaway faction Fedemu.

Contacted for detailed comment, Gen. Tinyefuza said there was no truth in the claims. 'It is not possible...I don't recall any of that. In any case, it is strange. All that is not true. Kayiira was killed by his true friend,' Gen. Tinyefuza said but did not name the purported killer.

Cpl. Sande said he does not know for sure if Brig Kerim was physically present during the operation. 'I don't know, because when we were called for fall-in at around 7 p.m., he [Kerim] came and told us that we were going for [an] operation and that someone would come and take us. Then he entered his short chassis Cross Country and drove to his residence in Kololo.'

In response to Sande's claims on Monday, Brig. Kerim showed no surprise at the Corporal's account, and went on to say that he had waited 20 years for a journalist to ask him questions over him questions over Dr Kayiira's death. Describing it as 'a terrible trend,' Brig. Kerim denied any involvement in the murder of Kayiira but said Cpl. Sande's account seemed to 'have good information.' But he said he was 'not supposed to talk much' since he was still a serving UPDF soldier.

Brig. Kerim, however, corroborated the historical aspects of Cpl. Sande's account and confirmed that he knew the names mentioned by the former kadogo. Recalling that Peter Nkola was a signaller and that David Kaboyo was an intelligence officer, Brig. Kerim argued that while he did not know about the Kayiira mission, it was possible that the execution could have been the work of intelligence operatives who did not have a duty to report to him.

Brig. Kerim said 19th Battalion was the biggest battalion under the Central Brigade, and that it was composed of many companies. He said the Brigade headquarters had 180 soldiers and that each company and platoon had its own commander. 'I don't know who commanded that platoon but what happens depends on individual commanders. If Kaboyo took Sande [for that operation], he took him illegally.'

'I do not remember anything about that mission. I don't

do secret missions…that is intelligence work…,' Brig. Kerim said. The Brigadier also denied any link with Maj. Gen. Rwigyema.

Asked whether he would feel hurt by this newspaper publishing this story, which names him, the apparently unperturbed Brig. Kerim said 'you seem to have good information.' Asked whether this reporter should proceed with the story, he answered, 'That is already a story, if a man has come out openly…'

After Kayiira's murder, the NRM government contracted Scotland Yard, the British Metropolitan Police, to investigate the case at a cost of $250,000. Uganda's tax revenue at the time was only $40 million. Scotland Yard was called in because of widespread suspicion in the country that Kayiira had been killed by Museveni's government. The government has never released the report to the public, resulting in a full-blown storm, 20 years later.

Last week the Democratic Party threatened to release the report at a rally at Constitution Square on January 6, but they did not succeed as police dispersed them with teargas and rubber bullets in running street battles that paralysed business in the city. They later said they would release the report on Saturday at another rally in Masaka. *Sunday Monitor* has however learnt that a decision was taken on Friday not to release the report at the rally.

Later in the day, DP, quoting from the said report, issued a press statement saying Kayiira's killers were drawn from the then Central Brigade under a top General.

In the statement, DP President Ssebaana Kizito said the report identified one of the killers as Suicide Brewery, a reference to the late Maj. Marius Katungi, who he said is named by Scotland Yard as having participated in the killing of Kayiira. The late 'Suicide' was known in the army for his spontaneous cruelty and was one of the NRA (now UPDF) bush war commanders.

In an interview published in *Daily Monitor* on

203

Thursday, Mr Gombya, in whose house Kayiira died, said the soldier who shot Kayiira was a Muganda officer who is now a Brigadier in the army. Brig. Kasirye Ggwanga, a Muganda officer, has denied any role in the murder but said Kayiira 'deserved death.'

Last week, at the height of DP's claims that there was evidence for the army's complicity in Kayiira's death, Security Minister Amama Mbabazi denied such a role by the army. The army spokesman, Maj. Felix Kulayigye, said he could not comment. 'Well, what can I say? No information, no comment,' he said.

Asked whether he wanted his story published, Cpl. Sande said, 'It is better if it is there on record (he accepted to be photographed and tape recorded) because even if you hear tomorrow that Sande Eddie is dead, you can then bring the tape. That's why I came here instead of going to *The New Vision* (a government-owned daily newspaper).'

He said he joined the NRA in 1985 at Mulima in Mount Rwenzori. 'I was under the protection of [Moses] Kigongo. We were there with men like [John] Nagenda and Jacob Asiimwe.' He said he was recruited into Brig Kerim's 19th Battalion (which he says was then still under the late Col Patrick Lumumba) by one Corporal Kalibbala.

Cpl. Sande claims he later attended the Mbarara Kadogo School and was trained in Libya. He does not remember his parents but says Cpl. Kalibbala, who recruited him at a tender age, told him his father used to deal in secondhand clothes and was a supplier to Kalibbala, who sold the clothes in Luwero, where he was also an NRA informer. Sande says during the war, he spent some time at Mulima (Mount Rwenzori) with other child soldiers.

Brig. Kerim told *Sunday Monitor* that most of his 19th Battalion recruits were child soldiers from the Rwenzori and Fort Portal region."

The assassination of Dr. Kayiira by NRA soldiers still

haunts Museveni's government and the ruling National Resistance Movement (NRM). It is also now and then used as a weapon by the opposition to discredit Museveni and his Movement.

Although Museveni continued to face opposition in the southern part of the country after he came into power, his biggest challenge was in the north, the ethnic and military stronghold of the Uganda People's Democratic Army (UPDA) which was fighting the National Resistance Army (NRA).

The Uganda People's Democratic Army (UPDA) was formed by Acholi soldiers under the leadership of Brigadier Odong Latek. The soldiers had left the national army – the Uganda National Liberation Army (UNLA) – after the government of Tito Okello was overthrown by Museveni. They fled north and sought sanctuary in southern Sudan. They returned to northern Uganda when the National Resistance Army (NRA) of Museveni occupied Acholiland in January 1986. They formed the Uganda People's Democratic Army in March the same year to push the NRA out of Acholiland which was also the homeland of the ousted Ugandan military head of state, Tito Okello.

The UPDA attacked NRA forces – who then, as now, constituted the Ugandan national army – in the north in August 1986 and got a lot of support across Acholiland. It was Acholi subnationalism at its best. The NRA forces, composed mostly of southerners, were seen by Acholis as an army of occupation by foreigners in Acholiland who had to be driven out.

It was nothing new but a resurgence of the same phenomenon, only in another form (armed resistance), that has been an integral part of Ugandan national life in a country where ethno-regional loyalties play an important role across the spectrum. Even the composition of the cabinet – as well as allocation of other posts – has to reflect regional balance for the sake of national unity and stability; that is also the case in many other African countries.

Northerners felt they were left out under Museveni, partly because of their support for Obote, their opposition to Museveni's leadership, and for simply being northerners who had little in common with southerners who were now in control of the government.

The National Resistance Army occupying Acholiland alienated the Acholi even further when they brutalised the people in retaliation for the attacks by the Acholi rebels of the UPDA. Many of them were killed, further encouraging them to support the UPDA fighters.

But the National Resistance Army proved to be too strong for the rebels. Although the rebels controlled most of the rural areas and knew the region well since it was their homeland, they failed to dislodge the NRA from the towns and started losing the war.

But they refused to concede defeat and many of them turned to the Holy Spirit Movement led by Alice Auma – better known as Alice Lakwena – who led her followers south in an attempt to take over the capital Kampala and end Museveni's rule. As they moved south, she and her followers got a lot of support on the way from other ethnic groups who, like the Acholi, were opposed to the national government under Museveni. But they were defeated by the national army in a forest near Kampala.

Other Acholi soldiers from the UPDA began to support other rebel groups including one led by Joseph Kony. Kony's group, also opposed to Museveni's rule, became the Lord's Resistance Army (LRA) which gained international notoriety through the years for attacking villages and killing civilians in northern Uganda – mostly in Acholiland itself – and for abducting children and turning them into child soldiers and sex slaves.

On 3 August 1988, the UPDA signed an agreement with the government to end the war. The agreement also called for an inclusive democratic government. But the

UPDA founder Odok Latek refused to sign the agreement and joined the Lord's Resistance Army. However, most of his officers gave up fighting. It was a final blow to the UPDA. The rebel group died out by early 1989, the same year Odok was reportedly killed by NRA soldiers in Nyono Hills in northern Uganda.

It is one of the tragedies of Ugandan history that ethnicity has always played a prominent role in national life – in the political and economic arenas, educational and sociocultural spheres and so on – to the detriment of national unity as has been the case in most African countries. The conflict in northern Uganda, and even the crisis in the Buganda kingdom in the sixties which led to the ouster of Kabaka Mutes II and his subsequent exile in Britain, would not have occurred if the people were allowed full participation in the political process on equal basis and if all the regions were equally represented in the government.

Unfortunately, the leaders themselves have exploited and continue to foster and exploit ethno-regional sentiments and loyalties in the post-colonial era the same way the colonial rulers did in the past to serve their own interests, not those of the nation. Their primary interest is domination from which everything else flows. Uganda is one of the countries which have suffered the most in this context. As Aaron Griffiths and James Katalikawe state in "The Reformulation of Ugandan Democracy" in *Can Democracy Be Designed? The Politics of Institutional Choice in Conflict-torn Societies*:

"Both the colonial and the nationalist governments failed to find structures to accommodate politicised ethnic group difference and the ambitions of 'tribal leaders' in a democratic polity. It is a problem that colonialism – both in the longer term and in the reforms it attempted in its dying hours – bequeathed to much of Africa, but in most places the experience led to less bloodshed and volatility than in Uganda.

Since independence, tensions have persisted between different parts of the country, especially the developed central part and and the undeveloped North.

Northern dominance in the military and inter-ethnic conflicts between different factions in the army only added to the strife.

Depending on who is in power, some consider themselves central to the country's mainstream political activity, while others feel marginalised and out of the reckoning.

The ethnic and tribal variation underlying Uganda's cleavages – 56 ethnic groups, four different linguistic categories and over 30 different dialects – does not mean that it is therefore impossible to forge a harmonious society within a stable nation state. Political institutions often failed in Uganda because they mediated these cleavages in a polarising rather than a cross-cutting way. The potential for Acholi Catholics to ally with Baganda Catholics, for example, thus reducing North-South polarisation, has rarely been realised, except in the early years of independence when the religious division of parties did give some cross-ethnic unity.

The roots of the problem must be traced to Uganda's colonial experience, which left damaging military, economic, religious and political legacies.

The British favoured recruitment from the 'martial races' of the northern Acholi and Langi, a tradition and military model which continued after independence. Northern soldiers, whenever trouble has erupted, 'were usually over-zealous in restoring order among the southerners' (Furely 1987: 2). On the other hand, the British preferred to grow their cash crops in the more fertile South, which developed the best infrastructure. The North and West did not share in colonial economic development.

Finally, the rivalry between the competing branches of

Christianity persistently materialised as violence. During the early crystallisation of political parties, the Democratic Party (DP) emerged as mainly Catholic, while the Uganda People's Congress (UPC) became mainly Protestant – both parties marked more by these characteristics than by any concerted ideology.

The political legacy of the colonial state was a narrow relationship with society, one of domination rather than representation, that left it unsuited to being a legitimate institution at the moment of independence. Further, the British formed differing relationships with the different tribal-political groups they encountered, and the governments they variously called kingdoms, territories and districts 'had no socio-political or economic network linking them to one another' (Odongo 2000: 33).

The British relationship with Buganda was to be particularly significant. The *Uganda Agreement 1900* had appeared to set Buganda apart from the rest of Uganda and conferred on the Kabaka – the King of the Baganda – and his chiefs 'special privileges' in return for their cooperation. It set the scene for the disunity of Uganda when in the 1950s the Baganda resisted reforms of the Legislative Council: instead of agitating for more African representation they sought assurances that the council would not affect the Agreement. This led to the abrogation of the latter, the declaration of a state of emergency in Buganda and the deportation of the Kabaka – who returned two years later.

The idea of a unitary form of government for Uganda, which the British authorities supported, was in shambles, and no mass nationalist movement emerged, as it did in Tanzania or Kenya, to counterbalance the sectarian nature of political groupings." – (Aaron Griffiths and James Katalikawe, "The Reformulation of Ugandan Democracy" in Sunil Bastian and Robin Luckham, eds., *Can Democracy Be Designed? The Politics of Institutional Choice in Conflict-torn Societies*, London: Zed Books,

2003, pp. 94 – 95).

The result is what you see today: a fragmented Uganda, divided along ethno-regional lines, although it has not fallen apart.

The two leaders who have had the most significant impact in trying to unite the country are Obote and Museveni. Especially during his first presidency, Obote formed a cabinet and made other appointments reflecting regional balance, north and south, and from all the kingdoms. But all that was counterbalanced, hence neutralised, by the army and security forces which were dominated by his fellow northerners – a colonial legacy – and who tipped scales in his favour.

Obote also divided the country during his second presidency when he rigged or allowed the general elections – which propelled him into office – to be rigged by his supporters.

He had the opportunity to make amends for the wrongs done by him and his supporters in the 1980 general elections by forming an inclusive government of national unity – embracing all political and ethno-regional groups – which should have included all of his opponents to avoid plunging the country into civil war.

He should have listened to them. He should have shared power with them on meaningful basis. He should have discussed with them on how to move the country forward after the disputed elections. And he should have conceded to their demands instead of listening only to his supporters in the Uganda People's Congress.

By locking out his opponents, he also locked out the majority of Ugandans because the majority did not vote for him.

It was a recipe for catastrophe. As Professor Phares Mukasa Mutibwa states in his book, *Uganda Since Independence: A Story of Unfulfilled Hopes*:

"Obote had promised to form a national or broad-based administration after a UPC victory, but once in power his group forgot this commitment and instead formed an administration composed entirely of UPC members, with the military as its ultimate source of support. Had Obote fulfilled his promise, it is possible that he would have mitigated some of the harm done in stealing the election. Indeed, had Obote formed such a broad-based government, it would have brought a measure of consensus to the confrontational style of politics that has existed in Uganda since independence. But power to Obote is like oxygen to a man, and there could be no compromise with those with whom he disagreed.

Thus, the UPC government did not have the support of those who mattered, particularly in central Uganda which was the heart of the nation containing capital. It soon became clear that, much as in the late 1960s, Obote's regime operated from within an enemy's camp, surrounded by hostile Baganda with whom he had now established a relationship of intense mutual suspicion and hatred. Thus it is important to understand the thinking of the Baganda and other southerners on the one side and of Obote and his military men, headed by Tito Okello and Oyite-Ojok, on the other at the start of Obote's second presidency.

The mere return of Obote from exile in Tanzania in May 1980 had cast a chill over a large section of the Bantu nationalities of southern Uganda who were not in the UPC camp; it was regarded as an ominous event.

When, on 11 December 1980, they saw on Uganda TV Obote taking the oath as President, the bad dream had come closer to reality. The people in Kampala and Buganda generally felt that they were in an occupied territory – mere local inhabitants who would be looked upon as hewers of wood and drawers of water for the ruling group. Lacking guns, they resigned themselves to what Obote and his military establishment would mete out to them....

Luckily for Obote, he still had many of his former lieutenants around, some of a younger generation than himself – men with whom he had lived in the sweltering tropical forest of Owiny Ki-Bul in southern Sudan in 1971 and then in the heated politics of Tanzania and who finally planned his return to the presidency during the UNLF (Uganda National Liberation Front) administrations.

Obote knew that he was disliked by the DP (Democratic Party), CP (Conservative Party) and UPM (Uganda Patriotic Movement) and the people they represented. It did not matter; what mattered was the power and influence he would use in the service of himself, his close lieutenants and the native regions of most of his supporters, both civilian and military. He did not ignore the political wrangles going on outside his encamped headquarters: time and guns, he mused, would take care of those problems and of those responsible for such misguided doings.

In this, perhaps, lies part of the real cause of Obote's failure in his second administration: his inability to accept that the Uganda to which he had returned in 1980 was very different from what it had been in 1971. Obote came back as a wounded buffalo, determined to crush all those whom he believed had supported Amin in the early days of his rule, and he was not prepared to offer any real reconciliation or compromise. If Obote ever knew what the English philosopher Thomas Hobbes taught three centuries earlier – that 'there is no valid reason for sovereigns to desire to oppress their subjects, for the strength of sovereigns is directly dependent upon the strength and wellbeing of their subjects' – he ignored it now.

To Obote there was no common ground, no common strength and well-being, between himself as a 'sovereign' and the people, his hapless and helpless subjects. It is for this reason that Obote is felt to have lacked a clear vision of his country's future when he assumed power for the second time in 1980; he was a fighter at a time that demanded conciliation, a short-sighted politician at a time that demanded statesmanship." – (Phares Mukasa Mutibwa, *Uganda Since Independence: A Story of Unfulfilled Hopes*, op. cit., pp. 149 – 150).

It is difficult to reconcile such short-sightedness with the astuteness of a politician like Obote. But it did happen. And the main reason was the quest for power: his determination to regain the presidency that was taken away from him by force in 1971 even if it meant using the same weapon, force, that was used against him although there was a better way, by democratic means, if the people really wanted him back in power. Professor Mutibwa goes on to state:

"Obote was able to defy his opponents because of the assurance he had received that the army – the UNLA (Uganda National Liberation Army), headed by the veteran soldier Tito Okello, with David Oyite-Ojok as Deputy Commander and the driving force behind its strategies – would support him. It was clear that Obote regarded the UNLA not as belonging to the nation but as his own and the UPC's army that would keep him in power at all costs. This was partly demonstrated during the 1980 election campaign, when Obote would challenge the DP leader to show him *his* army.

Obote knew that although he did not, like the DP, have a civil constituency, his own military constituency was solidly Nilotic. He knew that the Acholi-Langi hegemony which provided the underpinning for his administration was sure and strong, and supported by other soldiers from the peripheral areas in the east – such as Teso – and some Bantu-speakers from the south and west.

As we know, confronted with the decision whether or not to join Obote and the UPC in parliament after the disastrous December 1980 election, the DP leaders grudgingly swallowed their pride – some say they also swallowed their principles – and decided to join parliament. It is said that after the UPC coup, the UPM leaders approached the DP and asked what course it intended to take. According to some sources, the DP leaders replied that they were joining the parliament because they had been rightfully elected. 'Not all votes were stolen,' they appeared to be telling Museveni's party; otherwise the DP would not have won fifty-one seats.

A staunch DP member has stated that there was a long debate on the issue of whether or not the elected DP members should take up their parliamentary seats. But they eventually did agree to take up those seats, perhaps in response to Obote's promise to give them the post of Deputy Speaker and the nomination of four of ten Specially Elected Members who would be chosen.

Obote, with 'magnanimity,' agreed to Paul Ssemogerere becoming the 'Leader of the Opposition' and Alex Waibale 'Opposition Whip.'

The DP parliamentarians would continue condemning the UPC government for its rigging of the elections, but Obote and his supporters saw the DP's presence on the Opposition benches in parliament as the party's acknowledgement of the validity of the 1980 election.

However, some Ugandans – prominent among them being Yoweri Museveni – refused to give support to a government that had obtained power through fraud.

Museveni has been blamed for rejecting the results of the 1980 election since he had been Vice-Chairman of the Military Commission that organised it. Indeed, one critic has even said that not only was Museveni 'a key person in ensuring that the election was not rigged...[but] if anything, he could have been in a position to rig the election in his favour.'

Such criticism is not only unfair, but also shows how some commentators on these events had little idea of what was actually going on in Uganda at that time. Those with eyes to see knew that Museveni was no more than a figurehead within the Military Commission, as indeed was reflected by the nature and size of the room he occupied on the third floor in the parliamentary building. The real rulers in the Military Commission at the time we are talking of were Paulo Muwanga and David Oyite-Ojok.

Be that as it may, the UPM refused to accept the election results and some of its members, soon joined by other peace-loving Ugandans in other parties but especially in the DP, decided to oppose Obote through the use of the gun, since that was the only language Obote understood. They started a guerrilla war against his regime. The outbreak of this guerrilla movement from the moment when he stepped into State House once again compounded Obote's problems right from the start of his administration." – (Ibid., pp. 150 – 151).

Thus, right from the beginning, Obote denied himself the opportunity to govern and implement his policies effectively by refusing to reach out to his opponents and offer them meaningful concessions. He refused to work with them and relied solely on his fellow UPC members and supporters at a time when the country was deeply divided after the 1980 general elections. He was, in a very tragic way, partly responsible for his own failure and destruction and tarnished his image as one of the leading African statesmen.

Unlike Obote during his second presidency, Museveni tried to establish a broad-based political movement and succeeded, to a limited degree, in bringing different groups together in pursuit of national unity. But he failed to mobilise support in the north and bring in northerners to the degree that he should have.

And he fell short of instituting democracy which he promised he would after seizing power, although his government was not a full dictatorship; it had redeeming qualities even if they did not amount to full democracy.

215

But it could not claim democratic legitimacy when the opposition was not allowed full participation in national politics and in the electoral process.

Chapter Five

Uganda under Museveni

YOWERI MUSEVENI became one of the most well-known political figures in Uganda after Idi Amin was ousted in April 1979.

In 1980, he formed a political party, the Uganda Patriotic Movement (UPM), to run for president.

Museveni's main opponents in the general elections in December 1980 were former president, Dr. Milton Obote, leader of the Uganda People's Congress (UPC) which led the country to independence, and Paul Ssemogerere, leader of the Democratic Party (DP).

The Conservative Party (CP), led by Jehoash Mayanja Nkangi, also took part in the elections. Nkangi once served as prime minister of the Buganda kingdom under Kabaka Mutesa II and was in office when the *kabaka* was ousted in 1966.

But the Conservative Party did not pose a major challenge to the other contenders because of its limited regional appeal. It was mostly a party of Baganda traditionalists and drew its support almost exclusively from the former Buganda kingdom.

The most formidable challenge to Obote's Uganda People's Congress came from the Democratic Party which was moderately conservative. Although it had roots in the Buganda kingdom and was predominantly Catholic and appealed to Catholic voters in the sixties, it broadened its appeal and became a major contender in the 1980 general elections. It was strongest in the south while Obote's UPC's stronghold was the north, his home region.

Although the Democratic Party performed better than Museveni's Uganda Patriotic Movement (UPM) in spite of electoral rigging by Obote's UPC supporters, it lost some credibility among many Ugandans when it became the official opposition in parliament, thus inadvertently legitimising Obote's "victory" at the polls. Other groups, including the Uganda Patriotic Movement exerted a lot of pressure on the Democratic Party to dissuade its leaders from joining parliament but were unsuccessful.

However, such intransigence cost the Democratic Party some valuable members including Andrew Kayiira who decided to launch guerrilla warfare against the government. They formed an urban guerrilla group, the Uganda Freedom Movement (UFM), which had spectacular success in some parts of Kampala before it was finally defeated by government forces.

The group which became Obote's fiercest and most dangerous opponent was the National Resistance Movement (NRM) led by Museveni whose name is synonymous with what came to be known as the Uganda Bush War, also known as the Resistance War or Luweero War, because he was the driving force behind it.

The war was fought from 1981 to 1986, first against

President Obote, and then against Tito Okello, the military head of state who replaced Obote after a military coup.

The military wing of the National Resistance Movement (NRM) which waged the war was the National Resistance Army (NRA).

After Museveni announced that he and his supporters were going to launch a popular rebellion to overthrow Obote, he and his followers sought a safe haven in the southwest, his home region, where they formed the Popular Resistance Army (PRA).

The PRA later united with the Uganda Freedom Fighters (UFF) led by former president, Yusuf Lule, to form the National Resistance Army (NRA). They also formed the National Resistance Movement (NRM) as the political arm of the NRA to articulate and propagate the ideals of the struggle against Obote's rule and against any other kind of unrepresentative form of government, with the underlying principle that the people, not the leaders, are sovereign.

There were two other rebel groups during that time opposed to Obote: the Uganda National Rescue Front (UNRF) and the Former Uganda National Army (FUNA). Both were formed in West Nile District, Idi Amin's home region. They were supporters of Amin and waged war against the Uganda National Liberation Army (UNLA) – which was the national army under Obote – in West Nile District.

The war by the National Resistance Army was formally launched on 6 February 1981 when NRA fighters attacked an army installation in Mubende District in the former Buganda kingdom in central Uganda. It was a war that would change the political landscape of Uganda and other parts of the Great Lakes region for years to come because of Museveni's role in other conflicts as well.

He supported the Tutsi-dominated Rwandan Patriotic Front (RPF) which launched its attack on the Hutu-dominated government of Rwanda from Ugandan soil with his approval and finally overthrew that government in 1994, ending the Rwandan genocide. He also, together with Rwandan RPF ruler Paul Kagame who was trained in Tanzania as an intelligence officer and who served as the intelligence chief of the Ugandan army after Amin was overthrown, helped overthrow President Mobutu Sese Seko of neighbouring Zaire. And the armies of both countries, Uganda and Rwanda, went on to dominate eastern Congo, former Zaire, for years on orders from Museveni and Kagame.

When the RNA started its guerrilla war against Obote's government, no-one knew how far-reaching its impact would be if Museveni won and became president of Uganda, although he already had ambitions beyond Uganda and knew that he would try to overthrow Mobutu, his enemy, one day and help Rwandan refugees – mostly Tutsi – living in Uganda return to their homeland by force.

He already had military experience fighting against Idi Amin. He was the leader of the Front for National Salvation (FRONASA) which he formed in Tanzania and which was one of the military groups that joined the Tanzanian army, the Tanzania People's Defence Forces (TPDF), to overthrow Amin. He also had some knowledge about guerrilla warfare after spending sometime with the freedom fighters of FRELIMO – Front for the Liberation of Mozambique – in Mozambique when he was a student at the University of Dar es Salaam in Tanzania. And he used that knowledge to mobilise forces in Uganda against Obote's government.

To mobilise forces and civilian support, he focused on the areas where Obote was not popular; Obote was in fact hated by many people in those areas.

His primary focus was on the rural areas of Buganda, especially the central and western parts of the former kingdom which became his operational base in an area near the capital Kampala; his home region of Ankole and

220

other parts in the southwest; and in Bunyoro also in the western part of the country.

He started his campaign in Ankole and continued to mobilise grassroots support in other parts of the southwest. The campaign included political education, not just military training. As Professor Joshua Rubongoya states in his book, *Regime Hegemony in Museveni's Uganda: Pax Musevenica*:

"His decision to attend the University of Dar es Salaam, a hotbed of socialist and Marxist political paradigms, further strengthened Museveni's *Weltanschauung* or worldview and convinced him of a need for a fundamental transformation of both the socioeconomic structure of the peasantry and the peasants' consciousness of it.

Drawing from his social roots,Museveni makes the observation that African societies are precapitalist – and in a sense patrimonial – based on identity rather than rationality and are, therefore, vulnerable to local or international elite manipulation.

Because of these characteristics he argues that peasant ideology is still guided by an insidious form of superstition that limits entrepreneurial capacities, thus, perpetuating backwardness.

Out of this thinking emerges Museveni's opposition to political parties in general and multiparty democracy in particular. He reasoned that Uganda's political history was replete with examples of political parties that served as conduits through which parochial, ethnic, and religious interests have subsumed national priorities. They have perverted the development of national unity and consciousness, thus, undermining the roots of a modern economic system.

Indeed, his reasoning is that superstition, sectarianism, and the absence of a capitalist class have slowed the development of modern productive forces and left the peasantry open to the machinations of uncouth, irresponsible political party elites. In order to deal with these pathologies, Museveni advocated and implemented what has come to be known as 'movement' or 'no-party' democracy (Nelson Kasfir 2000). This explains his Johnny-come-lately advocacy for multiparty politics.

Nonetheless, when Museveni announced his desire to bring about 'fundamental change' on (his inauguration day) January 29, 1986, he meant not only restructuring society but also changing the political culture of Uganda's political elite. He campaigned for a shift from, in his words, the cheap, backward, and myopic forms of leadership to principled, disciplined, and scientific management of the state (Museveni 1997, 2000).

In practical terms, Museveni exhorted NRM leaders to mobilize and educate the masses, which explains why he personally went around the country teaching, lecturing, and debating issues pertinent to his political vision and philosophy (Museveni 1997, 2000). This form of communication earned President Museveni the label of democratic populist because it blends well with the local cultures in which consultation and talks between leader and the citizens is widely accepted and is, therefore, legitimizing. Indeed, much of Museveni's early popularity hinged on his virtuosity in combining paternalistic and populist elements in his leadership style.

The charismatic authority flowing from these elements has allowed Museven to inspire, *inter alia*, local community development projects and volunteerism, especially by LC committees and Local Defense Units (LDUs) that complemented national law enforcement and security units.

Museveni's leadership style appeared to reflect an intimate acquaintance with the everyday life and experiences of the masses. To ignore this background is to miss an important trajectory in the growth of his thinking and leadership, both as a guerrilla fighter from a peasant background and as president of Uganda since 1986. Indeed, much of what sets Museveni apart from his predecessors is rooted in the particularities of his social background.

Some have argued that Museveni was never an ally of the peasant/working classes, but a good political tactician. Be that as it may, Museveni's social roots cannot be divorced from the character, nature and outcome of the bush war or from the political vision he projected after assuming state power – these form the normative foundation for the early period of *Pax Musevenica*. Indeed once in government, these same political values became the springboard from which he would launch sweeping changes to the political, social, and economic landscape of Uganda.

What were the challenges that redirected Museveni's vision for Uganda? What political choices did his leadership make, and why? Which ones were imposed on him? What were the missed opportunities during this very pivotal moment in Uganda's history? And central to this study, how much democratic legitimacy did the NRM gain and to what extent was it used to further state institutionalization." – (Joshua B. Rubongoya, *Regime Hegemony in Museveni's Uganda: Pax Musevenica*, New York: Palgrave Macmillan, 2007, pp. 61 – 62).

There was also the question of how Museveni was going to become Uganda's president in order to implement the values and policies he had in mind probably since his student days at the University of Dar es Salaam in Tanzania.

He could have tried to seize power through a military coup. He already had military training and experience and took part in the ouster of Idi Amin. He also had contacts in the military since he had once served as defence minister under Obote after Amin was overthrown. But there were several factors which militated against a military takeover had he and his colleagues decided to attempt that to oust Milton Obote soon after Obote regained the presidency.

Museveni also ruled out other options which did not include right from the beginning participation of the masses, especially the peasants in the rural areas, in the struggle against Obote's government which he described as undemocratic since it came into power after the 1980 elections were rigged by Obote's supporters. As Rubongoya states:

"When Museveni left for the bush in 1981, as he had promised he would if the previous year's elections were rigged, Uganda was in the grip of Obote's second dictatorship.

The decision not to organize a possible coup against the now newly formed government of Obote was critical in shaping the future of the Museveni revolution. The success of a possible coup against Obote was in doubt, considering that over 1000 Tanzanian soldiers were still in Uganda following the overthrow of Idi Amin.

The other alternative was to appeal to the international community to annul the election results, but foreign election observers had already declared the elections 'free and fair,' thus, lending the all-important external legitimacy to the outcome of the polls.

The third alternative would have been to wage an urban campaign using assassinations of ruling elites and the destruction of state institutions as the main methods of opposition.

Museveni rejected all of these options, favoring instead the more protracted and arduous process of launching a grassroot, peasant-based guerrilla war. Not only would this option mobilize the support of peasant/working classes, but it would also ultimately lead to the Movement uprooting the elites and institutions of neopatrimonial governance. This decision was initially important in shaping the dynamic and ideological orientation of the

Movement because the latter was freed of external obligations. Peasant- and working-class participation would provide the strongest foundation both for the revolution and for the post-Obote system of government, especially at the local level.

The first and critical component of Museveni's revolution was the institutionalization of a force that would impose military resistance to the Obote regime. Museveni started with a military 'force' of twenty-six men and hardly any ammunition. The February 8, 1981, attack on Kabamba Military Training Wing would be the first of many such raids on military installations inside Uganda. Since the expected consignment of arms from foreign sources did not materialize, these raids were absolutely vital – as weapons supply sources – for an internal, incipient guerrilla force. But more, more importantly, during this initial phase, Museveni was faced with two challenges, namely, to be self-reliant in weapons acquisition and to find and train recruits for his embryonic army.

Furthermore, Museveni was determined not to repeat the mistakes of both the colonial and the previous postcolonial states in their policies of recruiting, training, and disciplining their militaries. Thus, the recruitment, partly out of necessity and partly out of a conscious decision, targeted both men and women – it sought to close the traditional gender gap in the military. The training of recruits included not only military discipline and know-how, but most importantly political education as well. While peasants involved in actual combat received more advanced training, the noncombatants underwent military training involving drills and gunhandling. Also included in the training courses were military songs, physical exercises, and group dynamics and cohesion.

But the popularity of these courses rested on the NRM rationale, namely, that such preparations would enable Ugandans to defend themselves in the event of a return to state-directed tyranny. And, in Buganda, in particular, this claim was poignant considering Obote's systematic slaughter of innocent citizens in the Luwero triangle from 1981 to 1984, for which his wife, Miria Obote, would later apologize." – (Ibid., pp. 62 – 63).

He goes on to state:

"Turning now to political education, the 'curriculum' consisted of 'daily lectures on topics such as African and Ugandan history, colonialism, law and justice, democracy, the practicalities of the LC (Local Council) system, civic rights and responsibilities, women's rights and economic development.' These courses – known locally as *mchaka mchaka* – were very popular because there was consensus among the peasantry that the acquired knowledge would cure the 'political immaturity' prevalent among the rural majority. The fact that this way of thinking among the rural masses fit perfectly with Museveni's paternalism contributed to his legitimacy early on, this was because the training – and the concomitant LC system – was seen as a democratization program that ran *with* the grain of local political culture rather than against it.

It was out of these mutations that that NRM/A was able to construct a social foundation upon which the basic political thrust of the anti-Obote movement would manifest, flourish, and lead to regime change. Even though *mchaka mchaka* programs later became propagandistic tools by which the NRM sought to exert state hegemony, in the beginning they were effective instruments for establishing badly needed regime legitimacy. Because such programs were unprecedented, NRM elites were able to distinguish themselves from previous regimes by strengthening their claims to fundamental change. But more importantly, by enabling ordinary Ugandan peasants to defend themselves against state tyranny, the NRM gained credibility and trust while improving value-based

226

reciprocity between state and society. It is from these early strategies that a governance realm would begin to emerge during this early period of power consolidation.

Museveni inculcated a new culture and ideology built around respect for civic virtue and the rights that flow from it. With these principles in place, the initial force of twenty-six individuals gradually expanded to include the mostly disenfranchised and alienated peasants and workers in the Buganda region that was later to be known as the Luwero Triangle. The latter became the geographic nucleus of Museveni's guerrilla movement.

The NRA itself was an amalgamation of Museveni's initial organization, the Popular Resistance Army (PRA), which was mostly made up of the Banyankore and the Baganda-dominated Uganda Freedom Fighters (UFF) led by Professor Yusuf Lule. This measure was undertaken to begin the construction of a non-sectarian military force in contrast to previous postcolonial armies that were dominated by northern ethnic groups. The institutionalization of a gender neutral and ethnically balanced military was a key decision not only in legitimizing the army, but also in turning it into an instrument for improving civil-military relations. The latter objective would become a key factor in the success of the guerrilla struggle itself." – (Ibid., pp. 63 – 64).

Whether or not Museveni truly identifies with masses – the peasants and workers – the way his political mentor Julius Nyerere did, is highly debatable. He undoubtedly projected the image of a populist when he mingled with the peasants during his preparation for guerrilla war that would later end Obote's rule. However, years later, after being in office as president, he does not seem to be the same Museveni the people knew earlier when he was mobilising forces in the rural areas to fight Obote.

Unlike Nyerere who remained humble and simple until his last days, Museveni is no different from other

African leaders who are known for their extravagance and lavish lifestyles and for dispensing favours to their friends and family members including sending them overseas for medical treatment and giving them high government positions as Museveni himself has done in spite of his claim that he identifies with the masses and lives modestly. He has even appointed his wife as a cabinet member.

In August 2012, Museveni outraged many Ugandans when he appointed his son to be the commander of special forces, a decision that was interpreted as a deliberate effort to prepare him to be the next president of Uganda. According to a report from Uganda's capital Kampala by Rodney Muhuza, "Uganda's President Elevates his Son's Army Powers," carried by the Associated Press (AP) on 27 August 2012:

"Ugandan President Yoweri Museveni made his son a one-star general and appointed him overall commander of the country's special forces, leading some Ugandans to conclude that the son is being groomed to succeed his father.

In changes announced on Monday, Col. Muhoozi Kainerugaba was made a brigadier-general, the latest promotion in the 38-year-old's quick rise through the ranks. Some Ugandans have long believed that Museveni, who took power by force in 1986, is nurturing his son to eventually take over from him when he retires.

Mwambutsya Ndebesa, a political historian at Uganda's Makerere University, said the promotion gives that credence.

'Museveni might now be confirming the rumors that he is preparing his son for succession,' Ndebesa said. 'It's just unimaginable that this is happening.'

In his new role Kainerugaba, who received some military training at the elite Sandhurst British academy, will be the chief protector of his father and resources such as oil wells. While he previously reported to the chief army commander, it appears that now he will answer directly to his father.

Some analysts say that Kainerugaba's rise through the army has been a source of resentment for the more senior army officers who see the first son as being shamelessly fast-tracked toward the point when he will assume firm control of the Ugandan military. Uganda's most senior army officers are veterans of the bush war that brought Museveni to power in January 1986, when Kainerugaba was not yet a teenager.

Nicholas Sengoba, a political analyst based in Kampala, said Kainerugaba's promotion had made it clearer that Museveni wants his son to have more say in the military going forward.

'It's been quite obvious that Muhoozi is headed for big things,' Sengoba said. 'This vindicates those who have been critical of Museveni. The doubts are being removed slowly.'

Throughout his political career Museveni has been dogged by accusations that he practices nepotism. His wife is a Cabinet minister and his brother used to be one.

Museveni, who was reelected last year, has not said if he will run again when his current term expires in 2016. But he faces pressure within and outside the ruling party to quit and preside over what would be the first peaceful transfer of power in Uganda's history."

As one reader, Mike, stated in his comment on the promotion, published in the *Daily Monitor,* Kampala, Uganda, 27 August 2012: "It is a custom with dictators who want to create dynasties. I'm not surprised!"

President Museveni's fellow countrymen have also been outraged by his lavish spending, including the purchase of an expensive presidential jet and sending his daughter to Germany to give birth, which cannot be reconciled with his image as a man of the people. According to a report, "Outrage at Ugandan President's Plan to Buy Himself £25 million Private Jet," subtitled, "Under Fire: Yoweri Museveni Wants to Blow Millions of Pounds on a Jet," in the *Daily Mail*, London, 19 December 2007:

"Uganda's president was today slammed over plans to spend £25 million on a private jet despite the average voter earning just £3 a week.

Members of poverty-stricken country's parliament claimed Yoweri Museveni's lavish gift would be a national asset.

But critics say Uganda, which has been devastated by AIDS with 2 million orphans from the disease, cannot afford the luxury Gulfstream jet.

'Why should a leader of a poor country fly a jet when leaders of some of the industrialised countries he begs from travel on commercial flights?' the *Weekly Observer* wrote in an editorial.

But a committee of lawmakers have endorsed the proposal to buy the plane which can comfortably fit up to 19 passengers.

'We believe this is not a luxury for the president. It is a national asset,' parliamentary committee chairwoman Mary Karooro said.

She also said the new plane would require less fuel than Museveni's existing presidential jet, need fewer inspections and stopovers on long-haul flights and be cheaper to maintain.

The government will either take out a loan from HSBC to buy the jet or borrow $28 million from the central bank, the rest of the cost being covered by proceeds from the sale of his existing plane.

Money-burning Museveni's frequent use of his presidential jet has sparked controversy in the past.

In 2003, he enraged critics by using it to fly his

daughter to a hospital in Germany so she could give birth, at a cost of $15,000 to the taxpayer."

The money spent to send Museveni's daughter to Germany to give birth also caused an outrage in Uganda and beyond. As Regina Jere-Malanda stated in her article, "Special delivery--the VIP baby: President Museveni has been trying hard to rebuff critics who have denounced his grandchild's costly birth at a German private clinic. But why did it happen?," in the *New African*, November 2003:

"President Yoweri Museveni has been under fire for flying his heavily pregnant daughter on his presidential jet to deliver her second baby in Germany at a reported cost of $90,000. But he has defiantly defended his action which his critics has condemned as needlessly uneconomical.

Museveni, who claims to live a 'modest lifestyle' and regularly condemns lavishness and wastefulness among Africans, says he had to send his daughter, Natasha, and an unnamed daughter in-law (due to give birth at the same time), abroad for the costly delivery--because he cannot trust local doctors and medical services.

'When it comes to medical care for myself and my family, there is no compromise,' he said in a defiant statement released to the local media who had widely condemned the action as an unnecessary wastage of limited public hinds, a view echoed by opposition politicians who only recently moved a motion in Parliament asking the First Family to trim down their 'luxurious lifestyle.'

In the statement, Museveni points out that he detests a wasteful lifestyle, but that as a leader, he is a constant target for plots to kill him and he believes some would-be assassins would not hesitate to use local doctors.

'I regard myself and my immediate family as a principal target for criminal forces,' he said in the strongly-worded statement which one of his senior advisors said the president wrote himself. 'He even described some doctors in Uganda as hostile, who cannot be trusted,' wrote the BBC's Will Ross.

President Museveni tried to dismiss the criticism even further by claiming that the whole affair cost 'only' US $27,000. But as one news paper reported, a Ugandan on the national average wage would take 85 years to turn that much.

The *Sunday Monitor* newspaper in Kampala, quoting a member of parliament with some knowledge of the aviation industry, broke down the cost as follows: it costs US$5,000 for every hour the presidential jet is airborne, and it takes--on average--Eight hours to any destination in Europe from Uganda's Entebbe airport. And it took the presidential jet on this special mission at least 18 hours to and from Germany—a whooping $90,000!

The two women were accompanied by an entourage of 10 other carers, including the First Lady herself, Mrs Janet Museveni. The expenses for their 10 days' upkeep – hotel, loud and probably shopping – while waiting for the babies to be born are not included in the above figure.

Apparently, however, nothing the president did here, is outside the law. In fact, according to Museveni's press secretary, Maria Karooro, the First Family in Uganda is perfectly entitled to such luxuries. 'The constitution says so.'

'The law provides for such a flight,' Karooro said. 'The Presidential Emoluments and Benefits Act provides that each biological or adopted child of the president shall be entitled to one trip abroad per year,' she told The *Sunday Monitor.* 'The law says such trips shall be at the expense of the State,' she added.

What prompted the president to send his daughter to deliver the baby at the unnamed private clinic has not been explained.

There has been speculation, however, that the president was concerned that rebel fighters or sympathisers of the

Lord's Resistance Army (LRA) had got wind of where Natasha was to give birth locally and planned an attack.

Normally, most airlines advise heavily-pregnant mothers against air travel--Natasha was only a few days away from her delivery date when she was flown out. She has another older daughter whom she gave birth to at a local private hospital and everything went perfectly fine then.

President Museveni's supporters have defended him as a humble and modest man who only gets an annual presidential salary of about 30,000 [pounds sterling]. 'Nobody who knows hint would describe him as a lavish man. His idea of a perfect meg would be a bowl of millet-meal washed down with a glass of milk,' says his senior advisor, John Nagenda. He adds: 'But as head of state, he has the right to do anything to protect his family if he has any reason to suspect they might be in harm's way.' However, critics say, the cost of having his grandchild delivered abroad could have paid for 1,200 Ugandan mothers to have a once in a lifetime chance of giving birth at a local private hospital in Kampala.

Most importantly, perhaps, $20,000 would have gone a long way in a malaria prevention programme – the country's biggest killer – of children or better still purchased basic medical supplies such as gloves and wound dressings which are routinely in shore supply in most local hospitals, but which come at a fraction of the cost of delivering the presidential grandchild."

That is in sharp contrast with Nyerere.

Museveni says he considers himself to be a disciple of Nyerere. But he obviously means not in terms of lifestyle.

Nyerere lived a very simple lifestyle and did not even carry any money in his pocket, according to those who knew him well and who were very close to him. Throughout the years when he was president, he did not live in his official residence, The State House. He used it only for visitors and for meetings. Instead, he chose to live in a very simple house, also of medium size, which he built after getting a loan from a bank in Dar es Salaam, Tanzania.

He was the lowest-paid head of state in the world, earning no more than $5,000 per year.

After he stepped down from the presidency, he returned to his home village of Butiama near the eastern shores of Lake Victoria in Mara Region in northern Tanzania to work on the farm as a peasant using simple tools – hoes, sickles and pangas (machetes) – and live in a simple house that was not even in good shape.

All that is unheard among leaders, let alone presidents. As James Mpinga stated – not long after Nyerere died on October 14th – in an article "With Mwalimu Gone, Free Bread for Butiama Children Goes Too," in *The East African*, Nairobi, Kenya, November 3, 1999:

"There is little to show that Butiama, the birthplace of Julius Nyerere, raised one of Africa's greatest sons.

Mud huts surround the Catholic Church where Nyerere used to pray, and both the church and the mud huts tell a story. From the mud huts came the children who knew exactly when Mwalimu would have his breakfast, and dutifully came to share it with him every morning, and in the church their parents shared a common faith and prayer.

'At first, it was bread and butter for both Mwalimu and the kids. Soon I couldn't cope with the increasing numbers of children joining him for breakfast, so I downgraded it to porridge and *kande* – (a boiled mixture of maize off the cob and pulses),' recalls Mwalimu's former housekeeper, Dorothy Musoga, 74, now living in retirement in Mwanza at a house built for her by Mwalimu.

I met Dorothy by sheer coincidence during Mwalimu's funeral at a pub put up by the Tanzania Peoples Defence Force (TPDF) building brigade at Butiama. Like all Mwalimu insiders, she was full of praise for the departed former president but, above all, worried about the future of his family and what she called Mwalimu's 'other children' who loved to share his breakfast.

'With Mwalimu dead, free breakfast for poor villagers will become a thing of the past,' Dorothy reflected, almost to herself, between sips of warm beer. The poverty of their parents remains, as does the lack of infrastructure at Butiama, which Mwalimu didn't want to transform into an edifice to be envied by Tanzania's 8,000 registered villages.

During the last week of October, vehicles thronged the dusty road to Butiama, which runs 11 kilometres from Makutano Juu along the Mwanza-Sirali highway. In fact, the road to Butiama was only made passable by last-minute grading. The net result, however, was a far from comfortable drive. The workmen had, in effect, only succeeded in increasing the circulation of dust.

The drive was a journey through abject deprivation and grinding poverty. On the way we saw small plots of cassava, much of it wilting under the searing heat. The land was mostly bare.

On Saturday, October 23, when Mwalimu was buried, Butiama may well have started to slip back into oblivion, to become what it once was, an unknown village in the middle of nowhere. With Tanzania's propensity for neglecting matters until they become a crisis, Butiama's transition from a collective shrine to an ordinary village is likely to be swift.

The process may, indeed, have started earlier, with Mwalimu's own house, which stands obscured from view by the relatively more affluent boma where the reigning patriarch of the Wazanaki, Chief Japhet Wanzagi, lives. By village standards, the chief's boma stands out as an island of prosperity in a sea of deprivation.

Many people take their first house as a proud possession, but the sewage system at the late Nyerere's first house bears marks of his self-denial. Children fetch water from a public standpipe and their mothers wash clothes in the open. The house itself could do with a fresh coat of paint. Nearby, and just as hidden, is the house where Nyerere's mother, the late Mugaya, lived.

However, judging from the relatively wealthier homestead of the chief, Mwalimu was no more than a peasant - which the Tanzanian government would want the world to believe. The truth is that the former president was in fact a prince who simply chose to shun the trappings of privilege out of his own conviction.

The day after the burial, October 24, I arrived at the village just as villagers in their Sunday best were leaving church. They behaved as if nothing had happened, a stark contrast to the day before when some of them had broken down, unable to reconcile themselves to a future without Nyerere. I was now seeing a different scenario; a people resigned to their common fate.

Only one person, Dr Ebenezer Mwasha, still remained in the past, eleven days after it had all happened. Dr Mwasha is among the scores of professionals who worked closely with Mwalimu both as individuals and as public servants. 'I always looked forward to Mwalimu's homecoming. I never thought I would have the misfortune to receive his body one day,' Dr Mwasha said ruefully a day before Tanzanians and their well-wishers buried Mwalimu.

I met Dr Mwasha again the Sunday after the burial, and he was still unable to believe the obvious. He and his wife were waiting to see Mama Maria, Mwalimu's widow, before he could drive back to Machame in Kilimanjaro region, where he now runs a non-governmental organisation dealing with primary health care. He told me he had been helping Mwalimu to put up an appropriate sanitation and water supply system at his new house, the one the Tanzania Peoples Defence Forces (TPDF) had built for him.

'It is sad that the old man didn't have much time to stay

in it,' Dr Mwasha said. Others at Butiama echoed his words. 'It was God's will, we cannot do anything' a primary school teacher, Gambiwa Masubo, said.

Gambiwa accosted me with poems for which he wanted me to find a publisher. 'Can *The East African* publish them, please?' he pleaded. Unfortunately, all them were in Kiswahili. In one of the poems, Gambiwa says Mwalimu has 'cleared the bush' so that the rest of Tanzania can move forward.

When I later visited the compound of Mwitongo, where Mwalimu was buried not far from the graves of his parents, only a few insiders and the late Nyerere's close family members had remained, among them his former press secretary Sammy Mdee and former aide-de-camp Philemon Mgaya. At the grave itself, TPDF soldiers from the army's building brigade were erecting a permanent structure.

The mood was still sombre, but noticeable was lighter than before. Some of the mourners took turns to have their pictures taken at the graveside. Was this some transition from mourning to a heritage industry? Now people had accepted the inevitable, Mwalimu's grave was already taking on the air of a world heritage site.

When Chairman Mao was asked what he thought about the French Revolution, a century and a half after it had taken place, he retorted: 'It's too early to say.'

Few in Tanzania can give a better answer about the impact of Nyerere's death. For the poor children of Butiama, however, the days of free breakfast with their beloved grandpa are gone. It is hard to imagine what will follow."

That is the leader Museveni says is his mentor and proudly adds that he is a disciple of Nyerere.

The contrast between the two is obvious.

Museveni greatly admired Nyerere not only as a great pan-Africanist committed to the unification and liberation of Africa including the liberation of Uganda from Amin's tyranny; he also greatly admired Nyerere for his humility and simplicity and uncompromising commitment to the well-being of the masses, the poorest of the poor.

He also greatly admired Nyerere as a great thinker, an assessment shared by other people including Nyerere's critics such as Professor Ali Mazrui who also at the same time always admired Nyerere and who stated in his work, *General History of Africa VIII: Africa Since 1935* :

"Julius Nyerere is the most enterprising of African political philosophers. He has philosophized extensively in both English and Kiswahili.

He has tried to tear down the language barriers between ancestral cultural philosophy and the new ideological tendency of the post-colonial era. Nyerere is superbly eloquent in both English and Kiswahili.

He has allowed the two languages to enrich each other as their ideas have passed through his intellect.

His concept of *ujamaa* as a basis of African socialism was itself a brilliant cross-cultural transition. *Ujamaa* traditionally implied *ethnic* solidarity. But Nyerere transformed it from a dangerous principle of ethnic nepotism into more than a mere equivalent of the European word 'socialism.'

In practice his socialist policies did not work – as much for global reasons as for domestic. But in intellectual terms Nyerere is a more original thinker than Kwame Nkrumah – and linguistically much more innovative.

Nkrumah tried to update Lenin – from Lenin's *Imperialism: The Highest State of Capitalism* to Nkrumah's *Neo-Colonialism: The Last Stage of Imperialism.* Nyerere translated Shakespeare into Kiswahili instead – both *Julius Caesar* and *The Merchant of Venice.*

Nkrumah's exercise in Leninism was a less impressive cross-cultural achievement than Nyerere's translation of

Shakespeare into an African language.

Yet both these African thinkers will remain among the towering figures of the twentieth century in politics and thought." – (Ali A. Mazrui in Ali. A. Mazrui, ed., *General History of Africa VIII: Africa Since 1935*, Berkeley, California, USA: University of California Press, 1993, p. 674).

Professor Mazrui also had this to say in *Governance and Leadership*: *Debating the African Condition*:

"(Nyerere's) great experiments and inspirational ideas are an indication that the mystique of Nyerere is not simply in his being an intellectual. It is also in his being a gifted and imaginative one.

Of all the top political figures in English-speaking Africa as a whole, Nyerere is perhaps the most original thinker....The originality of Nyerere consisted not in the policies advocated but in the arguments advanced in their defense." – Ali A. Mazrui in Alamin M. Mazrui and Willy M. Mutunga, eds., *Governance and Leadership*: *Debating the African Condition*: *Mazrui and His Critics, Volume Two*, Trenton, New Jersey, USA: Africa World Press, 2003, p. 85. Ali Mazrui's assessment of Nyerere and his policies, cited here, was first published as an article, "Tanzaphilia: A Diagnosis," in *Transition: A Journal of The Arts, Culture and Society*, Vol. 6, No. 31, June – July 1967, Kampala, Uganda, pp. 20 – 26. The article was also republished in Ali Mazrui's book, *Violence and Thought: Essays on Social Tensions in Africa*, London: Longmans, 1969. See also Ali A. Mazrui, *On Heroes and Uhuru-Worship: Essays on Independent Africa*, London: Longmans, 1967).

Mazrui was also interviewed by Professor Seifudein Adem on a wide range of issues about Africa including leaders such as Nyerere, Nkrumah and Mandela, and stated the following in that interview which was published in *The Gambia Echo*, 25 July 2008:

"The fact that Nkrumah had a greater positive impact on me than has any other leader does not necessarily mean that I admire Nkrumah the most.

Intellectually, I admired Julius K. Nyerere of Tanzania higher than most politicians anywhere in the world. Nyerere and I also met more often over the years from 1967 to 1997 approximately.

I am also a great fan of Nelson Mandela. By ethical standards Mandela is greater than Nyerere; but by intellectual standards Nyerere is greater than Mandela."

And in his lecture on intellectualism in East Africa entitled "Towards Re-Africanizing African Universities: Who Killed Intellectualism in the Post-Colonial Era?" in Nairobi, Kenya, on 14 September 2003, Mazrui had this to say about Nyerere:

"The most intellectual of East Africa's Heads of State at the time was Julius K. Nyerere of Tanzania – a true philosopher, president and original thinker....

In Tanzania intellectualism was slow to die. It was partially protected by the fact that the Head of State – Julius Nyerere – was himself a superb intellectual ruler. He was not only fascinated by ideas, but also stimulated by debates....

In my own personal life I was respected more as an intellectual by Milton Obote in Uganda and Julius Nyerere in Tanzania than I was by either Mzee Kenyatta or Daniel arap Moi in Kenya.

Even Idi Amin, when he was in power in Uganda, wanted to send me to apartheid South Africa as living proof that Africans could think. Idi Amin wanted me to become Exhibit A of the Black Intellectual to convince racists in South Africa that Black people were human beings capable of rational thought."

Nyerere was admired even by some of his most ardent critics. As Jonathan Power, who was highly critical of Nyerere's policies and one party-rule, stated in his article, "Lament for Independent Africa's Greatest Leader":

"Tanzania in East Africa has long been one of the 25 poorest countries in the world. But there was a time when it was described, in terms of its political influence, as one of the top 25. It punched far above its weight. That formidable achievement was the work of one man, now lying close to death in a London Hospital....

His extraordinary intelligence, verbal and literary originality... and apparent commitment to non-violence made him not just an icon in his own country but of a large part of the activist sixties' generation in the white world who, not all persuaded of the heroic virtues of Fidel Castro and Che Guevara, desperately looked for a more sympathetic role model.

Measured against most of his peers, Jomo Kenyatta of Kenya, Kwame Nkrumah of Ghana, Ahmed Sekou Toure of Guinea, he towered above them. On the intellectual plane only the rather remote president of Senegal, the great poet and author of Negritude, Leopold Senghor, came close to him.

Not only was Nyerere financially open, modest and honest, he was uncorrupted by fame or position. He remained throughout his life, self-effacing and unpretentious....

Many of us will mourn Julius Nyerere when he is gone. He was, without any doubt...the most inspiring African leader of his generation." – (Jonathan Power, TFF Jonathan Power Columns, "Lament for Independent Africa's Greatest Leader," London, October 6, 1999).

Kenyan journalist and political analyst, Philip Ochieng'

who worked at the *Daily News* in Dar es Salaam, Tanzania, in the early seventies also had a lot to say about Nyerere. As he stated in his article, "Africa's Greatest Leader Was A Heroic Failure, " *The East African*, Nairobi, Kenya, 19 October 2009:

"It takes extraordinary personal strength for a leader to admit in public that he is a failure.

Julius Nyerere is the only one I know who has ever done it.

Some time towards the end, he stood on a podium to announce that he had failed to achieve the social goal that had driven him into leadership.

But if you have genuinely tried, failure is to be respected.

Julius Nyerere is among the extremely few world leaders who have selflessly attempted great things for their national peoples.

Other African leaders -- notably Leopold Senghor and Tom Mboya -- have spoken of 'African socialism' as a means of restoring human dignity to the African person after a protracted era of colonial brutalisation and dehumanisation. But none has ever offered a plausible definition of 'African socialism.'

Mwalimu Nyerere was the first -- probably the only -- African nationalist leader to cast a serious moral and intellectual eye upon Africa's 'extended family' tradition and weave a practical national development philosophy around it.

Ujamaa had two basic components.

The Ujamaa Village was an attempt to revive traditional rural communalism -- bringing groups of villages together, investing collectively in them and running them through modern democratic precepts.

Since the turn of the 21st century, Kenya's own leaders have divided and sub-divided what used to be called districts into veritable village units, claiming a purpose similar to 'Nyerereism' -- to bring utilities and social services 'closer to the people.'

The second component was much more theoretically shaky -- a series of nationalisations intended to bring urban commerce and industry under state control, the state purporting to be the public's trustee.

But the 1967 *Arusha Declaration* in which this doctrine of 'socialism and self-reliance' was enunciated opened a Pandora's box of ideology. Ideas ran from the extreme right to others that were so leftist that, in the circular prism of ideas, they actually bordered on the right!

In a single-party system, all these ideas were forced to contend with one another within that party.

It was no wonder, then, that Marxist-Leninists, Bepari (capitalists) and even Kabaila (feudalists) held central positions both in the party and in government.

This, indeed, was where Nyerere began to reveal his greatness.

In other 'socialist' situations -- such as Sekou Toure's Conakry -- every thought and activity deemed dangerous would simply have been banned, often on pain of death.

Nyerere encouraged even his bitterest opponents to express themselves freely and without fear.

And he often took them on -- not by means of such state machinery as our Nyayo House basement, but intellectually, replying to each critic point by point.

The Nationalist (the party's own organ) and *The Standard* Tanzania (the government publication on which Ben Mkapa and I worked – later renamed *Daily News*) routinely published news, features, columns and letters expressing the most diverse views.

Nyerere demanded only that his detractors produce the facts and figures and weave these into cogent thought.

'Argue, don't shout!' he once admonished his equivalents of the loudmouthed but empty-headed coalition that rules Kenya.

No, Mwalimu was not a revolutionary in any Marxist

sense.

Like all of Africa's petty bourgeois radicals in power at that time -- Ben Bella, Kaunda, Keita, Nasser, Nkrumah, Obote, Toure -- he rejected outright all of Marx and Lenin's theories on class, revolution and party organisation.

His, said he, was a national mass movement in which every Tanzanian must participate.

Such a policy might sound noble, but it was what finally proved Dr Nyerere's Achilles heel.

You cannot implement any 'socialist' programme except through a committed vanguard.

For his Ujamaa Village projects, he relied on the peasantry, a property-owning class whose members, as a rule, are interested only in their small individual property.

For his nationalisation programme, he relied on another property-owning class, what the Kiswahili Academy called vibwanyenye.

This propertied urban class was led by the educated elite who monopolised the civil service, the police, the provincial administration, the army, the classroom, the shrine -- a social stratum deeply drilled right from the classroom in liberal Western individualism and self-pursuit.

In 1972, goaded by Idi Amin's overthrow of Milton Obote -- the ally across the Great Lake -- Mwalimu issued a set of ruling-party 'Guidelines' called *Mwongozo*, which, among other things, introduced an elaborate leadership code.

But to no avail. Soon the Ujamaa Village administrative network, as well as the two custodians of nationalised property -- the National Development Corporation and the State Trading Corporation -- were drowning in a well of corruption deeper than Lake Tanganyika.

Mwalimu reacted by decentralising the leaderships of both those bodies and the central governance system --

succeeding only in spreading bureaucratic ineptitude thinner on the ground, thus making corruption much more difficult to detect.

By replacing the colonial educational structure with what he called Elimu yenye Manufaa ('functional education'), he enabled Tanzania to kill up to five birds with one stone.

Tanzanian is the only African country that has totally banished illiteracy, and the Three Rs are solidly linked to vocational interests.

In the process, Tanzania became the African country with the highest degree of national self-consciousness and -- through it and through Kiswahili -- has almost annihilated the bane of Kenya that we call tribalism.

But, as a rule, internal policy is what guides a country's foreign policy.

Any nation that tries to cultivate self-sufficiency, self-efficiency, self-respect and self-pride will find it morally compelling to share these ideals with other nations the world over.

Ujamaa inspired Tanzania into spending much of its meagre resources on liberating the rest of Africa and the world from the colonial yoke.

At a time when Nairobi was drowning in crude elite grabbing, Dar es Salaam was a Mecca of the world's national liberation movements, and a hotbed of global intellectual thought.

From this perspective, it is justifiable to say that Mwalimu Julius Kambarage, son of Chief Nyerere, is the greatest and most successful leader that Africa has ever produced since the European colonial regime collapsed 50 years ago."

Another Kenyan journalist Barrack Muluka also stated the following about Nyerere in the *Standard*, Nairobi, 15 October 2011: "It shall take Africa ages to produce another philosopher like Nyerere."

Unlike most leaders, Nyerere not only mingled and identified with the masses who paid him the highest tribute after he died by saying "he was one of us"; he was also comfortable exchanging ideas with intellectuals, including some of the best like Professor Ali Mazrui, unlike many African leaders who are intimidated by them.

And probably more than any other East African president, it is Museveni who has tried to fill Nyerere's shoes and assume the mantle of leadership as the eminent leader in the region.

He may not be of Nyerere's calibre as a leader and as an intellectual. But he has harboured ambitions to be the the next Nyerere in the region and on the continent as a whole. And he wants to achieve what Nyerere failed to achieve by establishing a political federation of the East African countries Nyerere attempted to do in the sixties.

Although President Museveni has not reached that level in East Africa as a leader of Nyerere's stature and calibre, he has distinguished himself in Uganda where he did an excellent job in the early years when he was preparing for guerrilla warfare against Obote.

He was able to convince the peasants in the critical areas where he mobilised forces and established operational bases that he was on their side.

He also had a clear vision for Uganda and policies which would bring about fundamental change if they were implemented properly.

He also had a guerrilla force which was inclusive and even had non-Ugandans, mostly Rwandans, who were ready to take part in the revolution to bring about fundamental change in Uganda but also with the expectation that Uganda would in turn help them bring about such change in their own country. And that is exactly what happened.

Tutsi refugees who had lived in Uganda for many years, many of them since childhood, were some of the soldiers who constituted the National Resistance Army. One of them was Fred Rwigema (sometimes misspelled as Rwigyema). He was the commander of RNA guerrilla fighters. Museveni's half-brother, Salim Saleh, was the deputy commander.

Rwigema was also a friend of Paul Kagame and both planned the invasion of Rwanda from Uganda as the main leaders of the Rwandan Patriotic Front (RPF).

The RNA fighters used typical guerrilla tactics, moving around in small units, ambushing government military vehicles and convoys, and using hit-and-run tactics, and then melting into the civilian population.

The national army composed mostly of Acholi and Langi soldiers from northern Uganda randomly attacked civilians, ostensibly to flush out the guerrillas as the Americans did in Vietnam, but mainly to terrorise and brutalise them simply because they belonged to southern tribes which were against Obote, a northerner.

Massive relocation of civilians by government soldiers in the area that was the main battleground in that conflict, the Luweero Triangle, led to further abuses and countless deaths.

RNA guerrilla fighters were also responsible for many atrocities although not equal to those committed by government soldiers. NRA fighters planted mines which killed many civilians in the rural areas. They also used child soldiers.

The national army (UNLA) – which really became Obote's army with fellow northerners, the Langi and the Acholi, constituting the vast majority of the soldiers and officers – fought well against the NRA guerrillas when it was led by Oyite Ojok. But internal wrangling split the army along ethnic lines, Acholi versus Langi, as the Acholi complained of discrimination by the Langi who were members of Obote's tribe and who constituted the majority of the army officers.

The National Resistance Army took advantage of the

internal dissension within the army and capitalised on the split between the Acholi and the Langi. When the Acholi soldiers overthrew Obote, Museveni and his fighters sensed victory. They knew it was only a matter of time before they could seize power from the military rulers who overthrew Obote and whose army was now weak because of internal divisions.

After Museveni signed a peace agreement with Uganda's military head of state, Tito Okello, in Nairobi, Kenya, in December 1985, he began counting days when he would seize power. He had no intention of honouring the agreement. He knew the NRA would have an easy victory over the national army which was now mostly Acholi without the support of their fellow northerners, the Langi, many of whom had left after their kinsman, Obote, was overthrown by the Acholi.

The following month, on 25 January 1986, the NRA fighters entered Kampala, led by Museveni's brother Salim Saleh. They met virtually no resistance as Tito Okello and his fellow Acholi soldiers fled north, to their homeland. The National Resistance Army became the national army. It was renamed the Uganda People's Defence Force (UPDF) probably in honour of the Tanzania People's Defence Forces (TPDF) who had played such a major role in ending Amin's tyranny and thus helping pave the way for Museveni's rise to power years later. It was probably Museveni himself who chose the name. The RNA was renamed UPDF in 1995 after the country adopted a new constitution.

After seizing power, Museveni began to consolidate his base of support in the south. He portrayed himself as a civilian and not as a soldier in power. He tried to mobilise the masses and university students by identifying himself as a man of the people, using socialist rhetoric and focusing on the well-being of the vast majority of the people most of whom were poor. He also emphasised law and order after years of lawlessness and tyranny under

Amin and Obote.

He also embraced the people of the northwest, Amin's homeland, and gave high government positions to a significant number of them.

One of them was Amin's sons. Another prominent figure from the northwest was Brigadier Moses Ali, former minister of finance under Amin, who was the leader of a rebel group, the Uganda National Rescue Front (UNRF), which first fought against Obote and then Museveni. Many UNRF fighters joined Museveni's National Resistance Army after Obote was overthrown in July 1985 and after signing a peace agreement with the government. They also, together with other UNRF members, joined the National Resistance Movement which was the country's ruling party under Museveni.

But Moses Ali had a somewhat tempestuous relationship with Museveni's government. He was given a number of high government positions including ministerial posts but was arrested for treason in April 1990. He was released in June 1992 after being cleared of the charges. Museveni brought him back into the cabinet and gave him other ministerial posts including that of deputy prime minister.

There was also a resurgence of the UNRF, that came be known as the Uganda National Rescue Front II, whose members broke away from the West Nile Bank Front in 1996. Some members of the first UNRF joined the group. The UNRF II did not sign a peace agreement with Museveni's NRM government.

The Uganda National Rescue Front II was led by Major-General Ali Bamuze and was supported by the Sudanese government in retaliation for Museveni's – NRM's – support for the Sudan People's Liberation Army (SPLA). The SPLA was led by Dr. John Garang, Museveni's friend. Museveni and Garang attended the University of Dar es Salaam in Tanzania during the same period and were active in revolutionary organisations on

249

and off campus.

The UNRF II had its operational bases in Arua District in southern Sudan where its fighters retreated after launching attacks against government soldiers and other targets on Ugandan soil.

The conflict between the two ended in December 2002 when the Uganda National Rescue Front II signed a ceasefire agreement with Museveni's government in the town of Yumbe in the northwest. A battalion of the UNRF rebel fighters joined the national army. The group also got a monetary reward from the government for renouncing violence.

Another rebel group was the National Army for the Liberation of Uganda (NALU), formed in 1988, which was active in the northern and western parts of the country fighting the national army. NALU later merged with the Allied Defence Forces (ADF) and established operational bases in neighbouring Democratic Republic of Congo (DRC), especially in North Kivu province and in the border region of the Ruwenzori mountains.

When Museveni's government offered an amnesty to rebel groups in 2005, less than 50 members of NALU accepted the offer.

Museveni tried hard to achieve peace and stability after years of chaos and war and made a lot of progress in those areas.

He was also pragmatic enough to realise that the world had changed and abandoned his socialist beliefs. He became one of the most ardent advocates of free-market policies to rebuild the economy.

Although he won the war, there were still a number of rebel groups which continued to fight for various reasons including self-determination. And he made an effort to absorb them into the army and the National Resistance Movement to pacify the country. The insurgencies were mostly in the north, east and west, especially between the mid-eighties and early nineties.

They were mostly among the Langi, Obote's fellow tribesmen, and the Acholi in the central north; among the Teso – or Iteso – in the east; and among the Kakwa, Lugbara and Nubians in the northwest.

Among the Acholi, the Uganda People's Democratic Party (UPDA) led by Lieutenant-Colonel John Angelo Okello was the most active and prominent group. The Uganda People's Army (UPA) was active among the Teso from 1987 to 1992. It was led by Peter Otai who once served as minister of state for defence under President Obote during his second presidency.

The Citizen's Army for Multiparty Politics (CAMP) led by Brigadier Smith Opon Acak was one of the groups active among the Langi.

A former army chief of staff under Obote, Brigadier Opon Acak also fought together with Langi rebels against Museveni's National resistance Army in Lira District, the home of former president Obote. He was killed in July 1999 near the town of Lira while fighting the NRA soldiers. He was 56.

All those rebel groups were no match for the National Resistance Army. But they waged prolonged fights.

The toughest fight was in northwestern Uganda, the regional and ethnic stronghold of former military ruler Idi Amin, because of the advantage the rebels had operating from across the border in southern Sudan.

Some of Museveni's major achievements in reconciliation were in 1988 when his government signed peace agreements with two rebel groups, the Uganda People's Democratic Army (UPDA) and the Uganda People's Army (UPA). In April that year, the government offered an amnesty to the UPA rebels and others.

They were mostly members of small rebel groups and agreed to surrender and support the government.

And in June 1988, the UPDA signed a peace agreement with the government.

A significant number of UPA and UPDA fighters and

other rebels joined the government's National Resistance Army. But thousands of others refused to sign a peace agreement with Museveni's government and continued to fight.

However, Uganda under Museveni has been relatively stable. The stability the country has enjoyed is comparable to life in Uganda in the sixties after independence. Those were the early years of the post-colonial period under Obote when the country enjoyed peace and stability except for the conflict with the *kabaka* when he was violently ousted and forced to flee to Britain.

The country remained relatively peaceful until 1971 when Amin overthrew the government and instituted a reign of terror, killing countless innocent civilians as well as Acholi and Langi soldiers.

It was not until 1986 when Museveni rose to power that Uganda again started to enjoy relative peace and stability in spite of the continued violence in different parts of the country by rebel groups who were opposed to his rule. As Professor Frederick Byaruhanga states in his book, *Student Power in Africa's Higher Education: A Case of Makerere University*:

"President Museveni and his National Resistance Movement came into power surrounded by massive popular support, especially as a result of his army's demonstration of high-level discipline. For the first time in more than a generation, Ugandans felt secure in their own country, an aura that has buttressed President Museveni's popularity, especially, in the rural areas.

Threads of political, social, and economic initiatives across the spectrum have punctuated his almost twenty years of power. On the political arena, the Movement government maintained – until this year, 2005 – its no-party – Movement – umbrella political stance, arguing that political parties had only served to divide the people mainly along religious and tribal lines.

252

Instead, a new form of democracy, reflected in bottom-up grassroots governance, was introduced. This democratic triangle begins on grassroots local councils – Local Council I, II, III – to city mayoral council – LC IV – then district – LC V – and ultimately, the national parliament and the presidency. All these positions are elective based on individual merit.

A new constitution was promulgated in 1994 and in 1996 Yoweri Museveni was chosen – by universal suffrage – as the first constitutionally elected president (Mugaju, 1999).

The second presidential elections were held in March 2001, which gave Museveni the presidential mandate for a second and last constitutional five-year term (he remained in power after that and was still in office at this writing in July 2012 – comment by Godfrey Mwakikagile).

In both presidential elections, constituency-based parliamentary elections were held a few months later, forming a British-style constitutionally mandated legislative branch of government.

Despite occasional imbalance caused mainly by rebel incursions from the northern and western parts of the country, and most recently, political instability in neighbouring Rwanda and Democratic Republic of Congo, Uganda has enjoyed relative political stability.

In regard to the economy, the Movement government has since 1980s abandoned its near socialist stance, and embraced the World bank/IMF-mandated Structural Adjustment Policies (Programmes). The economy has for the most part been liberalized, resulting in considerable institutional privatisation....

Other reform highlights include decentralization of governance, allocating more power and resources to district leadership; educational reforms as exemplified by the introduction of free Universal Primary Education; various public civil service reforms; and the women's empowerment movement (Mugaju, 1999)....

Other challenges, however, remain. These include but are not limited to the alarming presence of corruption in high places; the need to forge a climate of lasting peace with neighbouring countries; the reality of poverty, especially in rural areas; and the HIV/AIDS epidemic, among other things." – (Frederick Kamuhanda Byaruhanga, *Student Power in Africa's Higher Education: A Case of Makerere University,* New York: Routledge, Taylor & Francis Group, 2006, pp. 12 – 13).

There is no question that Uganda has achieved economic success under Museveni. The country is not the same as it was under Idi Amin or during Obote's second presidency which is often identified as Obote II.

And the achievement is significant when one takes into account the fact that the country was devastated by Amin's reign of terror and by civil war under Obote. It was hard to revive the economy.

It is this achievement which has earned Museveni credit and accolades from his fellow countrymen and from donor countries. He has also used it to justify his long tenure as if he is the only leader who can sustain peace and Uganda's economic growth. He has also used it to insulate himself from criticism by donor countries about his authoritarian leadership under which freedom is curtailed and the people are denied other human rights.

He also uses it as shield against criticism by his own people, reminding them, even if indirectly, that if it were not for him and his National Resistance Movement, Uganda would not be where it is today as a relatively prosperous country which is also stable and peaceful.

The danger is that, by using such achievements to claim credit for good leadership, Museveni and his colleagues in the National Resistance Movement seem to be saying that denial or curtailment of human rights is justified or is the price Ugandans have to pay in order to enjoy economic growth, peace and stability; human rights are not that important, or denying people their rights is not a problem at all.

People in Uganda do enjoy some rights, including freedom of movement which many critics of Museveni have used to flee the country. But no amount of economic progress, peace and stability can be used to justify violation of human rights or be used as a substitute for democracy. There is no substitute for democracy. And that includes appeasing political opponents or manipulating local systems to co-opt critics in order to perpetuate Museveni in power:

"A polarization between good political leadership and long-term political institutionalization is occurring (in Uganda). Museveni and his contemporaries are deriving legitimacy from the international arena rather than by securing it internally through genuine political competition and participation.

Sophisticated manipulation of the political arena ensures a certain degree of compliance and stability. For example, Museveni has also developed a broad-based inclusionary system, bringing political leaders from all the political parties, regions and ethnic groups into the government by using both the 'carrot and the stick.' Increasingly, however, Museveni and the army have become less tolerant of criticism from members of parliament (MP) and the cabinet. Cabinet shuffles have become an effective way of silencing dissenting MPs and promoting loyal 'movementalists' and 'Musevenists'....

Uganda has achieved impressive economic growth and relative political stability – with the major exception of the instabilities in the North, the West and increased terrorism in Kampala. The LC (Local Council) system has allowed for limited participation and community self-help, but there are clear limits to popular participation. Economic liberalization is occurring at an accelerated pace, while political liberalization has encountered clear roadblocks. It seems as if Museveni still believes that he is the only one that can lead Uganda out of its difficult past. He has clear control over the military and clear support from the West, but decreasing control over the country.

It is, however, questionable how long he will be able to control the political process from above. Although political parties are divided, they are united in their resolve to bring back freedom of association, political pluralism and to rid Uganda of Museveni. The population may wish to avoid the turbulence of the past, but undermining the development of a viable opposition will only create more extrajudicial movements like the WNBF (West Nile Bank Front), the LRA (Lord's Resistance Army) and NALU (National Army for the Liberation of Uganda formed in 1988 and engaged in fighting the Uganda People's Defence Force – UPDF – in the north and in the west).

Although one could argue that Museveni's 'no-party democracy' has allowed for significant economic and political stability, the degree of freedom in Uganda, measured by such indicators as freedom of association, elections, political participation, separation of power, respect for human rights and the rule of law indicates that Uganda is far from a transition to or consolidation of democracy." – (Robert A. Dibie, ed., *The Politics and Policies of sub-Saharan Africa*, Lanham, Maryland, USA: University Press of America, 2001, pp. 181 – 182).

For a leader who talks so much about broad-based grassroots democracy, and who even established local councils whose legitimacy was derived from direct participation by the masses in elections at the village level, it is inconceivable that he would believe such democracy can be built and be consolidated from the top instead of starting at the bottom by letting the people decide what kind of political system and what form of government they want.

He dismisses such criticism by saying Westerners who

believe that there is only one kind of democracy, or that it can only be patterned after Western democratic institutions, are wrong because they don't know Africa, a continent where the vast majority of the people live in traditional societies and don't have the slightest idea of what democracy is.

To most Africans, he contends, formation of political parties means consolidation of tribal divisions and rivalries because any political parties which are established will be formed on tribal basis. So he wants to control everything from the top, telling the people what to do instead of the people – whom he claims are "sovereign" – telling him what they want:

"Political participation is present in Uganda, in fact actively encouraged, but through the LC system. In other words, political participation is controlled and channeled through state establishment structures....Unfortunately for the NRM regime, however, its consensus from above cannot be successfully imposed throughout Uganda. The North, Northeast and Western portions of Uganda have been in a state of virtual civil war since 1986, although relatively speaking; Uganda is still considered one of the more stable countries in the Great Lakes Region.

Museveni has successfully implemented its ERP, receiving considerable accolades from the West and the IMF. A positive investment climate has been encouraged and substantial economic growth has occurred in Uganda, even though the gaps between the rich and the poor, the urban and the rural have been increasing rather than decreasing. All in all, Uganda is still considered a relative 'success' story, mainly because it is on the road to economic recovery.

The key to Museveni and the Movement's success in ensuring economic restructuring and limited political liberalization while securing Western support rests on their ability to control consensus from above. Similarly,

Museveni's success and popularity are contingent to economic success, which is based on the whims of export prices, international aid and recognition, which are for the most part, beyond his control....

The regime still ensure(s) its continued position of power by...using intimidation when necessary and overall controlling the speed and timing of political liberalization. The whole issue of whether the Movement has been 'successful' and whether it is a 'durable' success story revisits the classic debate over whether strong-man rule is necessary in developing societies, and whether economic growth must precede competitive, political participation.

Exclusive Movement rule from 1986 – 1996 may have been necessary to stabilize the political and economic arena, but Museveni and the Movement have missed their window of opportunity to make Uganda a truly democratic nation....Uganda under Museveni can be characterized as a 'soft authoritarian' system which is increasingly resorting to not so soft methods of holding onto power.

Too much rests on one man as the messiah of Uganda. International donors and institutions may currently perceive Uganda as a successful story, but the long-term sustainability of Uganda as a success story to perhaps emulate, will depend on the institutionalization of power, the opening up of political competition, and the move away from glorifying one man as the savior or in contrast, the enemy of Uganda.

Ultimately, there are no 'quick fixes' for democracy and development in Africa. Uganda may well be stuck with an imperfect but reasonably effective and functioning alternative that is a compromise between dictatorship and democracy." – (Ibid., pp. 182 – 183).

Museveni has also been accused of dividing the very same country he fought so hard to free from tyranny and domination by northern tribes, the Langi and the Acholi, who controlled the army and the security forces.

It should be remembered that although he mobilised forces across ethnic lines when he started his rebellion against Obote, his focus was almost exclusively on the south inhabited by Bantu tribes, contrasted with the North which is Nilotic. Therefore he won support on ethnic and regional basis. The south became his stronghold even if it was for logistical reasons, as indeed was the case.

But even in the south, there were divisions along ethnic lines. Museveni may have consolidated those divisions after he assumed power.

It is a tragedy that ethnicity continues to play a major role in national life. It is an enduring phenomenon and a major problem.

Ethnicity fosters identity politics and makes the transition to democracy – under which people should be judged as individuals and not as members of a group – extremely difficult. Politicians use it to perpetuate themselves in power by exploiting ethnic and regional rivalries, thus weakening the opposition by indirectly encouraging members of different ethnic and regional groups not to work together.

A strong opposition can be established only if it cuts across tribal and regional lines, thus presenting a formidable challenge to the government.

Although Museveni is seen as a nationalist and as a Pan-Africanist, he has sometimes exploited ethnic sentiments to the detriment of other groups, probably northerners more than anybody else.

But there are complaints even among southerners. His critics contend that people from western Uganda, Museveni's home region, hold most of the key posts in the government and in other areas including the ruling National Resistance Movement (NRM). Thus, while the country was dominated by northerners, the Langi and the Acholi, when Obote was in power because they controlled the army and the security forces tipping scales in his favour; and by the people from the northwest, especially the Kakwa, the Lugbara and the Nubians when Amin was in power; under Museveni, it is his fellow westerners, especially from his home region of Ankole, who dominate the country:

"Museveni appointed a government broad-based politically and ethnically, although recently it has been accused of giving Ankole disproportionate jobs and influence.

Prominent members of the various political parties and the different regions and religions in the country gained positions in the administration, even if the balance favoured the Western and Central regions." – Jeni Klugman, Bilin Neyapti and Frances Stewart, *Conflict and Growth in Africa, Vol 2: Kenya, Tanzania and Uganda*, Paris: Development Centre Studies, OECD Publications Service, 1999, p. 25).

Charges against Museveni that he favours members of his tribe, the Banyankole – or Ankole – have also come from some of his colleagues in the ruling National Resistance Movement (NRM). According to a report, "NRM NEC: Museveni Accused of Tribalism," by Edris Kiggundu in a Ugandan newspaper, *The Observer*, Kampala, 13 January 2010:

"A member of the ruling NRM this week rattled the National Executive Committee (NEC) meeting, which concludes today at State House Entebbe, when she suggested that President Museveni had no moral authority to preach against tribalism yet he's wont to appoint largely tribe mates to senior government positions.

Sources have told us that Angella Kebba, a delegate from Adjumani known for her boldness, made her submission during a session that debated Museveni's opening speech.

'You are saying we should not be tribal but you have

appointed many people from your region in government compared to other regions,' our sources quote her as having said candidly.

She was responding to Museveni who said in his opening speech that people pushing for the creation of new districts were being motivated by tribalism and other selfish reasons.

'As all of you know I rear cattle and I do not mind which tribe the people who buy my milk come from as long as they give me money,' Museveni, who is also the NRM chairman, had said.

Kebba's submission caused excitement among delegates, sources attending the meeting told us. Many stomped their feet and clapped their hands, momentarily bringing proceedings to a halt. For some time, Museveni who appeared to have been caught flat-footed, remained seated at the high table but shortly took the floor to respond.

'This is a small issue,' Museveni began his defence, as the hall fell silent. 'I have heard this for a long time but the problem with people is that when you appoint a Munyoro, Mukiga and Mufimbira to Cabinet, they say they are from my place. Many people cannot tell the difference.'

Because of its delicate nature, Secretary General Amama Mbabazi cut short debate on the matter and pleaded with members to discuss other issues in Museveni's speech. Indeed, no other member appeared willing to further the debate. Kebba too did not push the issue.

Indeed this is not the first time the President has been accused of favouring people from a particular region by members of his own party.

A couple of years ago, Mike Mukula, a former minister of state for Health who is currently NRM vice chairman, eastern region, said in a Central Executive Committee (CEC) meeting that people in eastern Uganda were unhappy with NRM because the President had mainly appointed people from the western region to influential positions in government.

Outside the NRM, the opposition has always claimed that some regions are favoured when it comes to sharing the national cake.

Makindye West MP, Hussein Kyanjo, for instance, caused a stir in Parliament last year when he said that Army promotions were not fair. He claimed that some officers from a particular region were favoured for promotion. He gave an example of the five generals in the Army who all hail from Ankole sub-region."

Other NRM members have raised the same issue on different occasions. According to a report by *In2EastAfrica*, 3 March 2012:

"The National Resistance Movement party National Vice Chairman for central region Hajj Abdul Nadduli has cautioned President Museveni and the party leadership against hypocrisy and tribalism, trends he said are growing and threatening to ruin the party.

'We as NRM members from the central region are increasingly getting concerned that a party that had national ideologies is now taking a direction that favours individual party members (on the basis of tribalism),' Hajj Naduli said.

'We are also aware that all the individuals singled out clearly pointed out that they were under instruction from the top man, who is the President. Why should our party be reduced to the level that highlights hypocrisy and favouritsm for particular individuals?' he asked.

Hajj Naduli was commenting on the Cabinet sub-committee decision and information that a section of NRM members have resolved not to fire Bank of Uganda Governor Emmanuel Tumusiime-Mutebile over his role in the compensation of businessman Hassan Basajjabalaba.

Two cabinet ministers, Syda Bbumba (Gender) and

Khiddu Makubuya (General Duties) were forced to resign their ministerial positions over the role they played in the irregular payment of the money.

'Why has Basajjabalaba who allegedly received this money been left to walk free? Any actions taken on these national matters should be held transparently and in the interest of the nation and not of particular individuals,' Hajj Nadduli told the NRM Katikamu South party members at Nyimbwa Sub-county headquarters on Monday.

It is reported that party members were divided during the Wednesday caucus meeting whether Mr Mutebile should be fired or not and it spiralled into a tribal contest, forcing the leaders to end the meeting prematurely.

In the meeting, the Buganda contingent is said to have questioned why Ms Bbumba and Prof. Makubuya, who both represent constituencies in Nadduli's Luweero District, were summarily dumped from Cabinet for their role in the same transaction."

Like President Museveni, the Bank of Uganda governor, Emmanuel Tumusiime-Mutebile, comes from western Uganda. But he does not come from Ankole, the home of Museveni. Still, pressure from the president to keep Tumusiime-Mutebile at his job as the nation's bank chief brought charges of tribalism – or call it sectarianism or regionalism – against the president for favouring someone from his home region: western Uganda.

The subject was addressed by other prominent Ugandan leaders including Ssemujju Ibrahim Nganda of the Forum for Democratic Change (FDC) political party and member of parliament for Kyadondo County East – Wakiso District, in his article, "Mutebile Saga Has Brought Out Real Museveni," in *The Observer*, Kampala, Uganda, 14 March 2012:

"I have taken long without writing about tribalism and

nepotism, not because it ceased, but my relentless efforts almost reduced me into one.

In fact, towards the end of 2010, *The New Vision* named me the second worst person of the year on account of being 'tribalistic.' After sacking two ministers Hajjat Syda Bbumba and Prof Khiddu Makubuya, both from Buganda, *bonafide* NRM supporters from this region, thinking like I always do, realised their party chairman, Yoweri Museveni, is practising tribalism. This is because the same Museveni has convened at least three NRM parliamentary caucus meetings and at each one of them asked MPs to save Central Bank Governor, Emmanuel Tumusiime-Mutebile.

Mind you, the three are accused of the same crime – giving businessman Hassan Basajjabalaba, a whopping Shs 142bn in compensation. That is the reason Buganda caucus chairman, Godfrey Kiwanda, summoned us last week. His view was that there should be no selective justice in the fight against corruption, and I believe many of you agree with him. Former Buganda caucus chairman, Latif Ssebaggala, called a similar meeting when former Vice President, Prof Gilbert Bukenya, was sent to Luzira after his committal to the High Court on charges related to abuse of office.

The reason Ssebaggala summoned Buganda MPs was because people accused with Gilbert Bukenya, including Sam Kutesa, John Nasasira and Mwesigwa Rukutana had not even been arraigned before the court by the Inspector General of Government. Eventually, the three ministers from Museveni's region were also arraigned and charged with some crimes. The government shockingly decided to bungle the Bukenya case and it was immediately and summarily dismissed. I think this was intended to pave way for the eventual acquittal of the three Ankole blue-eyed boys.

Already, the three have won round one against the IGG in the Constitutional Court, courtesy of the Attorney

General. If I remember well, the court has already found some errors in their prosecution. Mutebile is not from Ankole, but from neighbouring Kigezi, from where Prime Minister Amama Mbabazi also hails. These two sub-regions compete, sometimes even recklessly, in giving Museveni votes. I personally think that although Museveni rigs elections and wins, in these two sub-regions, his support is about 55%.

Maybe this is the reason Museveni has never humiliated a senior leader from there. Dr Samson Kisekka who hailed from Buganda was sacked while away on an official trip. Prof Gilbert Bukenya was not only sacked, but made to suffer the worst humiliation of being sent to Luzira. But the bigger point many may have missed in this Mutebile saga is not the tribalism, but the contempt and arbitrariness of Museveni. First, Museveni appoints a ministerial sub-committee to look into the whole Basajjabalaba compensation saga. The committee is supposed to scrutinise the Public Accounts Committee report and advise government on what to do.

The committee is chaired by Defence Minister, Dr Chrispus Kiyonga. Members of the committee include Gen Moses Ali, the Second Deputy Prime Minister and deputy Leader of Government Business in Parliament. Moses Ali, by virtue of his appointment, is Kiyonga's senior, but here is a situation where the junior is supposed to call a senior to order!

The institution that has suffered the worst humiliation is the military, and now the police under Lt Gen Kale Kayihura. What Ugandans need to know is that sometimes people are appointed to higher positions and deliberately denied authority. That is why the Security ministry has only functioned while Amama Mbabazi was there. The previous security ministers like Betty Akech and subsequent ones like Muruli Mukasa are just occupying shells. Real power and authority is transferred elsewhere before someone outside the ruling class is deployed there.

265

But most important is the issue of skills and capabilities. Dr Kiyonga is a decent person and many MPs will give him a hearing. In this case, he's appointed to head a sub-committee in order to give it a human face. Although senior, Kiyonga is not considered to be part of the 'eating clique.' He, therefore, attracts sympathy and respect from many MPs that Amama doesnít. If he's the only one who can deliver results in tricky missions like saving Mutebile, why not appoint him Prime Minister? Another such person is Dr Ruhakana Rugunda.

Three critical issues: tribalism, failure to appoint people according to their skills and refusing to elevate scandal-free personnel to higher offices are what the Mutebile saga has helped unmask about Museveni."

Museveni has discussed the problem of tribalism in a broader context with regard to multiparty politics, although that has no deflected criticism directed at him that he favours people from his home region in western Uganda.

With regard to multiparty politics, his refusal to allow party politics is justified – by him and by his colleagues in the National Resistance Movement – on the grounds that having political parties encourages sectarianism, tribalism and regionalism and could easily take the country back to its dark past when such divisions plunged the nation into chaos and civil wars.

His critics say he uses this argument to suffocate dissent, perpetuate himself in office and ensure that his National Resistance Movement (NRM) continues to have hegemonic control of the country to the total exclusion of other parties – even if he doesn't call the NRM a political party but a national movement.

In a country with intense regional rivalries, especially between the north and the south, Museveni seems to have a valid point.

But his argument is refuted by what he himself said

266

when he assumed power that "the sovereign people must be the public, not the government."

And his "no-party" or "movement" system is no more than a poorly disguised excuse to justify and institutionalise one-party rule during his tenure and under his successors whom he hopes he will be able to choose or recommend to perpetuate the National Resistance Movement in power.

In that sense, he is no better than the other African leaders, the "big men" of the 1960s and 1970s, who became life presidents or instituted imperial presidencies to perpetuate themselves in office.

He has not shown much interest in broad-based democracy which embraces and accommodates divergent views including those which are in sharp contrast with his position and the policies of the National Resistance Movement. That is why no political parties can contest elections on equal footing, although they are now allowed to field candidates unlike before.

Even democracy within the National Resistance Movement itself is questionable. No-one can challenge Museveni. That is why he has been in power for 26 years now and may still be at the helm for more than 30 if nothing is done to remove him from office.

His view of democracy as a system that can function only within the parameters or boundaries of the National Resistance Movement undermines the very basis of a democratic society in which everybody has equal say. And that includes opponents of the National Resistance Movement and people who belong to different political parties regardless of how repugnant their views may be. Let the people decide.

While his argument that political parties can divide the nation along tribal, religious and regional lines may have some merit, it is not valid in all contexts. Parties can transcend ethno-regional loyalties. Any party which does not do that should not be allowed to operate.

Also, to broaden support across ethnic and regional lines, there should be only a few parties – with significant membership in every part of the country – which are allowed to compete in elections on equal basis instead of having only Museveni's National Resistance Movement as the contestant – virtually against no other party.

If there are only a few truly nationalist parties, people who are interested in voting will be forced to join or support one of those parties because there won't be any others to join. Even historical or tribal enemies will end up joining the same party cutting across ethnic and regional lines. Any parties which are regionally entrenched, if they are not outlawed, should merge with other parties to broaden their support across the nation.

A broad-based consensus transcending ethnic and regional loyalties should be the basis for forming any political party. Museveni has not allowed that.

He thinks only the National Resistance Movement (NRM) is capable of bringing the people of all regions and ethnic groups together; a view shared by his colleague next door, President Paul Kagame of Rwanda, who also thinks that only the Tutsi-dominated Rwandan Patriotic Front (RPF) should rule the country and is the only party – may be even "movement" – that is capable of maintaining peace and stability and uniting all Rwandans even if it means under Tutsi domination as has been the case since 1994 when the RPF seized power after ending the genocide by the Hutu-dominated government which ruled for 32 years at the expense of the Tutsi.

That is the case in many other African countries including my own, Tanzania, where the ruling Chama Cha Mapinduzi (CCM) – the Party of the Revolution – having ruled for decades, acts as if it has divine mandate to rule. It uses state resources and agencies including the police to frustrate the opposition in an an attempt to neutralise it. The primary target is Chama Cha Demokrasia na Maendeleo (Chadema) which means the Party for

Democracy and Progress. It is the strongest opposition party in the country.

Chadema rallies and demonstrations are broken by the police for no apparent reason, using flimsy excuses to do so. Its leaders are harassed and arrested. The party is often denied permission to hold rallies and does not get equal time on state radio and television. And its victory at the polls has been nullified in a number of cases in an attempt to weaken it.

Voters in some election strongholds were not allowed to vote or their names were not even on the voters' list. Some ballots were destroyed or rejected by government agent overseeing the polls.

There were even some reports stating that Chadema won the 2010 presidential election but was denied victory by the electoral commission – whose members belong to the ruling party, are appointed by the president and are therefore beholden to him – and by some members of the Tanzania Intelligence and Security Services (TISS) specifically assigned to the task of changing the results in favour of the ruling party.

Some of those reports, that the election was rigged and and that the vote count was manipulated by some members of the intelligence service, came from some of the intelligence officers themselves who had inside knowledge of this nefarious scheme by the ruling party to give the president, Jakaya Kikwete, victory for a second term instead of Dr. Wilbrod Slaa who was the presidential candidate of the main opposition party, Chadema.

Therefore this phenomenon – of the ruling party denying the opposition equal opportunity to articulate its position and mobilise support, and of rigging elections and even arresting opposition leaders – is not peculiar to Uganda under Museveni or Rwanda under Kagame. It is common in most countries across Africa where leaders don't value democracy. They are afraid of democracy.

Museveni has had remarkable achievements through

the years since he has been in power. But he also risks tarnishing his legacy by repeating the same mistakes his predecessors made. Obote was one of them.

Obote was accused of favouring and of being overly reliant on fellow northerners, the Langi and the Acholi. He was also accused of being a dictator. Amin favoured his fellow tribesmen and eliminated his ethnic rivals, especially the Langi and the Acholi. He was also a brutal dictator.

Museveni seems to have fallen into the same trap, with regard to his kinsmen from western Uganda, and of being an authoritarian ruler who has no respect for true democracy. As Ugandan journalist Andrew Mwenda states in "Personalizing Power in Uganda," in *Democratization in Africa: Progress and Retreat*:

"With Museveni...set to stay in office indefinitely, the future of democracy in Uganda looks bleak....

In 1996, he expanded his cabinet from the constitutionally prescribed 40 members to 67. Since most cabinet officers are Members of Parliament (MPs), and since the army has ten seats in the legislature, this meant that nearly a quarter of all MPs belong to the executive branch. More direct ways of keeping legislators in line exist as well: In October 2004, soldiers arrested and brutally beat four northern MPs for trying to hold a political rally in one of their constituencies....

On November 14 (2005), the government jailed (opposition leader Kizza) Besigye. When his supporters attempted a peaceful demonstration, soldiers crushed it with tanks and armored personnel carriers, leaving three people dead. Kampala looked like a war zone; newspaper headlines began comparing it to Baghdad.

Besigye was taken before the High Court and charged with treason plus a rape allegedly committed in 1997. When the High Court granted bail, the military accused Besigye of terrorism and placed him in the custody of a court martial. Foreign diplomats whom the minister of internal affairs had accredited to attend the trial found themselves ejected and locked out of the courtroom by soldiers.

In one especially macabre incident, the government sent hooded gangs sporting sunglasses and brandishing automatic weapons into the High Court to kidnap 21 of Besigye's codefendants in the event that they received bail. Looking on the thugs waved their guns at jurists and diplomats, the terrified detainees decided to remain in custody. The courts later released Besigye himself, but only after almost two-thirds of the campaign period had gone by.

On election day, the *Daily Monitor* opened a tally center to monitor results, which the paper's radio affiliate KFM began to broadcast. As this independent effort was starting to make it clear that Museveni would not get the 50 percent required to avoid a runoff, the president's men moved in to close the tally center, jam its radio signal, and block its website. It was amid circumstances such as these that the Electoral Commission announced Museveni's first-round reelection with 59 percent of the vote." – (Andrew M. Mwenda, "Personalizing Power in Uganda," in Larry Diamond, Marc F. Plattner, eds., *Democratization in Africa: Progress and Retreat*, Baltimore, Maryland, USA: Johns Hopkins University Press, 2010, pp. 234, 236).

Although Museveni may have an instinctive aversion to democracy, his contempt for democratic institutions is sometimes attributed to his revolutionary past shaped by a strong belief in the imperative need for violence as an instrument for fundamental change. As Mwenda goes on state:

"Looking back over Museveni's career, it is fair to say that he has never been a friend of liberty. He scorns the rule of law, shuns due process, and is always willing to run roughshod over people's rights. He believes in violence as a legitimate instrument to bring about 'revolutionary' political change and in the army as an important pillar of political power. At the University of Dar es Salaam in Tanzania, Museveni wrote a bachelor's thesis defending Frantz Fanon's calls for the use of violence. Both before and since Museveni became president, the themes of violence and the military have played central roles in his speeches and writings.

After claiming that President Milton Obote had stolen the 1980 election from them, Museveni and his party took to the bush as the National Resistance Army (NRA). Their goal was always to seize power by force of arms. In order to keep itself in funds and supplies, the RNA robbed banks, looted stores, and raided hospitals. Nor did it shrink from terrorism, blowing up petrol stations and mining roads in order to destroy ambulances.

Impunity thus lies at the very foundation of its bid for power.

Can anyone seriously think that a group which seeks to rule by the gun and stoops to pillaging hospitals will, once it captures the state, stay its hand from plundering the public fisc or brutalizing political foes?

From its inception, Museveni's army-turned-party has been informed by the logic of authoritarianism. The leader wears all the hats and pulls all the strings.

During his time in the bush, Museveni was the chairman of the NRM as well as commander of the NRA, sitting atop both the Army Council and the High Command. He also presided over the legislative National Resistance Council, all the while acting as his movement's chief theoretician and philosopher. Checks and balances to guard against the abuse of power can mean but little when so many levers rest in one pair of hands. When in January 1986 Museveni's forces took Kampala and made him president, he gained the resources of a state to help him rent or if need be coerce political support from the distressed body of his wounded country." – (Ibid., pp. 236 – 237).

He goes on to state:

"At first, the authoritarianism did not seem so bad. Museveni's forcefulness helped to promote economic reform. The various organs of the shadow state that he had created as a guerrilla had the potential to become partners in an internal debate. Yet Museveni never truly tapped that potential. Instead, he adeptly manipulated these organs to project the illusion that consultation was occurring even as he was effectively ruling by decree.

A close look at what was happening could often reveal the sham. Many times in the late 1980s and early 1990s, for example, if Parliament was slow to pass some measure that Museveni saw as important, he would put on his uniform and chair a closed legislative session until his bill had been rammed through.

The desperate situation that Museveni inherited in 1986 required a strong and dynamic leader. Amin's depredations – he had killed somewhere between 80,000 and a half-million people and had expelled the country's Indo-Ugandan merchant class *en masse* in 1972 – were followed by seven years of savage infighting that came in the wake of his ouster. Uganda was on its knees, its government and economy alike in ruins. Iron-fisted tactics appeared necessary – and even legitimate – since the country needed a leader who could take quick and decisive decisions where institutions were too slow or inept. Thus did Parliament swiftly approve Museveni's plans to restore the traditional local monarchies, privatize state enterprises, allow Indo-Ugandans to return and reclaim their property, cut back on the civil service, and the like.

Yet as institutions recovered and fresh economic growth produced new interest groups, Museveni's

273

penchant for informal methods and arbitrary decision making became increasingly counterproductive.

In 1986, not long after it seized power, Museveni's government restricted political-party activities on national-healing grounds. At the time, this sounded reasonable. Museveni appeared magnanimous as he invited leaders of other parties to join him in a national-unity – or as the president called it, a 'broad-based' – government. Yet even as the situation improved, Museveni held fast to the ban on political parties, letting go of it only under considerable pressure in 2005.

With the benefit of hindsight, we can understand the subjective motives for his seeming magnanimity.

The NRA was the strongest armed force in the country by the mid-1980s. But Museveni's political vehicle, the NRM, was unseasoned and rested on a narrow, unsteady base. Museveni, a brilliant student of Uganda's politics, reasoned that the no-party, 'broad-based' approach offered several advantages, including: 1) a viable alternative to the counterproductive expedient of open military rule; 2) a boost to his own NRM's political appeal nationwide; and 3) the means to make rivals and potential rivals from other parties serve at his beck and call.

To improve his chances for success, Museveni not only used his soldiers, police, and security agents to stop other parties from organizing, but also exploited local councils to build the NRM's organizational infrastructure, cajoled leaders from other parties to join the NRM, and systematically rid official ranks of all those who remained loyal to their old parties.

The decentralization of the budget process gave local officials reason to work with the NRM; the continued use of armed coercion made them fear what would happen if they broke with the president's movement.

Evidence that Museveni never had any intention of building a democracy may be gleaned from the NRM regime's conspicuous refusal to repeal any of the many

274

repressive laws – including some of the worst of Idi Amin's decrees – that remained on the books in 1986. in fact, Museveni's time in power has seen draconian statutes hampering freedoms of organization, expression, assembly, and publication not only retained, but reinforced.

The only signs of nascent democratization appeared in the constitution-making process. Even there, however, enabling acts to give effect to many of the 1995 basic law's provisions were not forthcoming, and activists from opposition groups, civil society, and the media had to sue in court in order to have repressive laws struck down.

The worst obstacle to democratic development in Uganda has been the personalization of the state. Arms and money are essential to this malign process. The arms belong to the military and security services, which the regime deploys selectively in order to suppress dissent. The money sluices through a massive patronage machine that Museveni uses to recruit support, reward loyalty, and buy off actual and potential opponents.

In his efforts to personalize the state, Museveni has skilfully undermined formal institutions of governance, preferring as he does to use highly arbitrary and informal methods of recruiting and rewarding officials. The destruction of the Parliament's will and ability to check executive power has been a keystone of his approach. Not surprisingly, the personalization of the state has gone hand in hand with its increasing arbitrariness.

Museveni has always sought to use the army to build his personal – less so the NRM's – political base. He employs violence sparingly and selectively – as an instrument of last resort when the political process fails to yield before his requirements or the opposition appears to need whipping into submission. Patronage, typically in the form of government contracts, tenders, and jobs, is his preferred tool and the one that he used to render Parliament ineffective.

Museveni's success at consolidating his power and stifling democracy flows from his knack for integrating large chunks of the political class into his vast patronage empire." – (Ibid., pp. 237 – 239).

Like most African countries, Uganda has never developed strong democratic institutions during the post-colonial period. The institutions it inherited at independence from the departing British colonial rulers were for domination just as they had been during the colonial era.

Even the press, which is supposed to be the guardian of truth and the watchdog for human rights, was used by the colonial rulers to serve their own interests, not to serve the interests of colonial subjects.

The judiciary may have been the only institution inherited from the colonial rulers which could have been used effectively to dispense justice and protect human rights. But it was used by the new rulers to serve their own interests and lost its independence under the strong arm of the government. That also has been the case under Museveni.

Uganda has gone through a lot of changes since the sixties when it was led by Dr. Milton Obote who also earned a reputation as one of Africa's leading statesmen during the era of the "big men" who laid the foundation for the modern African state in the post-colonial era. Then came the reign of terror under Idi Amin when the law meant absolutely nothing. All institutions, except the military, were destroyed.

During Obote's second presidency, the civil war made the country virtually ungovernable. Chaos reigned, with both the national army and rebel groups wreaking havoc across the land.

Museveni, who himself was partly responsible for the chaos that reigned during Obote's second presidency since he is the one who started the civil war, closed that chapter after he assumed power.

Under his regime, chaos ended except for some insurgencies in the north, northwest, east and west. A combination of military might and diplomacy ended those rebel activities.

What did not end was suppression of human rights. Museveni's National Resistance Army and other security forces including the police and the intelligence service did not refrain from using torture, imprisonment and other tactics to suppress dissent and punish government opponents. As Mary Anne Fitzgerald stated from Kampala in her article, "With Chaos Ended, What About Rights?" in *The New York Times*, 9 October 1992:

"One of the National Resistance Movement's most notable achievements has been the restoration of order. For a decade and a half, Ugandans had experienced levels of state-authored persecution and chaos that were extraordinary even for a continent known for its unreliable rule of law.

Visitors to Uganda in earlier years recall nocturnal fusillades, routine roadblocks manned by not always courteous soldiers, deeply pockmarked streets and hotels bereft of running water. On at least two occasions during a period of interim government in 1980, Western diplomats engaged in gun battles with intruders to defend their homes.

Today, people walk the streets safely at night and drive along Kampala's resurfaced roads without fear of being harassed by armed men. And as a barometer of the new confidence, in the marbled lobby of the Sheraton Hotel businessmen and aid officials sip coffee while they watch CNN news. The five-star hotel opened in November 1987 after undergoing a $35 million restoration.

Last month, the hot item of conversation in Kampala was a report on Uganda by Amnesty International, the London-based human rights organization. It alleges torture

277

and unlawful arrest, particularly by the National Resistance Army (NRA), and government failure to safeguard human rights.

Ominous as this sounds, officialdom's reaction to the publication of the report contradicts the picture of a decline in basic constitutional freedoms. Politicians and bureaucrats were open to frank discussion of the report. Many had a copy lying on their desks. In most other African countries, Amnesty publications are considered seditious literature and their contents hotly denied.

'It's in a way grossly unfair,' said Augustine Ruzindana, inspector general of government. 'It gives the impression the human rights condition is very bad and deteriorating, which is not true.'

The inspector general's office was created by the National Resistance Movement parliament to investigate human rights abuses and corruption under the present government. The office says that it was never consulted by the Amnesty authors when drafting the report. During a three-hour interview in Amnesty's London office on June 26, the existence of the report was not mentioned, Mr. Ruzindana said.

Politicians, bureaucrats and Western diplomats concur that while there have been recent incidents of violence and lawlessness perpetrated by NRA soldiers, Uganda's record is markedly better than it was some years ago. This year there has been a clear effort to correct abuses of the law. The Amnesty report contained only two instances of such abuse so far this year, in which seven suspected rebels were arrested by the army and executed without trial.

There have been further unsubstantiated allegations of mistreatment at the hands of government forces from lawyers based in Gulu, the seat of a rebel insurgency. At Palengo, 12 miles – 19 kilometers – south of Gulu, three suspected rebels were arrested by soldiers and buried from the neck down in holes they had been forced to dig themselves. All three died. Another three men were allegedly tortured to death while in custody, according to the lawyers.

Last month, 59 followers of the Uganda Democratic Christian Army (UDCA), led by Joseph Kony, were released. They had been awaiting trial for treason since October last year. Treason charges, which preclude the possibility of bail for 480 days, have in the past been used as a mechanism for dampening rebel support.

On coming to power in 1986, the National Resistance Movement faced a rebel insurgency in the north from a group called the Uganda People's Democratic Army (UPDA). It consisted of soldiers who had served under previous regimes. After a 1988 peace agreement, the UPDA was disbanded and incorporated into the NRA. Some remnants joined Mr. Kony's less effective UDCA.

Meanwhile, in the east, the Uganda People's Army, another rebel movement, was blamed for hundreds of killings. Thousands subsequently took advantage of a 1987 amnesty and presidential pardon to join the NRA. This conciliatory move by the government effectively undid the rebellions. Following a major military operation last year, armed opposition has disintegrated into banditry by small groups.

Observers say arrests for treason have now abated. In many instances, treason cases have been dismissed in court for lack of evidence.

Rebel atrocities, however, continue to occur. Last year, followers of the Uganda Democratic Christian Army cut off the noses, ears and upper lips of several women suspected of being government sympathizers. Hacking victims to death or mutilating them is common among rebel forces.

Last March, treason charges were dropped against 18 northern leaders arrested the previous year. The accused included the state minister for foreign affairs, Daniel Omara Atubo. Prior allegations of assault were investigated by the inspector general's office. A report on the incident has yet to be released, but Major General David Tinyefuza, who ordered the arrests, was relieved of his northern command.

In August, President Yoweri Museveni ordered the release of more than 1,500 political prisoners. The majority had been rounded up by the army last year during a counterinsurgency operation in northern rebel areas. They were sentenced *en masse* to serve jail terms of five years or more for desertion from local units. The International Committee of the Red Cross claims that at least 500 detainees are still being held. By comparison, in 1988 the NRA admitted to the existence of over 4,000 detainees.

The improvement in legal procedure has, to some extent, resulted from pressure by international aid donors. The month before the release of Mr. Atubo and others accused with him, the United States and European Community members lodged an official protest with the government over their detention.

'If the government senses a real concern, it behaves more responsibly,' a diplomat said. 'There's no doubt about that. The arrests happened in the context of heightened insecurity, which should be taken into account.'

JUDGED against the background of its recent past, Uganda has made progress in instilling moral probity in the military and its political leaders. Both Idi Amin and Milton Obote, former heads of state, were responsible for some of the grossest violations of human rights in modern history. All told, more than half a million Ugandans died at their hands.

'There was abuse of power by all levels of public officials,' said Mr. Ruzindana. 'There were no limits to their authority so ordinary people were very much at their mercy.'

'We have replaced the vicious circle of violence by accommodating everyone,' said First Deputy Prime Minister Eriya Kategaya. 'No group should be hunted for its past deeds. We don't need the West to tell us how to safeguard our human rights. It's our duty to do it.'"

So, while peace returned to Uganda, democracy did not. In fact, there has never been full democracy in Uganda.

And that is the biggest challenge the country faces in its transition to a stable, vibrant and just society where every individual has equal rights without fear of being punished or killed by the authorities for simply speaking up and telling the truth.

Many problems Uganda continues to face can be attributed to lack of democracy. For example, one of the biggest problems the country faces even under Museveni is corruption. But corruption cannot be solved without transparency. And transparency is impossible without democracy to enable the people to tell the truth without fear and to expose those who do wrong.

There can be no accountability where there is no transparency. Laws mean nothing. Therefore the rule of law itself is impossible without democracy.

Therefore, the biggest challenge Uganda and the rest of Africa faces is the establishment of strong democratic institutions which guarantee transparency, accountability and good governance in order to achieve peace, stability, and development. And the people themselves must be full participants in the process in order to secure their rights and hold leaders accountable for their actions.

Dictatorship or authoritarian rule cannot guarantee prosperity for Africa because the people who should be the primary focus are not allowed to participate in making decisions which affect their lives. Dictatorship cannot last forever. It carries seeds of its own destruction.

Appendix I:

How Mutesa shot his way to safety

In his book, *Desecration of My Kingdom*, Sir Edward Mutesa vividly describes the May 24, 1966 attack on his palace and how he made his escape. Here are some extracts:

It was not yet dawn – about 5.30 in the morning – when I was awakened suddenly by the sound of gunfire: quite near, I reckoned, certainly inside the wall that surrounds my palace and grounds.

As I hurried into a shirt, some trousers and a pullover, and sat on my bed to pull on some suede boots, I tried to work out more precisely what was happening and where the shots were being fired. Somewhere beyond the garages, it seemed; perhaps 200 or 300 yards away. I strapped on a webbing belt with a heavy automatic in the holster, grabbed a carbine, and dashed into the cool, dark garden to look for the commander of the bodyguard.

Troops from the Uganda Army were attacking my palace on the orders of the Prime Minister, Dr. [Milton] Obote. So much was clear. Nor should it have been in the least surprising. We had been suspecting such a move for weeks, and I myself had been surprised when nothing happened the previous evening.

Yet I was filled with a sense of outrage now that it was happening. The Constitution allowed me a bodyguard of 300, but I only had about 120, and many of these were absent.

Each man had a Lee-Enfield rifle and we managed to get hold of three carbines, half a dozen Sterling sub-machine guns and six automatic rifles. There was, unfortunately, no hidden arsenal, though Obote said later that that was what his soldiers had called at this early hour to collect.

Photographs of this cache tried to make something of an ancient German Spandau, a machine-gun, which bad been rusting gently on my veranda for years, and my brother Henry's ceremonial R.A.F. sword.

Nor was the palace designed as a fortress. The main gate is indefensible, and the two buildings, which are separated by gardens, are easy to approach under cover....

First man down

I quickly collected a few men and we made off to the west. I had in mind a group of trees from which we could command a clearing and possibly defend one of the bottom gates, Nalongo, if it had not already been breached.

We did not get there. A light fence surrounds the garden, and suddenly we saw two or three men standing in a half-opened doorway, peering cautiously in. We dropped one and the others made off. That was the first of many unfortunate deaths I saw that day.

We made that first foray with no idea as to how many men were attacking or from which angle. Now friends approached in the half-light and told me something of what had happened and what was happening, though still we did not know how many had been sent against us.

Perhaps that was just as well, as it would scarcely have raised our spirits to know we were faced with over 1,000, odds of ten against one, with our equipment much inferior.

However, my men were the more experienced in service, and a great number of the enemy were occupied in surrounding the wall. This high brick wall encloses an area much larger than the palace and gardens.

Inside are school buildings, white bungalows with corrugated iron roofs, football pitches, many houses with mud walls and thatched roofs that were to burn easily, and above all, dividing the open, grassy spaces, plantations of banana trees.

With our knowledge of every inch of the terrain, there was enough cover, confusion and resistance for us to elude our pursuers indefinitely, deployment plans having previously been sanctioned by myself.

Treasure hunt

The Special Force that had been sent against us was not very subtle. They had foolishly used lights to burn some thatched huts just inside the wall, and, thus lit up from behind, made themselves into very easy targets.

When one lot did break through the gate called Kalala, they ran across an open sports ground to join others who had come through the main gate. A pocket of my men commanded the open ground and held up their much larger force for some time, inflicting heavy casualties.

We had done as well there as we could have hoped, and now fell back. Another entrance had been forced through the southern gate, Sabagabo, and it was those men that had awakened me. The western corner was still ours, or at least disputed throughout the action.

It was well known that I preferred to live in the old palace, which stands smaller, darker and more African behind the gleaming white European building, which is used mainly for formal functions.

For the time being, this newer palace was left alone while they closed in on the rooms I used. It began to look as if it was me personally that they wished to destroy.

I heard someone shout, "Has he a safe?" as they entered the far side, and saw through a window my papers being torn up and my filing cabinets smashed with rifle butts.

We had not the strength to counter-attack, but we took up a position amongst some eucalyptus trees, which covered Nalongo, a white wooden gate, and held on. Nobody ever came through that gate.

As the sun got up, dispersing the morning mists, our gloom increased. There seemed to be an endless follow-up supply of enemy soldiers, many of whom were occupied with destroying my rooms.

I think they believed their own stories about hidden supplies of arms, and even indulged in fanciful ideas that a king must have hoards of treasure buried beneath his palace.

I was sustained throughout the morning by anger. I had known that an attack was probable, but I had not foreseen the random, pointless quality of their violence. Huts were burned for no conceivable tactical reason and I heard the screaming of an old woman as she burned.

Kabaka shoots 'looter'

The captain of my guard, Major Kibirige, disappeared and must have become a casualty. Once I was overwhelmed with emotion, and foolishly returned to the palace garden alone. There, I selected a looter and shot him out of honest rage. I felt calmer and somewhat uplifted as I made my way back.

Someone had loosened the horses, and they added to the atmosphere of disorder as they galloped to and fro in a frenzy of fear.

Though firing of small arms and mortars was almost continuous until midday, and though we held our position, it was getting desperate. I decided to abandon the trees and defend a cattle kraal with the same arc of fire, though it had mud walls and a thatched roof that might be fired. We were there when it started to rain.

It rained, as it can in Uganda, with a violence that made fighting impossible. For an hour visibility was reduced to a minimum and the main noise was the water thudding on to the roof and hissing in the trees.

Though the kraal would have been a useful place to hold, to save ourselves from being encircled, we decided we were not strong enough, and moved out into the rain to go a little to the north.

Many thought we had escaped at this time and it would have been an opportunity, but we were surrounded and had not prepared a route. Nor had we yet taken the decision.

At first I had thought it was to be merely a skirmish. We saw now that it was more serious than that, but still hoped that in the face of such prolonged and successful resistance the troops might call off the threat. Otherwise we hoped to resist until evening and escape in the dark.

Wife detained

Soon after the rain, a scout called for us to watch a sight which horrified me. From the palace a strange procession of women emerged, my sister and wife among other relations and maids.

I had not seen them during the fighting, but could imagine their feelings. Now they walked slowly towards the gate we were defending. I piously hoped they would stop, but they did not hear me and continued out of sight.

A moment later, there was a burst of fire and I exclaimed, "It can't be true," certain that they had been massacred. I am still not sure what happened, but they were allowed through and later put in prison.

As they disappeared, there was a new attack on the gate, which was already surrounded with corpses. We beat it off yet again. Our own ammunition was low and there was no indication of the troops pulling out.

Nor was there a chance of driving them away. I began to plan an escape as the decision was clearly forced. To the north the bandmaster and another group of the guard were firing gallantly, and with their protection behind us we moved a little to the south and started to attack some vehicles which were on the road outside the wall.

For a time our attack seemed to have little effect, though we gave them all we had and their counter-fire was feeble. Then at last a truck moved off and a minute later two more disappeared. We had made that area a little too lively and now there was a gap. How long it would remain open we could only guess.

As nine of us made for the red-brick wall, there was a shout and a girl rushed up to us from the direction of the enemy. She was Katie Senoga, a kindergarten school teacher.

"What on earth are you doing?" I asked her, but there was no time to do anything but take her with us. Poor girl, she was crying and trembling all over. I remember thinking that, if she had had a gun, in her excitement she would probably have tried to kill us all.

Window of death

We wasted ten valuable minutes, trying to open a hatch in the wall. There is a tradition that no [dead] body save that of the Kabaka should leave through the palace gates, so if a commoner dies inside the walls there is this opening through which he may pass. Unfortunately, it was locked and we could not break the lock. So we had to climb.

The wall, which had seemed quite low as a defence, suddenly loomed large when we stood beneath it. It is in fact ten or twelve feet high. Luckily, the bodyguard are trained to scale such an obstacle, and by standing on each other's shoulders we could haul ourselves on to the top, still slippery from the rain.

Speed was essential. I threw my rifle down, and as I jumped I eagerly bent over to reach it. It was a mistake I was to regret every day for a month. Landing unevenly, I dislodged a bone in my back from its place and I felt a sharp pain.

here was no time even to swear then, and we ran across the road into a plantation of banana trees, horribly aware how conspicuous we had been on the wall and unsure whether we had been seen.

Several bodies had been left on the ground, but there seemed to be no living opposition. For a moment we waited, with the rain still dripping from the leaves and the irregular firing behind us.

In less than five minutes, the most curious incident of the whole escape took place. Two taxis driving without particular urgency came into sight. After a momentary qualm as to whether they were full of soldiers. I waved them down.

They behaved as if it was the most normal event in the world, and if this was because we were armed to the teeth, they gave no sign.

We clambered in and asked them to drive us a couple of miles to the White Fathers near the Roman Catholic cathedral. Huddled on top of one another, we felt far safer, though in fact we must have been very lucky not to have been stopped. The Fathers received us, calmly accepting the unfamiliar clatter of rifles on the refectory table with aplomb.

The Kabaka eventually escaped by walking and hitch-hiking for over a month to Burundi through Congo. He later continued to England where he died on November 21, 1969.

Source: Excerpt from King Freddie, *Desecration of My Kingdom*, London: Constable & Co. Ltd., 1967. "How Mutesa shot his way to Safety," Uganda's 60-Year Old Conflict, Part 5, The Observer Media Ltd., Kampala, Uganda, 13 January 2010.

Appendix II:

Obote speaks

I did not sabotage East African Federation

Trouble at home

Immediately after independence, we faced three major challenges: the East African federation, the organisation of the army, and the lost counties of Buyaga and Bugangaizi.

Regarding the East African federation, there have been claims from people like Museveni that I am the one who frustrated it because I wanted to be a big fish in a small pond.

The East African federation could not have been sabotaged by me. We were talking about two federations at the same time, Buganda federation within Uganda, and the East African federation. There were problems in Kenya and Uganda which frustrated the drive towards the federation.

I do not remember the factors in Kenya. However, in Uganda, the UPC had come into government in an alliance with KY (Kabaka Yekka) which was rabidly opposed to the East African federation. Remember that the first time the British proposed an East African federation, there was a standoff with Mengo and the Kabaka was deported.

I find Museveni's reasoning myopic because he tends to personalise obstacles to decision making in Uganda under my administration to me personally. As prime minister of a political party in a coalition government, I could not make decisions without bringing different interests into agreement.

In fact even within the UPC itself, there was no consensus about the East African federation. For example, Adoko Nekyon, Felix Onama and Cuthbert Obwangor were opposed to the idea but I now forget on what grounds.

The second challenge was the army.

Immediately after independence in 1964, the army mutinied. We had to call in British troops to cool it down. Secondly, within a few years of independence, Grace Ibingira with Edward Muteesa began working closely with Brig. Shaban Opolot, the army commander, to overthrow the government. Ibingira had his own brother, Maj. Katabarwa in the army.

Ibingira accuses me, in his books, of refusing to promote people like Major Karugaba because they were Catholics. But I promoted many officers like Brig. Okoya who were Catholics. It was Ibingira in the UPC government of 1962 who had ideas about the army. Ibingira had started in London to pick up boys from Ankole and send them to military schools including his own brother Maj. Katabarwa. Ibingira picked up about five

Ankole boys to go to military colleges.

In 1964, I supported Muteesa to become president. Muteesa knew very well that the constitution of 1962 mandated the government to hold a referendum in the lost counties for people to decide whether they wanted to remain under Buganda administration, return to Bunyoro or become an independent district.

So Muteesa wanted Buganda to retain the counties. He began to frequent the counties and settle Baganda ex-service men there with the hope of increasing the numbers of Baganda in order to create an artificial advantage.

To ensure fairness, government declared that only those who were on the voter register would participate in the referendum. In fact Muteesa one time went to one of the counties and shot people, Banyoro, dead.

Although some unscrupulous authors have accused me of promising both Muteesa and the king of Bunyoro to help them win, in a game of double dealing, that is entirely untrue. I published all my positions, even in the UPC manifesto of the 1962 elections on the issue of the referendum. Muteesa was not a fool. Neither was Omukama a fool to see a referendum and they say Obote said "I will do this for you". The referendum was held as per the constitution towards the end of the second year into independence and people voted by overwhelming majority to go back to Bunyoro.

I understand the difficulty such a referendum presented to Sir Edward. Although he was president of Uganda, he was also Kabaka of Buganda. Under the constitution, he was supposed to sign the results of the referendum in order to bring them into legal effect. His dual role as president of Uganda and Kabaka of Buganda made this more difficult and he refused to sign. I do not blame him at all. The constitution also said in the event the president fails to ascent to a bill, the prime minister can. So I signed the results because I knew that was the best way to help Muteesa out of a difficult situation.

How could a Kabaka of Uganda sign away part of his kingdom to go to another kingdom? Some people have written saying this was the beginning of the break-up of the UPC-KY alliance. The UPC-KY alliance did not break-up. It ended in a marriage because by 1965, 16 out of 21 KY members of parliament had crossed to UPC. Therefore by the time the dissolution was officially announced, there was little left of KY. Muteesa and Ibingira deliberately encouraged KY members in parliament to cross to UPC in order to increase the number of UPC parliamentarians who would support a plot by Muteesa and Ibingira to get rid of me. So it was not done out of good faith.

I want to comment on the 1964 UPC delegates' conference which has been a subject of much writing and much misrepresentation. I have been accused of siding with Ibingira to remove John Kakonge from the office of Secretary General. I was sick. I don't know if Dr. Gesa is still alive but he will tell you that I did not attend the conference. I opened the conference and I went to bed. William Nadiope who was vice president of the party in collusion with Ibingira decided to have delegations which they financed. Nadiope took the whole of Busoga, thousands of people, to Gulu. Kakonge did not know that this group had been financed by the CIA. Kakonge's group was accused of being communist with me in it, but Kakonge did not know. They even gave him a CIA girl, Peace Corp volunteer to date so that they could spy on him.

When it came to the conference, Nadiope and Ibingira had filled it with their supporters and they used this numerical strength to defeat Kakonge. That is how Ibingira used CIA money to become secretary general of the UPC. If you read Ibingira's writings, he admits that he was plotting to remove me also from being party president so that Nadiope could take over the leadership of UPC.

Formation of OAU

In the meantime, we had other foreign affairs issues to deal with other than the East African federation.

This was the height of the cold war and the world was divided between east and west. I took a strong Pan African position in favour of a continental union. In May 1963, I arrived in Addis Ababa where the first conference of leaders of newly independent states was going to take place. Africa had been divided between two groups: the Monrovia group composed of conservatives, and the Casablanca group composed of the progressive radicals.

The Monrovia group was opposed to Nkrumah's proposal for an immediate creation of a union government for the whole of Africa. On the first day I arrived, my friend Kwesi Ama, a Ghanaian, came to me and said Kwame Nkrumah, the president of Ghana wanted to have lunch with me and that I should 'expect a bomb shell'. I had met Kwesi Ama in London. He was my friend and was Nkrumah's ambassador to London.

Nkrumah was the leader of African progressive opinion. We all admired him immensely. I personally admired Nkrumah immensely. He was an illustrious leader. He shaped African liberation and gave Africa a voice in world affairs. He supported liberation struggles all over Africa. So meeting him was a great honour and opportunity. People like Patrice Lumumba, Julius Nyerere, Kenneth Kaunda, all progressive African leaders looked to Nkrumah.

When we sat down to lunch, Nkrumah told me there was no conference. "You should go back home." He said the Monrovia group had already sabotaged the conference. I told him that we should not go back home. We should put our case to the conference on the need for African unity. And I told him that as far as I could see, there was possible success if only we could reorganise what we wanted the conference to do. Nkrumah said we wanted All-African

Union Government. I told him that given the polarisation, we could not achieve that. Although we could present our case for immediate African political union, we had to be careful because we could not get the majority needed to see it through.

So we had to argue our case as a bargaining tool to get the conference to form an organisation that would work towards the creation of a continental government. I also told Nkrumah that while a continental union was a great idea, we could not wish it. We had to put in place an organisation to work towards it. During the conference, Nkrumah made a great speech on the need for a union government for Africa. He called for a constitution for an African continent government, a common market, an African currency, an African monetary zone, an African central bank and an inter-continental communication system.

I stood up in the conference, called for the creation of a strong Pan African executive and an African parliament to which all African governments must be prepared to surrender their sovereignty. This position was supported by Modibo Keita, president of Mali; Sekou Toure, president of Guinea; and the president of Egypt, Gamer Abdel Nasser. All these were my friends.

My call for immediate unity was tactics. We used the Nkrumah stand to bring others opposed to African co-operation to agree that a compromise meant building an organisation to promote the ideals of unity. Later in the conference, I suggested that since African unity cannot be achieved overnight, let us put in place an organisation to work towards the realisation of that goal. This was a compromise position between 'unity now' and the extreme position by people like President Tsiranana of Malagasy Republic (now Madagascar), Balewa and others against African co-operation.

Then Ahmed Ben Bella of Algeria took to the floor with a moving call for African liberation. He pledged

10,000 Algerian volunteers to free African nations still under colonial oppression and white minority rule. "A Charter will be of no value to us," he said, "and speeches will be used against us if there is not first created a blood bank for those fighting for independence."

I stood up and offered Uganda as a training ground for African troops to be used to liberate African countries from colonial rule and white minority rule.

Then Sekou Toure suggested that we fix a date after which "if colonialism were not ended, African states would expel the colonial powers."

Leopold Sedar Senghor of Senegal and Nyerere stood up and made strong recommendations on building capacity to liberate the whole of Africa.

Finally we agreed to the formation of the Organisation of African Unity (OAU) whose mandate it was to end colonial rule and work towards unity.

Marriage to Miria

At the end of the conference, Nkrumah was impressed by my contribution and he cancelled his flight back to Ghana and instead came with me to Kampala where he planted a tree. That same year I married Miria and we spent our honeymoon in Ghana with Nkrumah. In 1965, I together with Nkrumah and Nyerere took a strong stand against Ian Smith's Unilateral Declaration of Independence in Southern Rhodesia now Zimbabwe.

I left Amin to pull the trigger

During the 1969 UPC delegates' conference, we invited delegations from other countries like Zambia, Tanzania, Congo and other countries. President Kenneth Kaunda of Zambia was there and so were Presidents Julius

Nyerere of Tanzania, Mobutu Sese Seko of Zaire, Jomo Kenyatta and Emperor Haile Selassie of Ethiopia. Some of them were my friends, very close friends like Kaunda and Nyerere.

On the last day of the conference I escorted the presidents back to Entebbe to take their flights to their respective countries and I returned to the conference to find that a resolution had been passed declaring Uganda as a one party state. At the conclusion of the conference I rejected the resolution because it was not part of the party programme. The party was solidly behind multipartyism.

After the closure of the conference, I walked out and I saw somebody aiming a gun at me. After that I do not know what happened because I was shot at: I broke my tongue, broke my teeth, then I was taken to Mulago hospital. At Mulago Hospital as I was walking in I met Rwetsiba coming out of the building, I did not greet him. I had no teeth, I had no mouth; I could not talk, but he did not know. I saw him clearly, he saw me clearly. Rwetsiba went to Uganda Club. He met some people who told him there had been an accident in Lugogo and I had been shot. He said "No, the president is at Mulago I met him there. He is okay and he is walking and it seems he had gone to see somebody there in the hospital."

It caused a hell of trouble because people wanted to lynch him. At Mulago a nurse nearly killed me! When I was waiting at Mulago, my sister-in-law Mey, came in my room. There was another nurse in the room. I know her but I won't mention her name. This nurse prepared an injection for me. Mey was looking at it. When this nurse tried to give me the injection, Mey jumped up from her chair, got hold of the needle and they fell down both of them, breaking the needle. My wife Miria was still at home in Kololo. I was operated on and now I still have a tongue to cause people like Museveni trouble.

I was in the hospital for about three weeks. While still in the hospital, my vice president, John Babiha, who was an excellent debater and the best Minister for Animal Husbandry ever in Uganda took charge of the country. He declared a state of emergency all over the country, because since 1966 it had only been obtaining in Buganda. The government also arrested many people like Dan Nabudere and Benedicto Kiwanuka. All those were done the very night of the (attempted) assassination by cabinet, under Babiha. I was in hospital, virtually not operating at all.

The state of emergency in Uganda was declared to be reviewed every three months. It was just natural to leave it for three months when parliament could review it. This was the time when we had declared a move to the left, and some people wanted to force me to stop the move to the left. The attempted assassination did not intimidate me. I am a politician. I do things I believe in. So I cannot just change course because someone tried to assassinate me.

After the attempted assassination, Idi Amin who was army commander went missing. He did not come to the hospital to see me. He did not attend subsequent defence council meetings. Later, there was a meeting of the defence council where I heard that his deputy, Brig. Okoya, accused him of cowardice and desertion. A few weeks later, Okoya was killed. Investigations in both the attempted assassination on me and the murder of Okoya were leading to Idi Amin by the time I left the country for Singapore in January 1971. In 1970, I reorganised the army, just an ordinary reorganisation, which took two years to implement, even to announce. This action was not aimed at Idi Amin. In my absence when I was at Entebbe Airport seeing off visiting presidents, Amin apparently made a very moving speech at the UPC conference. I was told about that and later I heard the recordings. It was very moving. It was in support of UPC.

But after the attempted assassination, Amin had disappeared! He was not to be found anywhere. When I retuned to office from Mulago, Amin came to my office and said the normal things: "Oh, thank you Mr President, glad to see you." I began to suspect that Amin was up to something. Why did he disappear the night of the attempted assassination? Before I left for Singapore, I called Amin and the minister of Defence Felix Onama to my office. The Auditor General had issued a report to the Public Accounts Committee of Parliament, where he said Shs2.6m in the defence budget had not been accounted for. So, I told Amin and Onama that I led a clean government; the AG had found money missing from the Defence ministry. I told them to find the money by the time I return from Singapore and restore the account.

David Martin, in his book *General Amin*, said I loaded the gun, put it on my head and left Amin to pull the trigger, which I suppose is correct. The Israelis were also involved in the coup of 1971. When Gen. Nimery came to power in Sudan in 1969, relations between Uganda and Sudan improved. The OAU had pronounced a new policy on mercenaries not being tolerated in Africa. The Israelis were using mercenaries to destabilise Sudan, which they considered the soft underbelly of the Arab world. So the Israelis were financing the Anyanya rebellion in southern Sudan in order to tie Sudanese troops down in the south so that Sudan could not play a major role in the Arab-Israel conflict.

In 1970, we arrested an Israeli mercenary, Steiner, and we deported him to Sudan where he was due to testify in court, a factor that would have exposed Amin's involvement. Another factor leading to the coup was the British. I did not want to go to Singapore. At that time there was what was called Mulungushi Club composed of Zambia, Tanzania, Uganda and we used to coordinate our policies, particularly foreign policies very closely. There was a conference in Singapore of the Commonwealth countries. Since I did not want to go to Singapore, I had to go and tell my colleagues why. I didn't want to go to Singapore because one, there was going to be elections in Uganda around April; two, I had to complete presentation or writing of the five year development plan. The second five-year development plan had been completed in 1970. 1971 was the introduction of the third five-year development plan.

I went and reported these things to my colleagues. However, during this time, the Labour Party under my friend Harold Wilson had lost power to the Conservatives under Edward Heath. Heath immediately announced that Britain was going to resume arms sales to South Africa, which arms would be used to fight the ANC who were fighting against apartheid. I did research on the nature of arms sales by Britain to South Africa and its likely implications on the liberation struggles in the whole of southern Africa. I presented the research to my colleagues who included presidents Julius Nyerere of Tanzania and Kenneth Kaunda of Zambia and the leader of the ANC, Oliver Tambo.

Having presented to them the research we had made on the British arms to be sold to South Africa, they understood my difficulties and requested that since the research could only be presented by me at the Commonwealth conference, I should go to Singapore and present the research. They also argued persuasively for the need for a united front of progressive African leaders in Singapore. I reluctantly and in the interest of African liberation decided to go to Singapore.

I left the country on January 11, 1971. In Singapore, I presented my case in a moving speech. Two or three days later, Edward Heath, the British Prime minister made a statement saying: "Those who are condemning the British policy to sell arms to South Africa, some of them will not go back to their countries," and I understood it to refer to me. I could see no country that presented a stronger case than I did about sale of arms to South Africa.

Secondly, events were unfolding in Uganda. First of all Chris Ntende who was permanent secretary in the Ministry of Internal affairs arrived suddenly in Singapore. His discussions with me could not give me exactly what was happening. So I rang Babiha, and rang Basil Bataringaya, the Minister of Internal Affairs. They said there was an attempted coup but they had incapacitated it. I asked what specific action they had taken. They said Amin had planned to assassinate me upon arrival at the airport, but they had taken care of that. Secondly they said they had alerted loyal army officers. I told them that was very little, too late. "Oh dear, Oh dear," I told them on phone, "it's already too late, it's already too late!" and two hours later, Amin's tanks surrounded parliamentary building and began to shell it. Later, Bataringaya rang me from Kampala and told me that the coup had succeeded.

Amin had said the army has asked him to take over government. I called my delegation to my room and briefed them about the situation back home. I said, "Loyalty to me personally ends here. When we are free either in Bombay or Kenya, you will decide for yourselves what to do, go back to Uganda or go to exile with me." I had decided to go back and handle the situation myself. So I flew to Bombay. From Bombay we contacted President Nyerere who was on a state visit to New Delhi. I was disgusted! It was a terrible shame! I was also worried about my family. In New Delhi, President Nyerere asked that I go and meet him there. So we flew to New Delhi. In New Delhi he told me: "You go to East Africa, from Nairobi go to Dar-es-Salaam, I will find you there.'

I got back to Bombay and flew back to Nairobi. In Nairobi, we were taken to hotels, I was given one hotel and my delegation was given another hotel. In my hotel, I divided my people into two groups. One group close to me, I directed them to ring various numbers in Kampala. Ring so and so, ring so and so, ask what is the situation of the coup, can it be altered? The result I got was that there were many reliable army officers and the coup could be altered. I started sending loyal staff to town to look for vehicles. I asked them to give me money so that we could pay for the vehicles. We had mobilised six vehicles to drive to Tororo when all of a sudden, Kenya authorities stopped anybody from leaving my hotel.

The key was to return to Eastern Uganda where we were assured that we could get into the barracks and we made plans to get into the barracks. But Kenya stopped us flat. Nobody left the hotel, our telephones were cut off. I decided to go to Tanzania quietly. In Tanzania, I was given a state welcome. Prime Minister Rashid Kawawa received us and took me to state house. A few days later President Nyerere returned and told me that what we lacked was manpower. If we could get manpower, he could train any number. I assured him that I could raise manpower.

Then I flew to Nairobi to inform President Kenyatta about the circumstances of the coup, then I flew to Addis Ababa to talk to Emperor Haile Selassie. I wanted their support to reverse the coup. Kenyatta just said he understood but that I should be careful about a war. Emperor Selassie also said the same thing. He said we should avoid a war. However, Siad Barre, the president of Somalia, even without consulting me, sent a delegation to Nyerere that the coup should not be left to consolidate. He said he was ready to send troops to Tanzania from where they could launch an attack on Uganda. I liked it very much and Nyerere agreed but somehow Somali troops never arrived in Tanzania.

Then in March I was woken up at night and told that a delegation from Khartoum wanted to meet me. I met the delegation and they told me that they had instructions from President Nimery that I should go to Khartoum. I packed up and we flew that same night to Khartoum. I remained in Khartoum for more than a year. I met President Nimery who was with his advisers. I presented my case that I wanted to use southern Sudan to enter northern Uganda, contact UPC members, raise an army send them in Southern Sudan and attack Uganda. They discussed it, and then said it was not possible because southern Sudan and northern Uganda areas were occupied by Anyanya under Joseph Lagu.

When they said that one, I said I wanted to meet the president alone. It was agreed. So we adjourned, afterwards I was allowed to meet the president, I told him my case. I said if one area is under Anyanya there was a possibility of raising an army through Koboko market which is in Southern Sudan but is attended by Uganda, Sudan and Zaire. A very big market! So I said I could go there with his staff, enter the Koboko market, meet Ugandans there and see whether we could use the facility as a way to get into northern Uganda, Arua in particular. This was agreed.

So we made preparations to go, and I flew with seven people to Koboko market. When we were there we nearly caused security problems. When Ugandans saw me, they were celebrating in the market on the Sudanese side of the border. I would send people to call them out. So I reported to the Sudanese and they found that it was possible to raise an army through Koboko market, send people through Koboko and bring people through Koboko, which I did and I raised 900 people. From West Nile, Acholi (Kitgum and Gulu), Lango, Teso, Bukedi, Bugisu, Bunyoro. In the next series, Obote talks about fighting Amin in the coup in 1971.

The Birth of a Republic

Let us come to the gold allegations motion introduced by Daudi Ochieng who was a KY (Kabaka Yekka) member of parliament and also a personal friend of Muteesa. Ochieng had introduced that same motion in October 1965 and the UPC parliamentary group and the cabinet had refused to support it because it had no substance.

In early 1966, he resubmitted the same motion. It so happened that I had organised to go to West Nile on tour.

Again the UPC parliamentary group discussed it and rejected it. I offered to cancel my going to West Nile and be present in the House to discuss the motion but my colleagues said I should go.

Now, up to that time, any resolution by the parliamentary group was never changed by cabinet, never! You don't have backbenchers saying one thing and the front bench saying another thing. I left for West Nile the next day, January 31, 1966. Ibingira and group waited for another cabinet meeting on February 4 where they agreed to support the motion.

That same day they contacted Ochieng to present it again in my absence. Ochieng accused me, Onama and Nekyon of looting gold and ivory from the Congo with Amin. He also accused Nabudere of organising an army to overthrow the government of Uganda, in collusion with Idi Amin and me.

The motion was presented in parliament, debated and passed on February 4. However, the resolution did not censure me as prime minister as some people have claimed.

It only called for the suspension of Idi Amin and recommended the appointment of a commission of inquiry by the prime minister into the allegations raised by Ochieng.

Most UPC parliamentarians were confused by the actions of the front bench, led by Ibingira, and abstained. Kakonge took a firm stand and in a moving speech opposed the motion and vetoed it. All this was illegitimate political action by Ibingira and group, and I would have handled it politically if something else had not happened.

On February 5, Onama who was Minister of Defence tried to suspend Amin as directed by parliament but found the action against the law and instead sent Amin on a short leave. While still in West Nile, Muteesa and Ibingira realised that parliament had not censured me. So they could not constitutionally use the resolution to remove me from office.

They decided now to use the army to change the government.

Working closely with the army commander, Brig. Shaban Opolot, the plotters sent Maj. Katabarwa, Ibingira's brother to where I was in West Nile with orders to bring me back to Kampala "dead or alive."

Unfortunately for the plot, it was leaked to me and when they reached me on February 6, they were disarmed and asked to deliver the message.

They said Opolot wanted me in Kampala urgently.

I returned to Kampala on February 12 and Opolot claimed that Amin, who was his deputy, had planned to kill him. Amin also accused Opolot of planning to kill him. There had been a number of plots involving Muteesa and Ibingira on the one hand and Opolot on the other.

I summoned Opolot and the Inspector General of Police, Erinayo Oryema and asked them what was happening. Oryema said he was summoned by Kabaka Muteesa, the president and told that something was going to happen. When Oryema asked Muteesa what was going to happen, the president replied, "You go and find out."

As Oryema left, I got a report that Moroto barracks was emptied. The army had left driving to Jinja. So I sent a word to Jinja. When they arrived in Jinja they were arrested. And they said they were going to Ankole to do a training exercise. I called Opolot who said he did not know anything about it. However, I knew that Opolot was the one who had ordered this army movement.

On February 9th, Muteesa called the British High Commissioner and asked for massive military assistance including soldiers, arms and ammunitions through a certain company.

When I asked Muteesa why he had made such orders, he said it was a precaution against trouble. I asked him, "Trouble from whom and against whom?" He just waved me to silence.

Although he was president, head of state and commander in chief of the armed forces, Muteesa did not have powers to order for arms. All these factors convinced me that Ibingira, Muteesa and group were not relying on constitutional methods in their political struggle against me.

On February 14th, I called a cabinet meeting and asked all those ministers who believed Ochieng's allegations against me to resign from cabinet and no one did. I proposed to cabinet that a judicial commission of inquiry be appointed to investigate the allegations and cabinet unanimously adopted the proposal.

Because Ibingira and Muteesa were using the army, I decided to take decisive action. On February 22 1966, I called another cabinet meeting, mainly with a view to get the coup plotters and arrest them since the best place to get all of them at once was at a cabinet meeting.

During the cabinet meeting, police (not the army) entered and arrested Ibingira and co-conspirators - George Magezi, Balaki Kirya, Mathias Ngobi and Dr Emmanuel Lumu.

On February 27, the Minister of Internal Affairs, Basil Bataringaya, appointed a judicial commission of inquiry consisting of Sir Clement de Lestang from the East African Court of Appeal, Justice Augustine Said from the High Court of Tanzania and Justice Henry Miller from the High Court of Kenya. Wako Wambuzi was secretary to the commission.

This was a truly independent commission since all the commissioners came from outside of Uganda. I personally testified to the commission as did Amin, Onama, Nekyon, Nabudere and all others.

The commission found Ochieng's allegations baseless. There was the problem now of Muteesa and his involvement in the coup plot. I sought the advice of my Attorney General, Godfrey Binaisa QC. Binaisa was among the best legal brains in the country and I trusted his

307

professional advice. He told me that given what Muteesa had done, asking for military assistance, I had to suspend him from being president of Uganda. Binaisa also told me that the only way I could suspend Muteesa was to suspend the constitution itself.

I had worked hard to hammer out the major compromises that made the 1962 constitution. I told Binaisa, "That constitution was my very child. I cannot become its killer. "You do not have to kill it," Binaisa advised, "it is already dead, as dead as a door nail, killed by Muteesa when he asked for arms from the British government unconstitutionally. All you have to do right now is to burry your dead child as decently as possible."

There was no constitutional way out, so on February 24, 1966 I called the press and suspended the constitution and hence the posts of president and vice president.

On April 15, 1966, I introduced the 1966 constitution in parliament whose only difference from the 1962 constitution was to merge the office of the prime minister with that of the president. There were 55 votes for it and only four votes against.

Events were moving fast at this time because six of the 21 members of KY in parliament refused to swear allegiance to the new constitution. On May 20, the Lukiiko met and passed a resolution saying that, "This Lukiiko resolves not to recognise the government of Uganda whose headquarters must be moved away from Buganda soil."

The motion was passed after intimidating everybody else at Mengo who wanted to oppose it by using the mob to lynch them. I retained calm amidst this extreme provocation from sections of Mengo. On May 23, we arrested three chiefs - Lutaaya, Matovu and Sebanakita and detained them for organising rebellion against the state.

There were reports of unrest in some parts of Buganda. I think some police stations had been attacked by thugs while others had thrown logs of trees to block roads in Makindye.

Later in the day, I was having lunch with Muwonge of Bugerere, Odaka's father-in-law Kavuma and Prince Badru Kakungulu, the uncle of the Kabaka discussing the situation. We heard gunshots. Oryema came and said that Amin was shooting at the Lubiri. I ordered for Amin who was called. He came and I talked to him alone. He told me there were reports that there were a lot of arms inside the Lubiri and when I sent an army contingent to verify the reports, they were shot at and they responded. I ordered him to stop immediately, but by this time Muteesa had fled.

For the next nine months, we worked within cabinet on proposals for a new constitution. In early 1967, these proposals were published for the public to make comments on them. The government revised the proposals by incorporating some of the reactions from the public.

Parliament then constituted itself into a constituent assembly and freely discussed the new constitution as the records of parliament attest.

The new constitution came into effect in September and abolished federalism, monarchies and made Uganda a republic.

Some time in 1960, a decision was taken to merge the UNC with the Uganda Peoples' Union led by Rwetsiba. A decision was made and the Uganda Peoples' Congress (UPC) was born.

When I joined the Legislative Council (Legco), it was a timid talking shop. I immediately set out to make it an effective assembly to voice the concerns of the African people. My first task was to link the members of the Legco with the wider community of the people of Uganda in the districts.

We started mobilising for a constitutional conference. Although I was new in the Legco, I immediately stood out because I had a message: Self Government Now! It was the Uganda National Congress (UNC) message, but my job was to exploit it, and I became its voice and people wanted to hear it. The Legco had great debaters like George Magezi from Bunyoro, John Babiiha from Tooro, John Rwamafa from Kigezi. There was also a conservative fellow from Buganda, I forget his name, he was a very great fellow, but he was not my friend.

There were very few black people in the Legco at the time. The majority were white and Indian. But we formed a formidable opposition. The white people would sit on the government side. Some Indians would sit with us on the opposition side, others on the government side. The Indians with us on the opposition side included Madhvani, Varghi and Patel. One issue dominated the Legco in the early years of my service there: the enguli issue.

People in Luwero and around Bombo were distilling Waragi from bananas. The British colonial government was totally opposed to this and were using chiefs to stop people from distilling or drinking enguli on grounds that it was crude. However, the real reason was to make Africans drink bottled alcohol from British companies. That is how colonialism had killed local African industry.

I immediately took up this issue. You can cross check with the records in the parliamentary records of the time. I stood firmly arguing that instead of ransacking people's homes, burning down their bananas plants and jailing those who drink enguli, government should instead refine it to remove its health hazards. I also promised that if an African government took over office from colonial rule, and if I were to play a key role in such an African government, we would build a factory to refine enguli into a healthy, non-crude drink and bottle it. And we did it. The first UPC administration built a factory and you can now drink Uganda Waragi.

Meantime, problems began within the UNC. Jolly Joe Kiwanuka wanted to lead the party. However, Ignatius Musaazi was the leader but Jolly Joe did not respect

Musaazi. Musaazi was a nationalist, a very intelligent man, but unfortunately he was a gentleman, he was not aggressive. Now Joe Kiwanuka went to Moscow and got some money. He went to Cairo and collected more money. Then he went to London and bought a lot of goods, presents for himself and his girlfriends. He had many girlfriends.

He put some money into in his newspaper, *The Daily Express* which we wanted very much, but he was using the paper also against the party and its leader Musaazi. Musaazi made a mistake when he said that is communism money. This gave Joe Kiwanuka an excuse to break up the party.

I had made a good impression in the Legco, so the elected members elected me to be their leader in 1958. The next year, the UNC called a delegates conference in Mbale. I was not in Mbale personally because my father was sick in Mulago. It turned out that the delegates did not want Musaazi because of the propaganda by Jolly Joe.

On elections day I was elected president of the UNC in absentia. Jolly Joe sent Paul Kiggundu and a lot of other people to take me to Mbale. So they came to my house at Naguru very early in the morning, said I was wanted by the delegates in Mbale. They did not tell me I was elected until we were on the way. I went to Mbale and the first thing I told Jolly Joe: "I want to talk to Musaazi first."

I was loyal to Musaazi and I respected him. I asked him if he approved me replacing him and he said he was happy about it but warned me against working with Jolly Joe. I went to the conference and accepted the post.

I immediately set out to organise the UNC from being a party of members of the Legco into a party of the people. My first task was to organise the office of the UNC itself because there had been no office. Together with Abu Mayanja, we set up an office in Number 1 Entebbe road building. Abu was the first secretary general of the UNC and we were very great friends. Up to now I consider Abu a great personal friend. He is a very brilliant man and I did not have a problem with him.

So together with Abu, we mobilised the party by taking it to the grassroots and people received us well. The colonial government tried to stop us when we began to open district, country and gombolola branches across the country. This was because when we called a meeting, people would turn up in thousands.

It was now time for the Wild Commission on the constitution of which I was a member.

We toured the country gathering evidence for constitutional advancement. I would send a message ahead in a district that, "The commission will be in your district on this day, I want you to organise yourselves, take the following demands to the commission," and it was very impressive. Members of the commission found that people were demonstrating.

John Kakonge had just returned from India and I had appointed him to conduct inquiries about what we were doing in the Wild Commission. He found that while the grassroots in the whole country supported UNC, UPU got members of parliament elected by district councils. Abu Mayanja had left us and gone to Mengo to be a minister. He had been invited for a tour of the US and while he was there, Muslims wanted him to be minister at Mengo. We wrote to Mayanja asking him not to accept. Mayanja wrote back and said this is a good thing, he will work from within.

Sometime in 1960, a decision was taken to merge the UNC with the Uganda Peoples' Union led by Rwetsiba. A decision was made and the Uganda Peoples' Congress (UPC) was born. Prior to the conference for the merger, I had been in office with John Kakonge and I began to feel sick. I was taken to Mengo hospital where they found I had been poisoned. So I did not attend the delegates' conference.

I was elected president of the new party in absentia and

George Magezi Secretary General. I do not remember how, but later Kakonge took over from Magezi.

Kakonge was a good brain and a committed nationalist. We began to prepare for elections leading to self government. Buganda had been a headache to the British, they insisted on indirect elections to parliament through the Lukiiko.

When the British refused the demand, Buganda boycotted the elections. When we went into elections, Mengo was effective in organising the boycott since less than 10 percent of the registered voters turned up. Although DP won the election with a majority of seats and formed government, UPC polled more votes and formed a vigorous opposition. Some DP MPs like Senteza Kajubi were elected with 80 votes. I regret to say that DP failed to make itself an effective government. They could not articulate their programmes.

We had powerful debating power with people like Aggrey Lanyoro, George Magezi, Rwamafa, John Babiiha, Mathias Ngobi, Cuthbert Obwangol, John Kakonge, Felix Onama, and me.

I must also say that Cuthbert Obwangol was a difficult man, but a very dedicated nationalist. I first met him in Nairobi when the British refused my scholarship in 1948. Onama was good when talking about an issue he understood well. Later we were joined by Grace Ibingira. He was a brilliant and articulate lawyer, but also a royalist who had a private agenda. In Ankole, for example, he thought UPC should win, but Bahima should rule. DP had failed to be an effective government.

I was determined that UPC should lead the next government. But first we had to ensure that there is another election before independence. Since Buganda had on instructions from Mengo boycotted the 1961 elections, we had a good argument that we cannot go into independence with a minority government elected by default.

I also realised that we had to listen to Mengo demands if we were to ensure a united Uganda into independence. Ben Kiwanuka (I do not blame him, but I blamed him at the time) said, "Look, the Kabaka knows where I am, if he has got any problem he should contact me." He said this to Uganda Argus Reporter. So we picked it up and said "A commoner saying Kabaka should go to him."

Although Ibingira in his books has claimed that he is the one who initiated talks with the Kabaka that is not true at all. The UPC-KY alliance was a matter of discussion between Muteesa and me only. Even UPC central executive committee did not discuss it. I used to report just the outcome.

I had known Sir Edward Muteesa for sometime, having been introduced to him for the first time by a member of Legco called Kisosonkole, now she is dead. She was Muteesa's mother-in-law and a South African married to chief Kisosonkole. She had been nominated by the governor to the Legco. I went to see Muteesa in Bamunanika with Abu Mayanja. This one Abu can confirm. That was the first time I met Muteesa and we became friends.

Ibingira did not play any role in the UPC-KY alliance that I know of. Later, Muteesa claimed that during the discussions I promised him that if UPC and KY came into government, I would resign my job as prime minister and let him appoint whoever he wished to become prime minister.

How can I, a leader of a national political party, make such a promise to a chief of a regional party?

Secondly, the constitution was clear: the leader of the party with a returned majority after an election would automatically become prime minister. Didn't Muteesa know the constitution? I did not promise Mutesa anything, if anything it was Muteesa who promised me everything.

UPC and Mengo had a common cause: we both wanted DP government out of office. Our dilemma was how we get rid of DP. Mengo wanted to have indirect elections to the Lukiiko, UPC wanted direct elections. By the time the talks began, KY had not yet been formed.

In fact KY was formed as a result of the talks so that Mengo can have an organisation structure to relate to UPC. I told Muteesa that KY is in Buganda, it will win parliamentary elections hands down, don't shame yourself with indirect elections. Muteesa did not want any vote to go astray. He wanted Mengo to have all the 21 seats in Buganda.

UPC did not even promise to support the proposal for indirect elections. We only promised we would not oppose it during the Lancaster House talks. At one time during the talks, DP walked out of the conference over this issue.

If there is any concession that UPC made to KY, it was that we would not field candidates in Buganda for elections to the Lukiiko. As a result of the UPC-KY alliance, UPC actually lost a number of seats in Toro, Ankole, Bunyoro and other places. In the April 1962 elections, UPC got 37 seats, DP gets 24, KY had 21. If UPC had not allied with KY it would have won more than 50 percent of the seats in parliament in April 1962.

I had been prime minister for only a few months when Governor Sir Walter Coutts asked me go to State House. He told me the story of the murder of the Turkana by one Lt. Idi Amin. Sir Walter told me about the inquiries made by the Kings African Rifles (KAR) in Nairobi about these killings and the case against Idi Amin. Sir Walter was the commander in chief of the KAR.

The GOC as I understand it found Amin guilty and sent the file to the commander in chief to confirm the sentence of dismissal. Sir Walter sought my opinion whether he should confirm the sentence or not. I regret to say to say that part of Uganda's suffering today can be traced to the opinion I gave Sir Walter.

Even now I cannot explain how I came to give that opinion for it does not fall into the various decisions involving loss of human life which I made subsequently or made before the opinion was given.

I advised that Amin be given a severe reprimand. After I had given my advice, Sir Walter told me that an officer like Lt. Idi Amin was not fit to be in the KAR; the case against him should have at least have had the sentence of imprisonment and that I was wrong to advise that Amin should not be dismissed. Then Sir Walter added "I warn you this officer could cause you trouble in the future." I remember that warning word for word except for the word "could" about which I have some doubt whether Sir Walter said would or could.

I come from royal ancestry

I was born on 28th December 1925. I grew up in Akokoro City in Lango. I call it Akokoro city because Idi Amin told Americans that Obote spent all the government money building a city in Akokoro. The Americans went there and did not find a city. They only found a village with destitute villagers.

My father was Stanley Opeto and my mother was Priscilla Aken Opeto. My father had another wife; she had three children, one son and two girls. My mother had five children with my father, and I grew up with two brothers. My mother's first two children were girls and they both died in infancy.

So when I was born, they wanted to organise a ceremony in order to undo what made the other two girls die. My grandfather, Ibrahim Akaki, said no. He was called Iburahimu Akaki. He was a Christian and all his sons were Christians. The one who made him Christian was called Isaac who married a woman called Rebbeca and his first son was called Esau.

My father was a Gomboloola chief. My grandfather Akaki was the King, who even served as a general in Kabalega's army. Initially, Akaki had his own army. Later, he went to Bunyoro and he became a general in Kabalega's army. So when the British came to look for Kabalega and Mwanga, my grandfather said, "You come to my place". So Kabalega and Mwanga came to Akokoro. My father fought alongside them against the British during the resistance to colonial conquest.

As you may have read from history, Kabalega was arrested in Lango. So you can see the unity of the African peoples' which the colonialists distorted and today's politicians promote divisions between northerners and southerners.

That is my ancestry. It is a royal ancestry as you can see.

I began school at the age of eleven when I joined catechism class to get baptised. I studied there for one year, got baptised and then went to Ibuge Primary School, 16 miles from Akokoro at the age of twelve years. I used to go for catechism class by bicycle.

Very near our home, there were leopards. One such morning we were going on two bicycles. The road was blocked by leopards. So we alighted, waited, but the animals were not moving. Then somebody came from behind and said: "Leave the leopards. Let us pass through the bush." We passed through the bush with our bicycles and we went to school.

On another occasion, I came back home on holiday. I had a friend called Lesley Okao who was very fond of animals. He was a trapper of animals. I was fond of animals because between my father's place and my mother's birthplace there were plenty of animals on the road. So every time I had travelled I used to see those animals and spend hours looking at them. I used to go with

Lesley Okao to the bush to trap animals.

One day I was going to his place, then I saw a waterbuck. I saw a python catch the waterbuck and was winding it's self around it. I went to Okao and reported to him. He came and killed the python, and took the waterbuck home for food!

Another time we were swimming at River Nile and standing next to me was a young girl of my age. She was taken by a crocodile!

I was also a trapper of birds. I would climb up a tree to trap birds and two incidents happened. Once, I fell from the tree and broke my right arm, I became left-handed. Another time I climbed the tree on top of a nest of an owl; the owl came and nearly did away with my eyes.

At my primary school at Ibuge, I did class one and class two. I did not do class three and class four. I was selected to sit class five entry exams and I passed and was sent to class five at Boroboro Primary School near Lira. In Lira, I stayed with my uncle, Yakobo Adoko, father of Akena Adoko who was county chief. I did class five and six.

In class six I was given a recitation on Parent's Day. I was the District Commissioner, so I did that recitation in English and all the Gombolola chiefs were there. The chiefs used to sit with the DC to select two boys to go to secondary school on a Lango scholarship. I was not selected by the chiefs. They said my father was a Gombolola chief, he could pay. The two chiefs, one was the chief of Maruzi which is part of Akokoro, the other was another chief from another part of Lango. They plotted to get rid of my father.

That same week they wrote a letter to the DC asking for my father to resign office. So my father lost his job because of my performance in primary six. When he was Gombolola chief of Akokoro, he used to produce cotton. And every January and December part he used to deposit part of his earnings with his brother, Yakobo Adoko. So when he lost his job, he told me, "Don't worry, I have been giving my brother money for years, let us go and see my brother, he will pay for your secondary school."

The father of Adoko Nekyon was Ezekiel Akaki. Nekyon's grandfather is the brother of my grandfather. He was number two to my grandfather. Nekyon's grandfather was called Opeto and my father was named after him. After Boroboro, I went to Gulu High School where I did Junior one, two and three. I performed very well because I was on top of my class every term. Even in primary I was always on top of my class every term. I was never number two or number three, I was always number one. I passed on top of my class at Gulu High and went to Busoga College Mwiri in 1946.

Gulu High School used to send students to Nabumali High School near Mbale. I did not want to go to Nabumali High School because in Lango they wanted somebody to pass and go to Makerere. The last Langi to go to Makerere was in 1941 when we were joining Gulu High School. That was the first Langi to go to Makerere. From there onwards they wanted someone to go to Makerere. Lango sent very brilliant boys to Nabumali but they did not pass to Makerere. So I wanted to change and go to Makerere, so I chose Nyakasura School.

However, that year Nyakasura had no teachers and could not take any students into secondary. We were all transferred to Mwiri and Budo. My headmaster at Boroboro was Stanley Owiny, and at Gulu High School, Stanley Moore.

My favourite teachers at Gulu High School were Elisa Lakol and Reuben Anywal. My favourite teachers at Mwiri were F. D. Cotts, the headmaster, Nabeta, Frick and Nsajja, our mathematics teacher.

But it is Cotts, who influenced me most. He was a very good man. He even taught me classics, Plato. We used to read Plato in secondary four.

Again throughout my stay at Mwiri, I was on top of my

class every term. It is only when I came late for secondary four, I became number two at the end of the term. I was again number two in secondary six, final term.

One day I was playing tennis when I saw my friend Wilson Aguma go to the dispensary. Then I heard a very great yelling then I ran and found Aguma down with the nurse crying, both of them were crying. The nurse had poured something in Aguma's eyes. I think it was acid. Frick came, put Aguma in his car we went to Jinja hospital and I was in Jinja hospital for two weeks. That term I was second in my class. That is why the head of the class in academics is written on the board, so I was not on the board. I was in Mwiri from 1946-1947 and then I went to Makerere. Only two of us passed from Mwiri to Makerere, Tibamanyire, a Munyoro boy and me.

My best friend in Mwiri was Zikusooka, and Luba both of whom later became engineers, Luba for Kampala City Council. Zikusooka remained my friend, and I even appointed him minister. My other classmate was Muwanga, who became a forester. I do not know where Muwanga is now. I went to do intermediate at Makerere and studied political science and geography although my favourite subject, history was not there. I was given a scholarship by Lango Local Government to do law at Khartoum University. I was the first Langi to pass to go to Makerere since 1941. That is why I won a scholarship to go to Khartoum.

I left Makerere voluntarily, although some people say I was dismissed because of a food strike. I was a participant in the food strike, but I did not lead it. I was given a scholarship starting with 1948, about June-July in Khartoum. When Makerere begun in March I did not go back because I was waiting to go to Khartoum. However, I got a letter from the secretariat in Entebbe written by the former DC in Lango saying that my scholarship could not be entertained. The British did not want me or someone from Lango to go and study law at that time. I rebelled. I went to Kenya.

The people I studied with at Makerere were Martin Aliker, who remained a close friend and was best man at my wedding. Others in my class were Lameck Luboowa and many others. I came back from Kenya and went to Jinja, got a job with Mowlem, an Italian construction company as a general clerk, accounts clerk. I was twenty-seven years old by this time. So I went to Jinja, I did this work. So 1952, they transferred me to Nairobi, exactly what I wanted.

Remember that in 1952 the Uganda National Congress (UNC) was formed. We from Jinja under Lubogo went to Kampala as Busoga delegation. I was therefore a founder member of UNC. When I went back to Jinja, I was transferred to Nairobi, I think of involving myself in politics. I worked in a place called Kabete near Nairobi. Then I was transferred to Mt. Kenya, a very cold place to work.

Then I decided to leave Mowlem because I wanted to do correspondence courses in Nairobi. I got a job with an oil company called Stanbak, which later changed its name to Mobil. By this time, I had a grudge with the British government. They refused me to take my scholarship in Khartoum. So I joined the Kenya Africa Union (KAU).

I had friends in KAU like Odede whom I had studied with at Makerere. I met Paul Gay, a Mukamba. He later became a minister in Kenya. I also met Argwings Kodek. I met Tom Mboya and we became great friends. Then I met Oginga Odinga. Jomo Kenyatta was in jail. Tom Mboya was later killed in 1969. I did not attend his funeral because I was in Zambia when he was killed. As a close friend who was head of state I got in touch with his family and they advised me not to go for his burial because it was suspected that there was foul play, that it was a political assassination.

In Kenya, I became the chairman of Kaloleni Social club. It was a social club of mainly KAU members mostly.

Our job was to do politics when politics was not allowed by Africans. We used to invite Europeans to lecture to us and then we put questions to them. That way we got around to discussing politics.

I decided to leave Kenya in 1956 because there was a movement in Uganda on land. The British government wanted to change land tenure in Lango from communal to private ownership. Lango people were very opposed to it. The UNC in Lango was very much opposed to it. So UNC got in touch with me and they said the minister was going to Lira to launch the private land tenure, and UNC had organised protests. They asked me to join in the demonstration. So I left Nairobi suddenly, without even saying bye to Kaluleni Social club. I went by train up to Tororo, then by bus to Soroti, then another bus to Lira. I was welcomed in Soroti by the Lango leaders of UNC including their chairman, Ben Otim, whom I had left at Gulu High School. From there we went by bus to Lango where I arrived after the demonstration had taken place the previous day.

Before I could even settle down, I got arrested the next day by the colonial police on accusation of leading the demonstration. I was handed over to the DC who decided to take me throughout Lango to address people about Land tenure. The British wanted me to promote private land ownership. I went throughout Lango with the DC but he did not know that I was well known in the district. I had been the last person from the district to pass exams and go to Makerere, so my name had been spread all over Lango.
Later the British released me and I joined active politics in Lango. I had saved some money from Kenya. Frederick Gureme said I went abroad and I got some money from communists, I never did. So I began preaching Self Government Now. I immediately became a key leader within UNC!

In Kenya just before I left for Uganda, I was the representative of UNC so they selected me to go to India.

So we went by ship to India to Bombay. From Bombay I went with some Kenyans by air to New Delhi where we met Nehru, who was very close to African politics. From there we flew to Cairo and I met Nasser. Nehru and Nasser were supporting the liberation struggle in Africa and the Third World. The UNC had a good policy of "Self Government Now; One Man One Vote". We left Cairo by ship back to Mombasa after which I left for Uganda.

Meanwhile in Lango, the member representing the district in the Legislative Council was Yakobo Omwonya, one of the Lango people who was the first to go to Makerere and did commerce. He wasn't effective in the Legco, so we put pressure on him to resign. He resigned and the district council had to elect a new representative. I stood against three other people: the late Okai, Okello Odong and someone else whom I cannot remember. I beat all of them hands down, and went to the Legco and I set it on fire. The records are all there, you can find them. I transformed the Legco from a timid talking shop into an effective assembly.

Obote tells how he escaped in '85 coup

KAMPALA - Former President Apollo Milton Obote says he was almost arrested twice by Gen. Tito Okello's troops as he escaped from Uganda during the 1985 coup.

Speaking in an autobiographical interview with The Monitor from his exile home in Lusaka, Zambia, Obote said his escape convoy was first stopped at Mukono and later at the River Nile bridge in Jinja by soldiers ordered by Maj. Gen. Bazillio Okello, who led the coup, to arrest him.

The former president says the Okellos had given instructions by radio call to all roadblocks to arrest him, which he had heard on his own radio call that was using the same frequency.

Obote recalls that when his escape convoy was first

323

stopped at a roadblock in Mukono, his personal doctor, Mr Henry Opiote, who was seated in the front car, lied that the convoy was going to pick Obote's wife, Miria, from Malaba.

"The soldiers did not know that I was seated in the next car behind," Obote says. "Surprisingly, they did not bother to inspect the cars to see who was in. At the bridge in Jinja, there was yet another roadblock, and we were again stopped. The soldiers there also allowed the convoy to continue without checking."

The story of Obote's narrow escape began on the morning of July 27 1985 with a telephone call from his trusted vice president and minister of defence, Mr Paulo Muwanga.

According to the former president, he was in his office at Parliament Building at about 1 am when Muwanga called him with the news that most soldiers had deserted them and a coup was most likely to succeed.

"I called (Chris) Rwakasisi who told me that Muwanga had called him and told him the same thing by telephone," Obote says. "I told Rwakasisi that this time I was not going back to exile. If there is a coup, they will have to come and kill me here."

The exiled former president says Rwakasisi, who was the state minister in charge of security in the president's office, advised him against staying.

Obote quotes Rwakasisi as saying: "No, we have to get you out of here, out of this country because if you are alive we can fight back, if you are dead we can not fight back. So we are going to drag you out of here."

Obote recalls that his convoy crossed the border at Busia at about 6 am. "At the border, a soldier tried to block our exit by closing the road because they had already learnt of the events in Kampala," he says. "Other soldiers just shoved him away and opened for us and we entered Kenya. We had no money, no passports, nothing."

The deposed Ugandan leader says he later met Kenyan

324

leader Daniel arap Moi, and called the Tanzanian leader Julius Nyerere who refused to return his calls.

Obote also talks about how he ended up in Zambia, where he has lived for the last 19 years.

Obote's party, the Uganda People's Congress (UPC), recently announced that he would be returning from exile on May 27.

Obote: More Reflections

Fighting Idi Amin: 1971-79

Upon meeting him, I found Museveni a consummate liar

Having raised 900 volunteers to resist the military coup by Idi Amin, we took the recruits to Owiny Kibul in southern Sudan for training. We had been given permission by Gen. Jaffer Nimeiri, the president of Sudan, to use his country's territory to train an army and launch an attack against Amin from Northern Uganda.

We expanded Owiny Kibul with farms and modern housing. After significant progress in our plans for an invasion, President Nimeiri entered an agreement with the Anyanya rebels led by Joseph Lagu to stop hostilities. Emperor Haile Selassie of Ethiopia had mediated the talks.

I must say that during my stay in Khartoum, President Nimeiri treated me very well. Whenever I wanted to see him, I would call state house or president's office in Khartoum and if he was in the country, I would meet GeneralNimeiri that same day or the next day. Whenever I went to see him, Nimeiri was always very kind, generous and understanding of our cause. I consider him to be a true African nationalist.

After the agreement, I was saddened when Nimeiri called me and told me that we could not stay in Owiny Kibul, because Anyanya wanted it to be their headquarters for implementation of the agreement. I reported this to President Julius Nyerere of Tanzania.

Then Nyerere sent a delegate to Nimeiri and it was decided that our recruits be transferred to Port Sudan to be taken by ship to Tanga in Tanzania.

We moved the recruits by road to Khartoum en-route to Port Sudan. I met them at an army barracks outside Khartoum and addressed them.

I left for Dar-es-Salaam by air and was received at the airport by President Nyerere. This time he did not take me to State House but to Musasani, a suburb in Dar-es-Salaam where Nyerere used to stay. He took me to a house only two blocks away from his, and that is where I found Mama Miria and the children. I had not seen my family since I left for Singapore and it was an ecstatic moment to see them again.

I had no hand in getting Mama and the children out of Uganda. I had heard that they were arrested and Amin nearly killed the children. I had been living in Khartoum from March 1971 to July 1972.

Back to our recruits, the men arrived in Tanga but they were very sick. The ship was contaminated with a disease called meningitis, many people died on the ship and they were buried at sea.

When they arrived in Tanga, I went to see them, I found them very sick but Tanzanian medical service did a wonderful job. In three weeks people who were very sick were now healthy.

I went again and asked them to do what they did in Owiny Kibul: start farming and build good houses, which they begun immediately.

A few days later, I got a shocker from President Nyerere and his security people. Nyerere came with his intelligence staff and they told me that a one Yoweri Museveni, who has been a student at Dar-es-Salaam and had later worked in my office as a research assistant had informed them that he had organised armies in Western

Uganda, in Masaka and in Jinja and Mbale.

This was not the first time I heard about Museveni. I had in fact heard about him before… even before I left for Khartoum in March 1971. Someone had told me that someone called Museveni had arrived and had gone to Morogoro where Tanzania had given us a camp for those Ugandans who wanted to be trained as guerrillas. I did not think much about him. Now it was 1972.

When Nyerere told me about Museveni and his troops in Mbarara, Masaka, Jinja and Mbale, I said, "Can you give me time Mr. President to check?" he agreed and said, "Take your time." I started working the telephones to people in Mbarara, Masaka, Kampala, Jinja and Mbale. I regret to say that I found no trace of recruitment and I reported this to Nyerere advising him that we should not trust that story. But Nyerere believed it because it was from his intelligence service. He trusted his intelligence very much.

Within a short time, Nyerere asked me to make preparations for invasion of Uganda. Amin had dreamt to expel Asians on the 17th September. I had a meeting with Nyerere and we calculated that the invasion should coincide with the expulsion of the Asians. I felt that the expulsion of the Asians may be popular with a few people but not the majority of Ugandans.

We started preparing for the attack. I went with Vice President Rashid Kawawa several times to the camp to prepare the recruits for the attack. But moving 700 men from Tanga to Mutukula became very difficult.

Anyhow, when they arrived at Tabora, in the middle of Tanzania, there was another group of people who had been to Morogoro to be added onto the 700 recruits.

The Morogoro people were not trained at all whereas the Tanga people had been thoroughly trained in Owiny Kibul. We moved them to Mutukula.

There were two segments to the planning: one group was to fly from Arusha to Entebbe and was commanded by Oyite Ojok. This group would capture the airport, and drive towards Kampala. They would find a contingent of troops from within Uganda's army with tanks along Entebbe Road.

Their combined armoured force would then march and capture Kampala and Oyite Ojok would make an announcement of Amin's fall and play a tape with a speech I had recorded. Tragedy befell this group when the tyres of the DC10 East African Airways aircraft burst while the plane was landing at Arusha.

Another group was to enter Masaka and Mbarara through Mutukula commanded by Tito Okello. It was to be an infantry invasion. Once it had entered Uganda, it was supposed to be joined by Museveni's army along the road to Masaka and Mbarara towns.

Museveni had told Nyerere he had trained an army in these areas which would be waiting to join and support the forces from Tanzania. If all this materialised, Nyerere had promised to send in Tanzanian troops to support our land invasion.

Everything went as planned on the infantry invasion, except for the usual problems of delayed take-off, bad roads and so on and so forth. However, when our troops advanced unto Masaka town, there were no Museveni troops.

The same applied when the troops advanced on Mbarara town. On Mbarara side, only one person, the husband of Frank Mwine's sister joined our troops. Museveni had lied!!

Whether Museveni had any troops at all, we never saw any. So, Masaka was a failure, Mbarara was a failure. Our troops fought gallantly but against heavy odds and were beaten. Many including Alex Ojera, Picho Ali and Capt. Oyile were captured and later executed by Amin.

Amin's army then went from House to house and picked up our leaders and killed them. Among those killed was Bananuka together with his three sons.

Later, I was told that the man whom our troops picked before Mbarara Town who was supposed to be part of Museveni's imaginary army, was the one who went house to house and made Idi Amin's people pick up people like Bananuka.

Obote's wife Miria and their children at Entebbe Airport in Uganda. Obote says he had no hand in getting them out of the country.

I do not have first class evidence, but this was what my informants told me.

Later, I met Museveni casually after the invasion was crushed. He was preparing to go to Moshi to be a teacher. I developed a very low opinion of him because I now knew him to be a liar.

My contempt for Museveni is based on my personal convictions as an individual shaped by my upbringing at home, and also on my institutional socialisation as a leader. I felt then, and still feel so now, that Museveni is a dangerous man.

First, to deceive an African government and its president that was risking everything to help us liberate our country from tyranny, that he had organised troops when he did not was a very bad and dishonourable act by him.

Two, to deceive us, his colleagues, who were prepared to fight the same cause with him that he had an army yet he did not have anything showed a callous mind that just wanted to kill people.

We were not prepared to send troops to Uganda if we had known that Museveni had no troops.

When the invasion was crushed, I asked Nyerere to give me a piece of land. He gave me a piece of land in Tabora district and I organised a very big farm of Ugandan exiles, of former guerrillas. And they became very rich through farming. Between September 1972 and 1978, we did not have much activity.

I felt that if I left our troops redundant, they would forget why they were in Tanzania. So I organised some of the men who were recruited from Sudan who were carpenters to be in Mwanza and to make boats so they could pretend to be fishing but spy on Uganda.

And by the time Amin attacked Tanzania in 1978, our boats were going as far as Masaka, as far as Busia to the east.

There were some incidents in Dar Es Salaam which are worth noting.

Sometime in the 1970s, Princess Elizabeth Bagaya of Toro arrived to celebrate Saba Saba Day (July 7th) in Dar-es-Salaam. She was Amin's foreign minister and I sat next to her, with Nyerere to my right and Kenneth Kaunda next to Nyerere.

Bagaya asked me to return to Uganda, saying that home was very quiet. She said Uganda was now a stable and peaceful country. I said, "My dear sister, I am inviting you to join us in exile. Amin is not a man to be trusted. This is an opportunity for you to run away before he kills you." Bagaya simply waved me to silence.

Few months later I heard that Amin had accused Bagaya of sleeping with white people in a lavatory at an airport in Europe.

Bagaya's story is sad because I had predicted Amin just right: he began looking for her to kill her but fortunately she escaped to Kenya.

When I heard that Bagaya was staying with Dr. Mungai in Nairobi, I phoned Dr. Mungai's home and I talked to Bagaya.

In retrospect, I think I was unfair to her because after exchanging greetings, I immediately said to her: "Didn't I tell you?" She said, "Ah, Dr. Obote, don't say that 'I told you so,' it does not help anybody." Later, I realised that that was too hard on her. I knew Bagaya very well. I had met her during the 1961-1962 London conferences.

Bagaya's father, King George Rukidi III of Toro was very a close personal friend and he introduced Bagaya to me. Rukidi had a son in the foreign office called Steven Karamagi whom he wanted to be his heir, but Bagaya wanted her own brother David Olimi Kaboyo instead.

I knew of this because the king told me and also because Bagaya used to tell us with Godfrey Binaisa.

In November 1978, I was in Lusaka where I had come to visit my friend President Kenneth Kaunda and I was staying at State House. Then I heard on BBC that Amin had attacked Kagera region in Northern Tanzania and annexed it to Uganda.

Immediately after that, Nyerere rang me. "Milton," Nyerere said with excitement in his voice, "this is what we have been waiting for. Please come back." I said, "I am a guest here, I cannot just leave." Then Nyerere said, "I have spoken to Kenneth and he is going to arrange for you to come back." However, it took about a week before President Kaunda found an aircraft for me.

Meanwhile, Nyerere was ringing everyday asking me to go to Dar-es-Salaam and Kaunda was failing to get us an aircraft. The day he got an aircraft for us to go, the Rhodesian army started bombing the airport at Lusaka. It was a very strange thing indeed because again we did not leave that day. We left the next day.

Immediately I arrived in Dar-es-Salaam, I went directly to my house in Msasani and Nyerere arrived a few minutes later. We were happy to meet again. We immediately began to discuss plans for an offensive against Amin.

Nyerere asked me to mobilise the Ugandans we had trained in Tanzania, and also raise more recruits inside Uganda. He also told me that "now we are going to fight Amin until we reach Entebbe and Kampala." I said "I will try." There was a mood of excitement. I started ringing everybody in Kampala, Fort Portal, Mbarara, anybody whose telephone number I could find, I rang and asked to send more men.

The UPC was very popular, because a lot of men were sent. I raised about 900 recruits. I went to the camp of the recruits we already had in Tabora and talked to the men and said now, our patience has paid off. Tanzania now wants us to get ready. Get into your companies and platoons and get into training quickly.

Then something happened; there was a group in Nairobi led by Robert Serumaga involved with a few other people and they got in touch. I think Museveni knew about them, because they got in touch with Tanzanian security which was close to Museveni.

They came to Tanzania, went to Tabora, were allowed to address the men in the training camp. They took 300 recruits to Musoma claiming that they were going to Jinja to attack.

Apparently, Museveni had claimed that he had an army in Jinja waiting to be supported. I did not know about that. In any case, I had lost trust in Museveni and his claims to having an army. The men were put onto two boats to go to Jinja. The first boat was big and collapsed in the middle of Kagera channel and people began drowning. A smaller one was behind, people were crying, very few people were saved.

Obote and his wife Miriam talk to Andrew Mwenda during the interview in Lusaka, Zambia, October 2004.

After returning from Lusaka, Nyerere had given me the task of bringing more recruits. He had also given me another task, to write papers on organising a conference, which I started drafting, and presenting to him through his intelligence service.

After I had done that I received an invitation from the organisers to go to a conference of Ugandan exiles in Moshi to discuss a post Amin Uganda.

I was happy about the invitation, which came to me through the director of intelligence. I accepted to attend, again through him.

Then Nyerere came to see me and said "Milton don't go. These people have done nothing. You are not of the same status as these people meeting in Moshi." Later, he wrote me a very beautiful letter with quotations from Shakespeare.

Unfortunately I have lost that letter. I hope someone who reads this article and has that letter can send it to me because it has fond memories.

Nyerere did not tell me the actual reason for stopping me from going to Moshi.

The reason he gave me above was unconvincing and to

be honest, I was not happy. However, in respect to him as a great leader, and to our friendship and comradeship, I accepted his decision.

Later, I learnt the actual reasons and understood why Nyerere stopped me. With hindsight, I could see how painful this must have been on him. Apparently, the British government was very scared of me returning as president.

They wanted Yusuf Lule to succeed Amin. The British felt that if I personally attended the conference, I would overshadow Lule.

The organisers, the Gang of Four were so scared of me that they even stopped Tito Okello, the commander of the Uganda liberation force, Kikosi Mwalum, from going to Moshi. Tito Okello was taken to Moshi by Olara Otunu.

Olara Otunu came with Godfrey Binaisa from America only to find that Tito Okello, his uncle, was not in the conference.

When Olara Otunu came to see me in Dar-es-Salaam, I briefed him why Tito Okello was not in the conference. The Gang of Four - Nabudere, Omwony Ojok, Edward Rugumayo and Yash Tandon, stopped Tito Okello, Chris Rwakasisi, Samwiri Mugwisa and many UPC people from attending the conference.

Even Paul Muwanga had been blocked until Olara Otunu said those people who are leading at the frontline should be at the conference. That is how Tito Okello and Muwanga were allowed to attend.

Meantime, I met Museveni again just before the Moshi conference. He came back from the front and met me on his way to Moshi.

He suggested to me that we form a joint front of the fighting forces between Kikosi Mwalumu, which was under Tito Okello and David Oyite Ojok, and his Front for National Salvation (FRONASA) on a fifty-fifty percent basis.

I did not think he had troops worth anything, and besides, the idea was to form a united political, not military front. He said he did not want to go to Moshi and find people who have contributed nothing to the liberation struggle to be pretending to organise a national front. He wanted us to have a front of those who had fighting forces on the ground.

Then Museveni asked me to form a military front with him against the Gang of Four. I told him that Nyerere had stopped me from attending the conference at Moshi. He asked me rhetorically, "Nyerere stopped you? Why?" I said, "Well, you go and ask him."

How Lule became president

How did Lule come about? When I returned from seeing the boat people who had survived the tragedy to Jinja, I found Lule in Dar Es Salaam. I said, "Oh Professor, have you come to join us?" He said, "No, no, I am a sick man, I have just come to acquaint myself with what was going on." I did not believe him because I had heard about the British who had supplied arms to the Tanzania to cross Kagera on condition that Obote does not replace Amin.

This plot to force Lule on the people of Uganda was so poorly executed at Moshi so that when the conference was delayed by one day from opening, the BBC and all the British press reported the Lule had been elected leader of Ugandan exiles in Tanzania - clearly showing that information about the manipulation of the vote had been leaked to the British.

In Moshi itself, there was a lot of haggling over who should lead the front.

At one time, delegates walked out protesting the undemocratic manner in which the organisers were conducting the conference and it took a lot of compromise to bring them back in.

Lule's nomination was bitterly opposed and UPC delegates supported Paulo Muwanga.

It is Tito Okello who suggested a compromise that Lule should become chairman of the National Executive Council and Muwanga, the chairman of the Military Commission.

That is how Lule became president of Uganda, with only a handful of votes from Ugandan exiles in Tanzania and only in the context where the organisers blocked many Ugandans from attending.

Liberation from colonialism was my greatest contribution

Upon arrival here in Lusaka, I immediately began plans to fight the government of the Okellos. Then Yoweri Museveni removed them and I transferred the efforts to another political struggle to liberate Uganda from Museveni's dictatorship.

I am now 79 years old and in virtual retirement. But I have got to continue for as long as I breathe to ensure that Uganda is once again a free nation. I do not, however, consider ever being president of Uganda again, no, never! I am old.

I am not like Ronald Reagan, former United States president who came for his second term in 1984 when he was eighty years old.

Even if Museveni's government fell, UPC is revived and they say we want you to be the presidential candidate, I would refuse.

Let me take stock of my life history as prime minister, later president of Uganda twice, and as leader of that great political party, the Uganda Peoples' Congress (UPC).

What have the UPC and I achieved in our life history?

My successes

When I look back, I see the liberation of Uganda from colonial rule and later from Idi Amin's tyranny as my greatest contribution to my country. The second pillar of my legacy is the economic development of Uganda.

In both my first and second administration, Uganda's economy grew impressively well: at an annual average of 5 percent in the 1960s and 6 percent in the early 1980s. These facts can be verified from the library of the Ministry of Finance in Entebbe.

In the economic sphere, by the time Idi Amin staged the coup, Uganda was a net supplier of ready made textiles and garment to major departmental stores like H&M, C&A, Marks & Spencer etc. Museveni does not know that Uganda by 1970 had reached a stage of the manufacture and export of industrial products and was competing very well in European markets, and was about to enter the US market.

As a result, throughout the 1960s, Uganda enjoyed an impressive trade surplus, as our export volumes and values increased considerably.

The share of industry and services increased, while that of agriculture to total GDP reduced. There was also a rapid expansion of the monetary economy.

The third pillar of my work is investment in social infrastructure to improve the quality of life of our people. We wanted our people to live well.

So we invested in housing estates for the upper and middle-income groups. Large-scale apartment blocks like Bugolobi, Bat Valley and Bukoto estates are a product of this effort.

The UPC administration made significant investments in health by building 22 rural hospitals in every district (then) and over 500 dispensaries in every sub country in Uganda.

Our investment in education in both my first and second administration was also significant and that is why UPC is popular all over Uganda.

We expanded existing schools like Budo, Mwiri, Nyakasura, Ntare, and all other A-class secondary schools

337

from 320 students to 760 by building more and better classrooms, dormitories and laboratories.

We expanded Makerere University and other institutions of higher learning, in terms of student in-take, physical infrastructure, academic facilities and student welfare.

Then we built roads, improved the rail system and expanded our air services.

My government established state enterprises and ran them more efficiently, more profitably and more effectively than many, if not most private enterprises in Uganda.

State owned banks, industries and other parastatal bodies attracted the most professionally talented Ugandans and increased the participation of Africans in their own economy.

We also promoted the development of private enterprises owned by Ugandans who competed effectively, just like state enterprises, against both multi national companies and Asian owned business.

It is Museveni and Amin who killed state enterprises and turned them into incompetent and loss making enterprises.

The fourth pillar of my achievements is in the field of international relations. I was a founder member of the Organisation of African Unity. During that conference, I played a major role in hammering out the compromise between the Monrovia Group and the Casablanca group, and personally suggested the creation of a body to drive Africa towards unity.

I am very proud of the role played by me personally and my government generally in the liberation of many African countries from the yoke of colonial rule.

We contributed money, logistics and diplomatic support to the different liberation movements in Africa in both my first and second administrations.

Uganda was among the countries that former South African President Nelson Mandela visited when he ran

from South Africa and visited other African states looking for support.

In his book *No Easy Walk to Freedom*, Mandela does refer to my meeting him and offering support.

Uganda, Tanzania and Ghana were the three major Commonwealth nations that opposed Ian Smith and his Unilateral Declaration of Independence in 1965.

It was because of my deep involvement in the struggle for South Africa's liberation that I went to Singapore to attend the Commonwealth conference there in January 1971, and caused the British to gang with the Israelis, South Africans and Amin to overthrow my government.

My failures

On the negative side, I consider control of the military as being my major failure. I regret ever having trusted Idi Amin. I should also never have left Tito Okello and Bazillio Okello in command positions in the army.

I am reluctant to condemn Paulo Muwanga because I am not very sure about his role in the coup. In any case, Muwanga remained a strong UPC until he died.

I also regret that my second administration was unable to stop the killings and massacres of innocent civilians in Luweero by Museveni and his insurgent army.

As head of government, it was my duty to ensure the safety of person and property in Luweero from all threats - be they from within government or from without.

I also regret the move to the left. With hindsight, I think we should not have attempted socialist or nationalisation policies.

Regarding the attack on the Lubiri, I regret it only in as far as I was the head of government. I had nothing to do with it.

I was having a luncheon at Kampala Lodge with Bulasio Kavuma, Badru Kakungulu and Elidad Muwonge of Bugerere when we heard at about two o'clock, a bomb

at Lubiri.

We later found out that it was Idi Amin's soldiers who were bombing Lubiri. I called for Amin, he came and we discussed it.

Amin tried to justify his action saying that the men who were in the Lubiri wanted to overthrow the government, wanted to overpower the army. I did not accept that one. I ordered him to return the troops to the barracks, which he did.

By this time, the battle of Mengo was over, although many authors have said the battle went on into the night. Unfortunately Mutesa was my friend. Regarding the current political situation in Uganda, I am not happy with the proposed cabinet White Paper because from the little I have read, it seems as though Museveni wants to manipulate the return to multi party politics without actually freeing political parties.

Regarding federo, I think Buganda should get it. In the 1960s we accepted it as the UPC government.

We found that federo virtually means division of work between two governments. We assessed the different institutional and resource capacities of the different districts/regions - Toro, Ankole, Bunyoro, Busoga and Buganda and we gave them different degrees of control of their own resources.

I regret to say that Buganda used federo to undermine the central government. The Kabaka was used to attempt to overthrow his own government when he was also president of Uganda, a very unfortunate development.

Also important to note is that at the time, ethnic loyalties were very strong in Uganda and the kingdoms did not help much in helping the young nation to develop a national identity.

One of the reasons why the government, and later the constituent assembly, decided in 1967 to abolish kingdoms was because of this problem.

Today, Ugandans have a strong sense of nationhood

and therefore kingdoms no longer pose a threat to national unity, at least not to the magnitude that we had to deal with in 1960s.

Regarding Buganda, the current Kabaka, Ronald Mutebi is a more understanding king than his father, with better judgement to avoid the pitfalls Mutesa led Uganda into.

In any case, although many people in Buganda may not accept this, the dissolution of their kingdom as a result of conflict with the central government in 1966/7 has taught them to be more careful in the future and therefore not to press unrealistic demands on the central government.

My return to Uganda

I hope I will return home, because Uganda is my country and I have spent the best efforts of the last five decades to the development of my country.

There is a time when Ruhakana Rugunda was Minister for the Presidency and he presented a paper to cabinet about my return. As it turned out there was no plan at all but a manoeuvre to try and lure me back to Uganda and perhaps to kill me.

Recently, Museveni asked a friend of his, an Indian here in Lusaka that he should like to meet me. And I asked the Indian, what for? I never received a reply and when the day of the meeting came, I sent a delegation to meet Museveni to get the message from him.

Instead, Museveni turned around and claimed I am the one who had called the meeting. Since he had nothing for my delegation, the meeting collapsed.

I am very reluctant to meet Museveni. I would not want to meet him. If in the unlikely event I found Museveni in the same room as myself, I would walk out. I hate Museveni very much because the man killed my parents; I would be inhuman not to hate him. The army attacked my father's home! He was a blind man.

341

My father told the boy who used to hold his stick to go and climb a tree. The boy went. My father was put in the courtyard in his chair. The soldiers came and they cut off his tongue.

They said they would not waste a bullet on him. He died bleeding. I built a house with a water-tank on top and had a borehole in front of my mother's house. So people who came to draw water would also fill the tank up. The tank served my mother in her house. They went and pulled off the borehole that it was built with government money. I had never used government money in all the years that I was in government to do personal work or to build my house or my father's house. In short I was never corrupt. Never! If there has been a Ugandan president who has never been corrupt, I am that president. So my mother got a heart attack and never recovered.

I would not want to talk to Museveni face to face. Museveni is a killer.

My conditions for returning to Uganda are simple. When the parties are operating, and there is no more dictatorship, I will return to Uganda.

I am the father of the nation. Whatever people may say, whatever Museveni says, I am the father of Uganda. I cannot live in Uganda when it is being ruled under a dictatorship and the army.

I would rather be out! Museveni being in government does not necessarily mean dictatorship and military government. Museveni can be under democracy. It depends on the situation.

One time I read that Museveni had offered to rebuild my house in Lira. I don't accept that. He destroyed it, now why would I want the taxpayer to do it for me?

If by accident of history I found myself in the same room with Museveni, I would poke him if I had a stick. That is how much I loathe and hate the man. He is a huge fellow I can poke him anywhere.

My message to him is that he should not bother me. I

am willing to come home provided there is no dictatorship and no one party rule.

He is punishing Ugandans for nothing and punishing himself for nothing. The man does not sleep.

I have been a president I know he does not sleep. He is worried that all the suffering he has taken Uganda through will come back to haunt him.

I personally was never worried about being overthrown when I was president the way Museveni worries about it.

This is because while I was president, I served the people. Museveni is president to serve his ego.

If I were overthrown, I would worry about the service to the people. If Museveni is overthrown, he would worry about himself. So what else would someone do other than overthrow me? You have got to replace me and do wonders that UPC did for Uganda. All those who replaced me failed to register my achievements.

I do not therefore miss being president because I never worked for it. I did not like titles like Your Excellency.

You remember in 1980 while we were campaigning I stopped UPC members who had been in the NCC from calling themselves honourables.

My days as president were days spent very well. However, there were days spent badly. My major preoccupation was working for the people of Uganda and the people of Africa. I would consider a day good if I spent it successfully designing or implementing a project that would improve the lives of the people of Uganda. A bad day would be a day spent without designing or implementing a good project.

So I would spend most of my time as president working on projects like the construction of hospitals, schools, roads, industries, water projects, electricity for the people and other economic projects.

One of the major problems of being president was being cut off from my family. Being president is a very demanding job. You cannot be with the family and be president successfully at the same time.

My greatest joy for being prime minister and later president twice was to be able to serve the people of Uganda.

Travelling abroad for international conferences was a great experience. I remember the time I travelled to London for a Commonwealth conference. It was 1963. When I arrived, Kwame Nkrumah then president of Ghana shouted to all other heads of state and said, "There is Obote!" I was very proud to be introduced by such a great man, to such a gathering of leaders. I was very proud.

The one person I admired most was Nkrumah who is now dead. He was a personal friend and an inspiration in the struggle for Africa's liberation and unity.

The other leader was Mahatma Ghandi. I never met him but I liked his philosophy. Nkrumah had ideas about Africa, which were good. But implementation was difficult.

He was not patient enough to cultivate implementation. He was in a hurry. But he was an illustrious leader. Africa has not had such a great man again. Nkrumah was frustrated by the western powers through the manipulation of the price of cocoa on the international market. They pushed it downward in order to cause him foreign exchange problems and when he was overthrown, the price went up in Ghana, which means that those who were responsible for it put the price down in order to undermine Nkrumah. Nkrumah thought African, governed African, lived African and died African.

Another leader who inspired me was Jawarha Nehru, first Prime Minister of India.

He governed a difficult party, the Indian National Congress, and a difficult country, India, and he did it democratically.

The other leader I respected a lot was Julius Nyerere of Tanzania. He was a personal friend and a very successful president. I admired and liked Kenneth Kaunda of Zambia and we were close friends.

One of the icons of Africa was Gamar Abdel Nasser of Egypt. The other was Ahmed Ben Bella of Algeria. I had also great admiration for Sekou Toure of Guinea and when I was overthrown in 1971, he sent me a message of support.

I like Nelson Mandela although his most productive time was spent in jail. After he left jail, he gave South Africa the best constitution for that country, which other African countries should emulate.

The American president I admired was John F. Kennedy. I visited Kennedy when I was prime minister and had a discussion with him.

I was impressed by his keenness to learn more about Africa and want to work in partnership with us for the advancement of the African peoples.

I did not have the opportunity to meet the other US presidents, so I cannot judge them. British Prime Minister Harold Wilson was a personal friend and we shared a common background of leading political parties with a strong base among workers.

Museveni is responsible for most of the killings in Luweero

During the campaigns for the December 1980 elections, one candidate, Yoweri Museveni repeatedly said that if UPC won the elections, he would go to the bush. That was a lie.

Museveni had been planning to go to the bush all the time. He had been training his own troops as Minister of Defence and placing them in units across the country.

His brother Salim Saleh, for example, was in Moroto barracks. So, immediately when we came into government, Museveni launched the war. Although he claims to have begun with only 27 people, he actually began with many more than that - even in excess of 2,000 rebels.

However, our first priority as government was to deliver the promises in our election manifesto. Remember that it is only the UPC, which produced a manifesto in the 1980 campaign. The promises in the manifesto were reduced into a government programme, The Rehabilitation Programme.

Later Museveni plagiarised our programme, renamed it the Recovery Programme in May 1987.

First, we withdrew the army from the streets of Kampala and thereby reduced insecurity in the city.

For security, we wanted to depend on the Ugandan Police; they were rather thin on the ground. But we depended on them to some extent and we reduced the scare of killings in Kampala.

The killings were at a time when we had the Uganda army and police and the Tanzanian army and Police were all in Kampala. Fortunately President Nyerere withdrew Tanzania Police and then later he withdrew the Tanzanian army.

Muwanga wanted Tanzanian army to remain. I was not too sure. Muwanga travelled to Tanzania to plead with President Nyerere to leave the Tanzanian army, the president refused.

When I travelled to North Korea, I asked Kim III Sung for assistance. He gave some arms, the Katushka, and some instructors to train our army. We now prepared to follow Museveni in the bush and defeat him there.

By the time of the coup in 1985, Museveni had been so thoroughly defeated that he personally ran away to Sweden while what remained of his insurgents fled to Toro.

I was contacted by the government of Zaire and told that some Ugandans had entered their territory. I was in the process of negotiating with President Mobutu Sese Seko of Zaire to hand them over to UNHCR when Bazilio Okello, Tito Okello and other senior Acholi officers in the Uganda National Liberation Army (UNLA) begun colluding to overthrow the government.

There is one accusation that has dominated all debate about my second administration, and that is the killings of innocent civilians in Luweero.

Although a lot of propaganda has been written accusing my government of orchestrating these massacres, the truth is that it was Museveni who is responsible. Museveni is a killer.

That is exactly what he has been doing in Gulu, in Kitgum, in Lira, in Pader, in Soroti, in Katakwi, Bundibugyo and Kichwamba for the last 19 years. Museveni would dress some of his insurgents in official army uniform and send them to attack villages, kill people so that the villagers would think it was the army.

Then he would send another group of his insurgents wearing rags and would go to the ransacked village and say, "What has happened? It is the UNLA doing that. If you stay here they will kill all of you. Please come with us and we will protect you."

I have hundreds and hundreds of testimonies from many families in Luwero who came to visit us at our home in Kololo when I was still president.

All of them told us these stories. I am very happy that Museveni's own senior colleagues in the struggle have begun to boast about these killings.

At the burial of Adonia Tiberondwa recently, Maj. Gen. Kahinda Otafiire, for example, revealed that the National Resistance Army (NRA) rebels used to wear UPC colours and then go into villages in Luweero and kill people in order to make the people think these were actions of the UPC government.

Otafiire was boasting of the "tricks" NRA employed to win support in Luwero, but was also revealing the sinister

347

side of Museveni and his insurgents.

My wife, Mama Miria, is a Muganda. She has many relatives in Luweero. They would come to my home in Kololo to see their sister. Unlike Museveni, I never used to live in State House when I was president.

I used to live in my small house in Kololo like all other ordinary Ugandans. We have testimonies of people from Luweero telling us how Museveni was recruiting child soldiers by first killing their parents.

Museveni has committed crimes against humanity. I could never allow the army to go to Luweero and kill innocent people.

Given that my wife is a Muganda, and my children therefore half Baganda, what type of muko would I be to kill Baganda?

The opposition led by Ssemogerere did not even help matters.

Instead of working with government to establish and expose the genocidal killings Museveni was conducting in Luweero, they began to accuse government of committing atrocities.

They even said they were writing a black book on government atrocities. I ignored them because, what is a black book? Where is it now? It has never surfaced because there was no such black book in the first place for the simple reason that there were no government atrocities to document.

Let me be clear: I cannot deny that individual soldiers in UNLA committed atrocities. That would be a lie. However, I had given clear instructions to Oyite Ojok to punish anyone who violated civilian rights.

Each time there was a reported case of mistreatment of civilians by the army, we arrested those responsible and punished them severely. The truth is that most of the soldiers in the army who were committing atrocities were Museveni's people. And whenever we zeroed in on them, they would run to join him in the bush in Luweero. Take the example of Pecos Kutesa. He had an interview with William Pike on Capital Radio in Kampala in 1995 in a program called Desert Island Discs. He told Pike that he was in UNLA but as an NRA infiltrator whose mission was to undermine the credibility of the army from within.

Pecos Kutesa's testimony is instructive of how Museveni personally orchestrated the killings of innocent people and the harassment of civilians not just in Luwero but other parts of Uganda as well during the 1980s.

His testimony is also important because it fits very well with what Otafiire and Lt. Gen. Elly Tumwine have confessed.

Let us listen to Pecos Kutesa, whose interview on Capital Radio I have kept as my evidence. He told Pike that he used to be at a roadblock in Konge. As a lieutenant, he was the man in charge of that roadblock.

According to Pecos Kutesa's own testimony on Capital Radio, Konge roadblock was the most notorious in harassing civilians, robbing them of their money and killing some. Kutesa says reports reached army headquarters of his harassment of the civilians and Oyite Ojok summoned him to Kampala for disciplinary action. He ran to the bush.

Kutesa's story on Capital Radio has many lessons, mainly because he gave it as personal congratulations for a job well done.

First of all it is a testimony that the army under my second administration officially did not condone harassment of civilians and whenever such cases were reported, soldiers were punished, just like he had been summoned to Kampala to be questioned and punished.

Second that it is Museveni who employs atrocities against civilians to achieve military victory, but in a more subtle way by ensuring that his adversary instead takes blame for Museveni's atrocities.

Kutesa's story directly fits into the same story I have illustrated above regarding the killings in Luweero - the revelations by Otafiire at the funeral of Tiberondwa and the testimonies of visitors and relatives of my wife from Luweero.

The more important lesson from Kutesa's story is that Museveni wanted to grab political power by the gun having failed dismally to convince the people of Uganda to vote for him. It did not matter what methods he employed to get power - cold blooded murders of UPC chairmen in Luwero, robberies of banks, mass killings of civilians; he employed all these.

People like Mugisha Muntu, Kiiza Besigye and Eriya Kategaya are going to find out, or have already found out, especially Besigye, how far Museveni is willing to go to hold and retain political power.

He will employ any level of violence, commit any amount of atrocities to block a democratic process that may get him out of power. That is what he did in Luwero to get power. That is what he is doing right now in Acholi to retain political power.

Museveni has for the last twenty three years fought different enemies in different regions of Uganda: Uganda National Liberation Army (UNLA) in Luwero, Uganda People's Democratic Army (UPDA) in the north, West Nile Bank Front in West Nile, Uganda People's Army (UPA) of Peter Otai in Teso, Allied Democratic Forces (ADF) in western Uganda, and the (Lord's Resistance Army) LRA.

In all these wars, the adversaries are different, the theatre of war different, the periods different.

There are only two elements that are constant: Museveni on the one hand and massive atrocities against civilians on the other.

What does this tell us? How can it be that all Museveni's adversaries in the different regions of Uganda, under different political organisations, and at different historical times fight the same way? Is it not logical that since Museveni and atrocities are the only constants, that it is Museveni who employs atrocities to win wars?

I think that Joseph Kony is only a very good student of Museveni's methods, and that is why he has survived longest.

After 1980 elections, the Commonwealth observer team gave the process a clean bill of health. Ssemwogerere made a lot of noise that he was going to high court, to question the election irregularities. He did not prosecute any of them. Up to 1984, he was not progressing.

We in UPC also filed 26 petitions. We did not prosecute any. It was difficult to prosecute any of the petitions. Amin had virtually killed the judiciary, the laws were bad, witnesses were difficult to find, and so the chief justice in 1984, threw away all the petitions, which had not been prosecuted including ours.

Ssemwogerere was a weak leader. Although I commend him for taking the right decision to go and challenge me in parliament, I condemn him because in 1985 and 1986, he joined gunmen, first Tito Okello, and later Museveni. In the process, he aided Museveni to cripple the Democratic Party.

I used to meet him as leader of the opposition. There was a time when he went to Gulu. He campaigned there.

He came back and wrote me a very good letter saying he wanted co-operation which I accepted and I gave the schedule to Otema Alimadi, the Prime minister to follow it up.

Now, problems arose in Ssemwogerere's party. Tiberio Okeny wanted to break off from the DP which he did and formed another party, the National Liberal Party.

Sometime in 1983, I was in India on a state visit and Paulo Muwanga rang me to say he was giving me sad news.

He said, "We have lost Oyite Ojok in Luweero, it is a helicopter crash". Then he explained the details. I stopped him.

I said, "Paul, stop there, go back to the beginning." So

he started again from the beginning. He explained, I understood.

Then he said, "I am sending you a cable," which he did. That same day I informed Indira Ghandi, the prime minister of India and a close personal friend and political ally that we could not continue with the state visit and she graciously accepted the state visit to stop and we returned to Uganda the same day.

I still think it was Museveni's guns that shot the aircraft, but other people think it was an accident. Even in government there were two views; there were people who thought it was Museveni's guns, there were people who thought it was an accident. Peter Otai knows the details better than me.

Then the Ministry of Defence did not immediately produce a replacement. I was not running the Ministry of Defence; the suggestions should have come from the Ministry of Defence for a replacement.

I used to write to them asking them to propose a name. Paulo Muwanga used to reply only informally, "You know I have only two names and I can not propose one."

There was only Smith Opon and Bazillio Okello both of whom were brigadiers. Muwanga used to say that he could not propose Bazillio Okello because he had been promoted above his level of education and training and Smith Opon was good on paper qualifications but weak in administration and command.

Later, after one and a half years, the two names were brought to the Defence Council, which I chaired, and included Otai, Samwiri Mugwisa, Tito Okello and Muwanga. In the middle of the vetting of the candidates, Muwanga and Okello asked to be excused to go out and consult.

They returned to the meeting and proposed that we drop Bazillio Okello and consider only Smith Opon Acak which we all accepted.

Some people then began to claim that I appointed Acak

because he was a fellow Langi.

My only contribution to his appointment was ceremonial i.e. that I chaired the Defence Council, and that it is the commander in chief who was the appointing authority.

I personally did not know Acak. At least I knew Oyite Ojok and he was a personal friend. I did not appoint Oyite Ojok as army chief of staff. I found him in that job just like I found Tito Okello army commander.

Tito Okello was an ignorant person, he should not have remained army commander. I accept that to have been a mistake, actually a fatal one, we made.

By the time Oyite Ojok died, the army had been stabilised and there was some understanding within the army that we have got to try civil administration rather than military administration, hence less likelihood of a coup.

On allegations of corruption during my second administration, the first thing Museveni did was to appoint a commission of inquiry of each minister. Have you ever seen any report? None! No minister was found to be corrupt. A commission was appointed for Obote alone. There was no report. None! I was not found to be corrupt.

People seem to forget that Museveni appointed a commission of inquiry about the corruption of each minister in Obote II. None was found to be corrupt. And Museveni had no liking for all those ministers including me.

A man like Emmanuel Cardinal Nsubuga supported insurgents. When Andrew Kayiira's rebels of the Uganda Freedom Movement attacked Kampala in 1982, his arms were hidden in Rubaga, I don't remember whether inside the cathedral itself. But it was within the vicinity of the Rubaga and when he withdrew through Rubaga.

So Nsubuga used the Catholic Church to support armed rebellion, give them sanctuary and even propagate their cause. We lived with that provocation from Rubaga.

353

I assembled a good team of ministers. I am not one of those who appoints ministers on the radio. I call a minister, and I offer him a job and I say you will have to do the following things, if they are a problem let me know.

Each one of them I discussed the portfolio with him and each one of them did not disappoint me. I would give them tasks and the time frame to achieve the tasks.

I also used to look at peoples' qualifications and experience. My economic team was the best in Africa: Ephraim Kamuntu, Richard Kaijuka, Yona Kanyomozi, Leo Kibirango, Robert Ekinu, Joseph Okune, Henry Makmot. Look at those names and tell me that Obote was a tribalist!

I appointed Oyite Ojok the chairman of the coffee marketing board because when we came to government, we found that Uganda government had no money. There was no fuel in the country and we needed foreign exchange, and coffee was the main foreign exchange earner.

I wanted a Coffee Marketing Board plant to work 24 hours, day and night. There was need for security at the plant, so I appointed Oyite Ojok as chairman of the coffee marketing board to give that security at the plant in Kampala for over night work, which we did and we immediately got fuel in the country. That is how I solved the problem of fuel.

With the African countries I wanted friendly relations and I started with Kenya because Kenya was our gateway to the sea and I found President Daniel Arap Moi accommodating. We contacted Mobutu and he helped us just like Juvenal Habyarimana in Rwanda who was very co-operative. It was only Burundi, which was a headache to us because its president, Jean Baptist Bagaza was supporting Museveni in Luwero.

Gen. Jaffer Nimeri of Sudan was becoming weak because the insurgency in the south had become too powerful.

I retained excellent relations with Julius Nyerere. I would visit him and he would visit me. I would call him on phone often and he would call me often. However, one time Nyerere wrote to me a letter, which was very surprising. The letter was brought by his brother or cousin called Joseph.

The letter said I should transfer $10m to Tanzania. We did not have that type of money and Nyerere should have known that we had no capacity to have in Uganda coffers $10m just sitting there.

The cost of war was always undermining the relationship between Uganda and Tanzania.

We used to pay US$ 5m or 2m every month through coffee sales. But it was not enough for Tanzania, they would ask for more.

There was a time when I thought we had paid the whole lot only to find a new bill, which returned the cost back to the beginning. Even Museveni has not finished payment I think.

Source: Obote was interviewed by Ugandan journalist Andrew Mwenda in Lusaka, Zambia in September – October 2004, about one year before he died at a hospital in South Africa on 10 October 2005. He was 80 years old.

He had lived in exile in Zambia for 25 years after being overthrown. Those were his last interviews. The interviews were published as a series in the Ugandan newspaper, *The Monitor*, in April 2005.

Party President Laid to Rest: President attacked as Dr Obote is buried at a private function

Hussein Bugere
The Monitor, **Tuesday 25 October, 2005**

Akororo – Former President Apollo Milton Obote was buried yesterday at a private function at his ancestral home in Akokoro, Apac, attended by only family, clan members, local clergy and senior officials of his Uganda People's Congress.

All the government officials and dignitaries who attended the last funeral service, including the tightly guarded Vice President, Prof. Gilbert Bukenya, were not allowed at the grave. They remained at the home of Obote's parents, about 200 metres from the grave.

Bukenya had arrived in Akokoro with three Mambas (battle wagons). UPC stalwarts like Lira Municipality Member of Parliament Cecilia Ogwal and Dr James Rwanyarare, who had fallen out with Obote before he died, also did not reach the burial grounds.

Dr Obote was buried at 4:50p.m. next to his grandfather Ibrahim Akaki as he had willed.

The tiles in the grave were painted in black, red and blue, the UPC colours. Obote died of kidney failure on October 10 in Johannesburg, South Africa, where he had been hospitalised. He had lived in exile for 20 years after his second ouster in July 1985.

The thousands who attended the funeral service witnessed first hand some of the acrimony that has characterised Obote's relationship with President Museveni and his government.

Bukenya condoles Miria Obote

Obote's cousin, Akhbar Adoko Nekyon, dismissed the President's speech, which was delivered by Vice President Bukenya.

The President had left for a four-day visit to the United Kingdom earlier in the morning.

Parts of Museveni's speech were a direct response to what Obote's widow, Miria, had said at the national funeral service at Kololo last Thursday.

She said the death of her husband in exile was "a national scandal" and that Ugandans should view politics that sends leaders into exile as "a scourge on our nation."

Death in exile

Museveni said, "It is, indeed, sad that Ugandan leaders have had to die in exile."

Obote was the fourth former president to die in exile, after Edward Mutesa, Yusuf Lule and Idi Amin.

"These unfortunate happenings are a reflection of our turbulent history that was caused by bad politics constructed around sectarianism and not adhering, meticulously, to the sovereignty of the voters..." Museveni also took issue with Miria's previous statements about Obote's role in the 1966 crisis.

"Our understanding of those unfortunate events is at variance with Maama Miria's understanding," he said. "However, we hope to say our piece at the right time in the right forum."

Museveni also said he would also have occasion to comment on repeated assertions "by various UPC spokespersons" that he was responsible for the killing of civilians in Luwero. "This is not the time to engage in controversies regarding the divergent understanding of our turbulent history," he said. "We have been mourning and paying respect to the late former President Obote, and we shall stick to that."

Taxpayers' money

But Nekyon could not take any of that. He said Bukenya had wasted taxpayers' money by travelling all the way to deliver Museveni's message. "I have read the message from Museveni, but I have failed to understand it," Nekyon said. "It was a waste of public money to travel up to here. He should have written the letter in the newspapers."

Nekyon said further, "Let's learn to honour our leaders when they are alive. Let's not wait for them to die in poverty and honour them, posthumously. Look at that contradiction. Yesterday Obote was a killer, ghost and swine. But today he is a hero and flags are flying at half mast!" Nekyon exclaimed.

President Museveni had in the past described Obote and other former leaders, as swine. He once called Obote a ghost on account of the former president's hair.

Nekyon said Obote had "never killed even a chicken or a goat." He said he would not be intimidated as he led the family's claims for compensation. "Nobody will ever intimidate me under this sun," Nekyon said. "All we are asking for is our right not privileges or patronage. We are a well-established clan."

Obote's widow Miria thanked former UPC youth wingers Tumusiime Mutebile, now Central Bank Governor, and Ruhakana Rugunda (now Internal Affairs Minister) who attended the burial ceremonies, saying that they had acted professionally. Dressed in a red Kitenge with a sash hanging on her shoulders, she said Obote died happy having groomed young people like Mutebile and Rugunda.

Ministers Betty Akech (security), speaker Edward Ssekandi also attended. Others were Former President Godfrey Binaisa, former minister Bidandi Ssali, Forum for Democratic Change leaders Salaamu Musumba and Maj. Gen. Mugisha Muntu, Justice Forum leader Kibirige

Mayanja and former Kampala mayor Nasser Ssebaggala.

There were also delegations from Kenya and Rwanda among others.

Binaisa denies

Binaisa earlier told mourners at the home of Obote's parents that he never advised the late Obote to abrogate the 1962 Constitution. Binaisa said, "We are here to discuss the future of Uganda. Let me clear some misunderstandings... I did not force the Parliament to change the Constitution. I did not have the powers nor did Obote."

Binaisa was Attorney General in Obote's first government.

He said Parliament had the power to change anything except turning a man into a woman. "You must understand that I didn't hate anybody but had to fulfil my work," Binaisa said.

"I had to work. It was the duty contracted to me by Milton. I did not intend to harm anyone, not even Baganda. I was born in Buganda." Binaisa said, "The thing I want to stress is that we should go forward," he said.

Appendix III:

Amin dies

Idi Amin, Murderous and Erratic Ruler of Uganda in the 70's, Dies in Exile

Michael T. Kaufman,
The New York Times, 17 August 2003

Idi Amin, whose eight-year reign of terror in Uganda encompassed widespread killing, torture and dispossession of multitudes and left the country pauperized, died yesterday in Jidda, Saudi Arabia, where he had lived for years in exile. He was believed to have been about 78 years old, though some reports said he was as old as 80.

Mr. Amin had been hospitalized and on life support since mid-July. He died from multiple organ failure,

Reuters reported.

For much of the 1970's, the beefy, sadistic and telegenic despot had reveled in the spotlight of world attention as he flaunted his tyrannical power, hurled outlandish insults at world leaders and staged pompous displays of majesty.

By contrast, his later years were spent in enforced isolation as the Saudi Arabian authorities made sure he maintained a low profile. Mr. Amin, a convert to Islam, his four wives and more than 30 children fled Uganda just ahead of an invading force of Ugandan exiles and Tanzanian troops that overthrew his government. They went first to Libya, and eventually to Saudi Arabia.

By the time he had escaped with his life, the devastation he had wreaked lay fully exposed in the scarred ruins of Uganda. The number of people he caused to be killed has been tabulated by exiles and international human rights groups as close to 300,000 out of a total population of 12 million.

Those murdered were mostly anonymous people: farmers, students, clerks and shopkeepers who were shot or forced to bludgeon one another to death by members of death squads, including the chillingly named Public Safety Unit and the State Research Bureau. Along with the military police, these forces numbering 18,000 men were recruited largely from Mr. Amin's home region. They often chose their victims because they wanted their money, houses or women, or because the tribal groups the victims belonged to were marked for humiliation.

But there were also many hundreds of prominent men and women among the dead. Their killings were public affairs carried out in ways that were meant to attract attention, terrorize the living and convey the message that it was Mr. Amin who wanted them killed. They included cabinet ministers, Supreme Court judges, diplomats, university rectors, educators, prominent Catholic and Anglican churchmen, hospital directors, surgeons, bankers, tribal leaders and business executives.

In addition to Ugandans, the dead also included some foreigners, among them Dora Bloch, a 73-year-old woman. She was dragged from a Kampala hospital and killed in 1976 after Israeli commandoes raided Entebbe Airport to rescue 100 other Israelis who along with her had been taken as hostages from a hijacked Air France plane.

As an awareness of spreading horror and suffering filtered out of Uganda, Mr. Amin began to address the criticism, choosing words that intentionally added insult to injury. He declared that Hitler had been right to kill six million Jews. Having already called Julius Nyerere, then the president of Tanzania, a coward, an old woman and a prostitute, he announced that he loved Mr. Nyerere and "would have married him if he had been a woman." He called Kenneth Kaunda, then the president of Zambia, an "imperialist puppet and bootlicker" and Henry A. Kissinger "a murderer and a spy." He said he expected Queen Elizabeth to send him "her 25-year-old knickers" in celebration of the silver anniversary of her coronation.

In other comments he offered to become king of Scotland and lead his Celtic subjects to independence from Britain. He forced white residents of Kampala to carry him on a throne and kneel before him as photographers captured the moment for the world to see. He also ejected Peace Corps volunteers and the United States marines who had guarded the American Embassy in Kampala.

Mr. Amin's flagrant brutality, coupled with his seemingly erratic behavior and calculating insults, aroused disgust but also fascination far beyond Uganda's borders. Some African nationalists cheered his insults of Europeans. Radical Arabs, led by Muammar el-Qaddafi of Libya, actively courted him as an ally, and for a time so did the Soviet Union. But there were others who questioned his sanity. Harold Wilson, the leader of the British Labor Party, called him "mentally unbalanced."

Mr. Kaunda described him as "a madman, a buffoon."

Many, however, who had observed him long and carefully from close quarters warned against such judgments. '"Capricious, impulsive, violent and aggressive he certainly is, but to dismiss him as just plain crazy is to underestimate his shrewdness, his ruthless cunning and his capacity to consolidate power with calculated terror," wrote Christopher Munnion, a reporter for *The Daily Telegraph*, after he was detained at the notorious Makindye military barracks, where four of his cellmates, former police officers, were killed with sledge hammers.

Like many African leaders including Mr. Nyerere and Jomo Kenyatta of Kenya, Idi Amin never knew the date of his birth. According to his army documents, he was born around 1925 in a remote northwestern region near the borders of Sudan and Congo, while Uganda was under British control. His father was a farmer of the small Kakwa tribe and his mother was from the linked Lugbara people. The region is ethnically distinct from the rest of Uganda, with many people, like the Amin family, having close ties to tribesmen in Sudan. Ugandans referred to these northern tribes collectively as Nubians, and it was upon such Nubians that Mr. Amin would later rely for his security forces.

Soon after his birth, his parents separated, and his mother took her child to live in Nubian settlements in Ugandan cities. At one point she worked as a cane cutter on a plantation that her son would, as president, appropriate from its Asian owners.

Her son joined the King's African Rifles in 1946 as an assistant cook. Later, after he had given himself the rank of field marshal and covered his massive chest with medals, he would claim that he had fought with the unit in Burma, but there is no record of such combat. Yet the powerful Amin, 6 feet 4 inches, quickly attracted the attention of British commanders.

As a young soldier he rose steadily through the ranks,

spending the mid-1950's fighting in colonial Kenya against Mau Mau guerrillas who used terror tactics to spread dread among white settlers in hopes of ending British rule. In 1957 he was promoted to sergeant major and two years later was singled out for the rank of "effendi," a new position for native noncommissioned officers judged to have leadership potential.

There were a few blots in his record book. He was charged with failing to obtain treatment for venereal disease. This might have been the basis of allegations that his erratic behavior reflected the mental degeneration of untreated syphilis. More serious were allegations that a unit under his command had killed desert tribesmen. Still, when Uganda became independent in 1962, Mr. Amin held the highest rank of any African in the Ugandan military.

He was on very good terms with Milton Obote, the country's first prime minister, who in 1963 approved his promotion to major. Mr. Amin was sent for special training to Britain and Israel, where he gained his paratrooper wings. In 1964 he was promoted to colonel and appointed deputy commander of Uganda's army and air force.

In February 1966, charges were raised in Uganda's Parliament that two years earlier Mr. Amin, carrying out Mr. Obote's orders, had misappropriated $350,000 in gold and ivory from guerrillas in Congo who he was supposed to have supplied with arms. Mr. Amin's forces arrested the five ministers who raised the issue and Mr. Obote suspended the Constitution. Two days later Mr. Amin was put in full charge of all the military and the police.

Two months later, Mr. Obote annulled Uganda's basic political formulation under which power was shared between himself and Mutesa II, the king of the Baganda, long the country's most powerful tribe. Mr. Amin sent tanks to shell the palace of the king, who escaped and fled to London.

In 1967, Mr. Amin was promoted to brigadier general and the next year to major general. As Mr. Obote declared a turning to the left and sought to remove influential Bagandas and replace them with his own ethnic kin from the Acholi and Langi tribes, he and Mr. Amin worked closely together.

But in 1971, Mr. Obote, believing that his top general had been plotting behind his back, sought to rein him in. As he left for a conference in Singapore, Mr. Obote ordered Mr. Amin to prepare an accounting of several million dollars in defense spending. Mr. Obote never returned to his presidential residence. On Jan. 25, while he was flying back from Singapore, Mr. Amin seized power. Mr. Obote eventually made his way to Tanzania, where he would later denounce his former ally as "the greatest brute an African mother has ever brought to life."

Inside the country, crowds danced and toasted the new leader. Outside Uganda, Mr. Amin was also applauded. In light of Mr. Obote's announced plans to nationalize British-held property, the reaction in London was favorable. The Israelis, who had large building projects in Uganda and who had worked closely with Mr. Amin, also believed they would benefit by the change.

Ethnic conflicts soon spread through the army, with Mr. Amin's Nubian supporters killing a few thousand soldiers from the Acholi and Langi tribes. The economy deteriorated as Mr. Amin ordered more money printed to cover expenditures. In 1972 he asked the Israelis for more money and jet fighters, saying he needed them to deal with Tanzania, where Mr. Obote was living. When the Israelis dismissed the request, he traveled to Libya and obtained promises of aid from Colonel Qaddafi. He then ordered 500 Israelis out of the country, ending several large building projects, and began his fulminations against Zionism and Jews.

On Aug. 5, 1972, with the economy continuing to falter, Mr. Amin announced that all Ugandans of Asian origin holding British passports, some 40,000 in all, would have to leave the country within 90 days. The majority of them were third-generation descendants of workers brought by the British from the Indian subcontinent. Most of those expelled left for Britain. They were allowed to take only what they could carry.

In the middle of the exodus, Mr. Obote's backers mounted an ineffective invasion from Tanzania. It was soon repulsed, but it provided a pretext for increasing terror, beatings and murders of Ugandans.

A special vocabulary of killing and torture was developed and used by Mr. Amin, according to his former associates who managed to escape. "Giving the V.I.P. treatment" to someone meant to kill, as did the instruction "Go with him to where he sleeps." "Giving tea" meant whipping and dismemberment.

On June 27, 1976, seven terrorists, two of them members of the German Baader-Meinhof gang, hijacked Air France Flight 139 after it left Tel Aviv for Paris. The plane landed first in Benghazi, Libya, and then continued on to Entebbe in Uganda, where it arrived early on June 28.

On the morning of July 4, Israeli commandoes killed the hijackers, rescued 102 hostages and destroyed eight Ugandan Air Force MIG's. The raid on Entebbe left Mr. Amin with few options for retaliation beyond killing Mrs. Bloch, who days before the rescue had been taken to hospital when some food stuck in her throat.

In 1978, Mr. Amin sent troops into Tanzania in an effort to annex the Kagera salient, a desolate spur to the west of Lake Victoria. By early 1979, they fled under the assault of Tanzanian forces and Ugandan exiles. Mr. Amin's army and its Libyan allies were unable to stop the counteroffensive, and on April 12 Kampala was taken. Mr. Amin fled, first to Tripoli in Libya and finally to Saudi Arabia.

He remained there until January 1989, when he slipped out on a false passport and flew to Kinshasa in what was then Zaire, where he claimed he would return to Uganda to

367

reclaim power. The Zairean authorities held him while he looked for someplace that would take him. The Ugandan government said it would accept him only to stand trial. No other country would take him, and ultimately Saudi Arabia, which had also sought to keep him from returning there, reversed itself and once more provided him with sanctuary. Since then he had lived in Riyadh, where he was occasionally seen driving a white Chevrolet.

Idi Amin

Patrick Keatley, *The Guardian*, London, Sunday 17 August 2003

Ruthless dictator whose rise to power was facilitated by the British colonial authorities, he went on to devastate Uganda.

Idi Amin, who has died at an age thought to be 78, was one of the most brutal military dictators to wield power in post-independence Africa.

While chief of staff of the Ugandan army, under Dr Milton Obote's civilian government, he seized power in 1971. He made himself president, with the rank of field marshal, and after eight years of power left Uganda a legacy of bloodthirsty killings and economic mismanagement. Parliament was dissolved; no elections were held; secret police - most of them in plain clothes - exercised absolute power of life and death; and the courts and the press were subjugated to the whims of the executive.

The death toll during the Amin regime will never be accurately known. The best estimate, from the International Commission of Jurists in Geneva, is that it was not less than 80,000 and more likely around 300,000.

Another estimate, compiled by exile organisations with the help of Amnesty International, put the number killed at 500,000.

For Tanzania's president, Julius Nyerere (obituary, October 15 1999), Amin was "a murderer, a liar and a savage." In the perspective of history he will go down as one who damaged the cause of African nationalism. His rule of Uganda became a synonym for barbarity.

Amin was neither well-educated nor particularly intelligent. But he had a peasant cunning which often outflanked cleverer opponents, including Uganda's civilian president Milton Obote, who was displaced in the 1971 coup.

He also possessed a kind of animal magnetism; a quality he used with sadistic skill in his dealings with people he wished to dominate. In his relations with women it brought him a succession of casual mistresses, longer-serving concubines, and six wives. Turned against men, this magnetism was used as by a snake on a rabbit; Amin soon learned how to exploit it to frighten, dominate and command. It explains the otherwise bizarre decision by his last British colonial regimental commander to select Amin as one of the first two black Ugandans to be promoted to commissioned rank, when his educational background was virtually nil.

That was in 1961. With independence the next year and the rapid Africanisation which followed, he was elevated to army commander by 1964. He claimed to have been the officer who, virtually single-handed, put down the army mutiny at Jinja, Uganda's second city, in that year. Whatever the truth of it, Obote trusted him enough to put him in charge of the highly political military operation two years later: the attack on the "new palace" of the Kabaka (king) of Buganda on Mengo Hill. There was no military glory involved - Sir Frederick Mutesa and his supporters had only a few hunting rifles - but the victory of this Moslem officer of peasant origins over the Christian patrician ruler of the sophisticated Baganda, hitherto the dominant tribe, invested Amin with a mystique that was to make him a legend and carry him to the heights of power.

The Battle of Mengo Hill, as he liked to describe it, was something he never ceased to describe to visitors like myself, in greater and more gory detail with the passage of the years. It gave him the conviction he was not as other mortals; that bullets could not touch him, that he was selected by God to walk with kings, presidents and prime ministers alike and, when directed by God in mystic dreams, to humble them. Indeed, the time was to come when, in the Denis Hills affair, he was to humble the foreign secretary of Great Britain, bringing him grovelling to Kampala to plead for a British resident's life.

Amin was born around 1925 - exact records were not kept for Africans in those days - in Koboko county in West Nile district, home of the Kakwa tribe. His father had spent much of his life in the southern Sudan, where the Kakwas, an Islamic people, had originated. His mother was from the ethnically related Lugbara tribe. Violence and bloodletting were observed, by early Victorian explorers, to be particularly marked among these Sudanic-Nubian peoples; the homicide rate there is still one of the highest in Africa to this day.

Amin's first foot on the ladder was the traditional one for poor boys with little training, seeking to better themselves: he joined the army. He became an assistant cook in the King's African Rifles. He claimed to have fought with the regiment in the Burma campaign in the war. This was true of many Africans who joined the British colonial forces, but in Amin's case was an audacious lie. His record file shows his entry into the KAR took place in 1946.

A mere 16 years later, after training in Wiltshire, as a commissioned officer, he was to command a battalion of the 4th KAR and, when in civvies, wore the KAR tie all his life.

His only distinction in terms of overseas service was to be identified as leader of a scrimmage among Ugandan troops stationed in Mauritius, which was put down by British-led police. The other black mark in his regimental book was an entry indicating, in 1955, that he had been repeatedly infected and cured of venereal disease. He is said to have acquired his taste for bordellos, and for variety in women, when serving in army posts in the sheikhdoms of the Gulf, from Aden northwards, in colonial times.

The first sign of his sadism came after the fatal decision to make him a commissioned officer. In 1962, commanding troops of the 4th KAR, he carried out the Turkana Massacre, an operation that began as a simple assignment to check cattle rustling by tribesmen in the Turkana region of Kenya. Complaints from villagers reached the British authorities in Nairobi; bodies were exhumed from pits and it became clear that the victims had been tortured, beaten to death and, in some cases, buried alive.

But Amin was lucky. The British authorities in Kampala, with Uganda's independence only months away, decided it was politically impossible to court-martial one of the country's only two black officers. The man who was later to be toppled by Amin, Dr Milton Obote, concurred.

In December 1969 came the mysterious episode when assassins, never identified, tried to kill Obote as he walked from a party rally. Badly wounded, he ordered an investigation while recovering in hospital. Amin could not be found but turned up later at the meeting where Brigadier Okoya, the deputy army commander, indicated that the net was closing in. A date was set for a second meeting, on January 26, when decisions would be taken and the guilty ones named.

At 11pm on January 25, shots were heard in the Kampala suburb where the deputy commander was living. Friends called police and went to the house, to find

Brigadier Okoya and his wife both dead from multiple bullet wounds. Nothing had been stolen.

Later in 1970, while the Obote government was still in power, police investigating an armed hold-up, arrested a gang of kondos, the local word for thugs in illegal possession of arms. Under questioning, one of them indicated he took his orders from Brigadier Amin. This was embarrassing, as Obote was about to promote Amin to chief of staff, so the police commandant, Inspector-General Cryema, took no action.

The kondos were released from detention and were killed in unexplained circumstances soon afterwards. Cryema was arrested and executed soon after Amin took power, in the coup of January 25 1971, while Obote was attending a Commonwealth prime ministers' conference in Singapore.

As this reign of terror got under way, the Chief Justice, Benedicto Kiwanuka, a former prime minister of Uganda, was arrested in his robing room and brutally killed by plain clothes thugs. The Anglican Archbishop, Janani Luwum, was killed in a simulated car crash in Kampala. Other leading figures were expunged in similar brutal circumstances, including the vice-chancellor of the university.

About six weeks after Amin seized power came the explosion at Makindye Prison in Kampala, when 32 army officers, crammed into a tiny cell, were blown up by a charge of dynamite. The group was made up of Christian tribes such as the Acholi and Langi, which had supported the government of the fallen President Obote. It now seems that two thirds of the Ugandan army's soldiers, out of a total of 9,000 men, were executed in Amin's first year of power. The pattern had been set for the mass blood-letting that was to come.

I myself had a glimpse of Amin's cruelty and cunning one morning in Kampala, when the police band were giving a concert as part of a major ceremony. The dictator,

372

in full uniform, stepped forward at a break between numbers, seized the baton from a quivering conductor and barged into action. The official police photographer appeared on cue to record this "spontaneous event." Then came a trap.

Spotting me in the crowd, Amin declared: "There is my best friend, Patrick; he will do the next number." With that, he signalled to the cameraman, who moved into position, ready to take the compromising photo that would have me standing next to the dictator. It was clever; it would make me immediately suspect in the media world.

I hastily resorted to a coughing fit, face in handkerchief, and scotted. When I recounted this over lunch that day, sitting on the verandah of the Speke Hotel with Anil Clerk, QC, the acknowledged leader of the Ugandan bar, he discreetly pointed out a plainclothes police officer.

"Patrick," Clerk said, "the time to leave Uganda is now, this afternoon." I took his advice. I never saw my distinguished lawyer friend again. His body was found a fortnight later, doubled up in the boot of a partly burned car, his throat cruelly bound with razor wire.

Some months later in Nairobi, I was tipped off by an old friend, an African airlines official, who advised me to avoid refuelling stops or even overflights in Uganda air space. My name had been added to the death list of those to be taken off any flight and shot.

According to Amnesty International, the ICJ, and exile sources, Amin deliberately created four rival and overlapping agencies to carry out his mass killings. These were the Military Police, the Presidential Guard, the Public Safety Unit and the Bureau of State Research. His bodyguards were drawn from his own Kakwa tribe and, with their special language and accent, they were well-placed to detect any attempt by an outsider to infiltrate their ranks. This, combined with Libyan security experts, and Amin's own good luck, headed off seven major

373

assassination attempts organised by dissident army and air force officers between 1972 and 1979.

Amin was a considerable linguist, and once explained to me that he was much more fluent in his own Kakwa or its two related northern languages, than in English, which he had mastered only after joining the army. He was fluent also in the language of southern Uganda, and in the East African lingua franca, Swahili.

In 1977, after Britain broke diplomatic relations with his regime and then withdrew the two remaining diplomats who had stayed on attachment at the French Embassy, Amin declared he had beaten the British and conferred on himself the decoration of CBE which, he said, stood for "Conqueror of the British Empire."

Radio Uganda then solemnly read out the whole of his title: "His Excellency President for Life, Field Marshal Alhaji Dr Idi Amin Dada, VC, DSO, MC, CBE." Frequently, when the national radio made an announcement, referring to "a military spokesman," the text had been dictated by Amin himself at the presidential lodge in Kampala, which he re-named the Command Post.

He was a man who acted on hunches and impulses. His decision to expel the 35,000 Asians of Uganda in the space of three months between August and November 1972 came to him, he said, in a dream. He expounded the dream the next day to troops at a military post in the north, and the policy came into effect before nightfall.

Until a bitter quarrel with Israel, when he ordered the diplomatic mission in Kampala to be closed, Amin was proud of the parachutist's wings which he wore above all his ribbons on his elaborate marshal's uniform. He brought back this badge from the course he took in Israel while still an army sergeant. Later another parachutist on the course, Reuben Cohen, declared that Amin had failed his tests but was given the wings for reasons of diplomacy at the time.

Then in 1976 came the hijacking of an Air France

plane bound from Athens to Paris, initially by two members of the Popular Front for the Liberation of Palestine and two from Germany's Baader-Meinhof gang. The plane was forced down at Entebbe and the crisis only ended with an audacious airborne raid by Israeli commandoes. But one passenger, the unfortunate Dora Bloch, who held joint Israeli-British citizenship, had been taken from the airport to hospital in Kampala.

After the raid, according to Uganda's minister of health at the time, Henry Kyemba, who later escaped into exile, Mrs Bloch was taken screaming from her hospital bed and brutally executed the same day. This incident did much to convince world opinion that, in Amin, the international community was dealing with a madman.

The Bloch affair loosened tongues in Israel and a doctor who had served in an Israeli medical aid team in Uganda told a newspaper correspondent in Tel Aviv: "It's no secret that Amin is suffering from the advanced stages of syphilis, which has caused brain damage."

When, in 1975, the then British foreign secretary James Callaghan, had to fly to Uganda to plead for the life of the British lecturer, Denis Hills, held hostage in prison after being given a death sentence by a military court, he was given a confidential file referring to the same theory: that Amin was infected and insane.

The Islamic religion became a fetish for this unbalanced man, and his uncouth espousal of it did great harm to the Muslim cause in Africa. Amin succeeded in enlisting the support of his Islamic near-neighbour, the Libyan leader Colonel Gadafy. But other Muslim leaders in Syria, Jordan and Iraq rebuffed him when he travelled to their capitals looking for alliances. However, contingents of Libyan troops and planes helped his regime survive, against the odds, on more than one occasion.

Amin's fanaticism came to a head in a bizarre telegram sent to the then United Nations secretary-general, Kurt Waldheim, when he purported to analyse the Middle East situation and focused his hatred on the Israelis.

The message contained these phrases, personally dictated by Amin to his secretary:

"Germany is the right place where, when Hitler was the supreme commander, he burnt over six million Jews. This is because Hitler and all German people knew that the Israelis are not people who are working in the interest of the people of the world, and that is why they burnt the Israelis alive with gas."

Reaction in black Africa was profound. Leaders like Nyerere and Zambia's Kenneth Kaunda, who had condemned Amin from the start as a dangerous, unbalanced man, were vindicated.

Amin's family life remains cloaked in mystery. He divorced his first three wives at various times. A fourth, Kay, disappeared and her body, butchered into chunks and then reassembled, was seen at a mortuary by one of Amin's ministers, who then fled into exile. There were two other wives, the sixth being a nightclub singer, Sarah, whom he married when she was 19 and he 50. He claimed to have fathered 32 children.

Amin's downfall came in 1979 after some weeks when Ugandan troops crossed the frontier into Tanzania, looting and wrecking in villages along the Kagera river. The Tanzanian president, Julius Nyerere, retaliated by despatching an armoured column, led by three tanks. Hundreds of Ugandan exiles volunteered to join it, and when it triumphantly entered Kampala, it was led by a young Ugandan army officer, Colonel Oyite Ojok.

Libya's maverick leader, Colonel Gadafy, had begun sending troops to help shore up the regime, but hastily reversed the airlift after some 400 Libyan casualties. Amin followed them into brief exile in Tripoli and then moved on to Saudi Arabia, where he was given a villa in Jeddah on condition that he remain incommunicado indefinitely.

The Saudi motive was to silence him because of the harm they believed he was doing to Islam.

In the subsequent 24 years, he gave no interviews and stayed close to home. His life appears to have been a dull round of sports events, gym sessions and massage parlours. He had a Range Rover, a Chevrolet Caprice and a powder-blue Cadillac for his aimless shopping trips, and visits to the airport to clear through customs the parcels of cassava and other food items sent by relatives in Uganda.

Amin brought bloody tragedy and economic ruin to his country, during a selfish life that had no redeeming qualities.

Idi Amin Dada, politician and soldier, born around 1925; died August 16 2003.

Appendix IV:

Obote dies

Milton Obote Dies at 80; Strongman in Uganda, Twice Overthrown

By Agence Frace-Presse,
The New York Times, 11 October 2005

LUSAKA, Zambia, Oct. 10 (Agence France-Presse) - Milton Obote, Uganda's former strongman, who was first toppled by Idi Amin and overthrown again after a second period in power, died Monday in a South African hospital, said his party. He was 80.

"Dr. Obote died today in the early hours of the afternoon" in Johannesburg, said Henry Mayega, an official with Mr. Obote's Ugandan People's Congress party, adding that the exact cause of death was not immediately known. Mr. Obote's son Ben confirmed the death.

Mr. Obote had been taken to south Africa from Zambia, where he had been living in exile. His death followed a series of strokes.

Mr. Obote maintained a low profile in Lusaka despite repeated calls from his supporters in Uganda for his return.

Born Dec. 28, 1924, in northern Uganda, Mr. Obote was expelled from college in Kampala in the late 1940's for leading a student strike and took a job as a construction worker in Kenya.

A naturally skilled orator, he later returned to Uganda and joined the independence movement there and became a member of the colonial legislative council in 1957.

A shrewd political operative, Mr. Obote first maneuvered his way into power in 1962 after striking an unlikely alliance with the King's Party of the powerful Baganda tribe to form independent Uganda's first government.

As executive vice president under the titular presidency of the Baganda party's leader, Sir Edward Mutesa, Mr. Obote clashed frequently with his partners as he voiced a particularly pro-communist line.

The coalition unraveled in 1967 when Mr. Obote declared himself president a year after scrapping the Constitution and replacing it with one giving the executive nearly absolute power.

He incurred the wrath of many by ruling large swaths of the country under draconian emergency laws adopted with the abolishing of the limited powers of the traditional leaders of Uganda's five tribal kingdoms.

Mr. Obote's socialist policies also made him anathema to the West and when his army chief, Idi Amin, overthrew him in 1971 while he attended a summit meeting of Commonwealth heads of state in Singapore, few were initially concerned.

Mr. Amin was accused of torturing and killing as many as 500,000 people before being overthrown in 1979.

Mr. Obote, who spent the Amin years in exile in Tanzania, returned to Uganda on May 27, 1980, and won disputed general elections a few months later to become president for a second time.

He was ousted five years later by forces led by the current president, Yoweri Museveni.

Mr. Obote, whose rule was marred by repression and who was accused of torturing political opponents, was granted political asylum in Zambia following his second ouster, in 1985.

An estimated 300,000 civilians died between 1981 and 1985 as Mr. Museveni's guerrillas, the National Resistance Army, battled Mr. Obote's government forces, the Uganda National Liberation Army.

But the responsibility for the killings is still disputed, with Mr. Museveni claiming that the former government was responsible and Obote loyalists saying it was the guerrillas.

Milton Obote

The first leader of an independent Uganda, he imposed virtual one-man rule, but was twice overthrown.

Julian Marshall

The Guardian, London, Tuesday 11 October 2005

Milton Obote, who has died aged 80, had that rarest of opportunities among deposed African leaders - a second chance - and he blew it.

One of the architects of Ugandan independence in 1962, he served as prime minister, and then president, before being ousted in a military coup by his military commander, Idi Amin. Seeking exile in Tanzania, he was helped back to power by President Julius Nyerere, whose forces invaded Uganda in 1979. Controversially elected president a second time in 1980, he was overthrown by the army yet again five years later, and his exile became permanent.

The horrors of Idi Amin's reign of terror did much in the early days of Obote's "second coming" to cover the excesses of his government, but it is estimated that more than 100,000 people died fighting in the guerrilla war waged by the ultimately victorious Yoweri Museveni, the country's current president. Museveni's government estimates that more than 500,000 people died during Obote's second presidency as a result of him trying to make people move from rural areas into cities.

Milton Apollo Obote was born in the village of Akokoro in the Apac district of northern Uganda, the third of nine children of Stanley Opeto, a farmer and minor chieftain of the Lango tribe. "I was born of a ruling family," Obote was fond of saying, which in time became a conviction that he was a man of destiny. Educated at a Protestant missionary school in Lira, he entered Makerere University College in Kampala in 1948, but dropped out after two years, completing his formal education with a number of correspondence courses.

After working in Buganda, in southern Uganda, as a labourer, clerk and salesman, he served his political apprenticeship in neighbouring Kenya, where he worked for an engineering firm. He became a member of Jomo Kenyatta's Kenya National Union during the troubled period of the Mau-Mau emergency. When he decided to return home, he founded the Uganda National Congress (UNC) in 1955, and three years later joined the pre-independence Uganda legislative council, as a full-time politician.

In addition to gaining a reputation for outspokenness with the colonial authorities, he soon became a canny political operator. He thus concluded an electoral alliance with the newly-established Kabaka Yekka, or King Only Party, so that his own Uganda People's Congress (UPC, following the splitting of the UNC) had a comfortable majority in coalition, with Obote as prime minister, at independence in 1962.

Four years later, in the wake of allegations of corruption - he and Amin were accused of involvement in gold smuggling - he suspended the constitution and had himself installed as executive president. Sir Edward Mutesa 2, the kabaka, or king, of Buganda, called the government's action illegal. Troops surrounded the kabaka's palace and many of the powerful Baganda never forgave Obote for ending the centuries-old kingdom and driving King "Freddy" into exile; he died in London in 1969.

Under Obote's virtual one-man rule, Uganda, for a time, experienced relative political stability and economic prosperity. He launched a "move to the left" in 1969, introducing a Common Man's Charter to create "a new political culture and way of life with the means of production in hands of the people as whole." Ruthlessly driven, he soon became the whipping boy of the western press, a kind of socialist ogre of the emergent independent Africa.

In fact, Obote's policies did not involve large-scale nationalisation, as was alleged. What he sought was a substantial, but not majority, shareholding in foreign-owned businesses, as was happening in other African countries at that time. It was a diluted form of socialism that he proposed to put before the electorate, but he was frustrated by Amin's coup in January 1971, carried out while Obote was attending the Commonwealth prime ministers' conference in Singapore.

At first the overthrow was welcomed by many Ugandans. Before long, however, Amin launched an eight-year reign of terror; while the number of dead will never be known, exile organisations put it at 500,000. From his exile in Tanzania, Obote issued regular denunciations of the "fascist dictator Amin who had transformed Uganda into a human slaughterhouse." But it was not until 1980 that he had an opportunity to regain power following the overthrow of Amin by invading Tanzanian troops. In elections marred by widespread and blatant irregularities - to their lasting discredit pronounced fair by a team of Commonwealth observers - Obote's UPC won.

Although power was again his, he had sown the seeds of dissatisfaction that in time were to flower into full-blown revolt and victory for the guerrilla leader Museveni. Those fraudulent elections, plus his miscalculated exploitation of tribal politics, proved to be his downfall. His Langi-dominated army took terrible retribution on civilians living in the Luwero triangle, just north of Kampala, where Museveni's National Resistance Army guerrillas were operating, giving Uganda one of the worst human rights records in the world at that time.

However, internal divisions arose within the army, and by July 1985 Obote was once again on the ignominious road to exile, first to Kenya, and then to Zambia, where fellow independence leader Kenneth Kaunda allowed him to stay.

Milton Apollo Obote was once quoted as saying: "I'd rather have Milton's brains than Apollo's good looks." In the event, it was brawn that kept him in power and muscle that eased him out.

He had four children by his marriage.

Milton Apollo Obote, politician, born December 28 1925; died October 10 2005.

A Founding Father Adored, Dreaded in Equal Measure

Timothy Kalyegira,
The Monitor, Kampala, Uganda, 11 October 2005

IT is impossible to compute the extent to which Apollo Milton Obote evoked the feelings of millions of Ugandans and hundreds of thousands of others further a field of Uganda's borders.

In many quarters, there was felt outright, almost hysterical hatred and fear; in the other, such adoration that parents named their boys "Milton" or "Apollo" after Obote.

Fittingly, his last full day of life was October 9, 2005, the forty-third anniversary of the independence that he ushered in that night at Kololo airstrip in Kampala.

Eloquent crescendo

His booming voice and eloquent crescendo of a delivery that echoed of the late British Prime Minister Winston Churchill made Obote an enthralling speaker to listen to.

He would become one of the most formidable political leaders Africa has ever produced.

The 80 year-old Obote has been living in exile in Zambia since he was deposed in an army coup in July 1985.

For many in the older generation, the return of Obote to the news headlines hearkens back to a period, both turbulent and inspirational, in East Africa's history when there was a greater sense of oneness than at any time since. Obote's standing in East Africa goes back to the 1950s.

After he left Uganda's then prestigious Makerere University (reportedly expelled during the second year of a Bachelor of Arts course), he got a job with the British engineering and construction company Mowlem.

He was transferred to Mowlem's branch in Kenya where he soon took up a keen interest in Kenyan independence politics.

The Grolier Encyclopedia states that Obote was one of the men who helped form the Kenya African National Union (KANU) party in 1960.

Obote originated from Uganda's Lango district and, like one of Kenya's leading political figures at the time, Tom Mboya, was an ethnic Luo.

KANU would go on to lead Kenya to independence in 1963. Obote was one of the founding leaders of the Organisation of African Unity in May 1963.

As one of the three East African leaders of the

immediate post-independence period, Obote strode the map of the region, involved in the move toward an East African federation which, in 1967, was created and named the East African Community.

This spirit of an East African troika abruptly came to an end in January 1971 when Uganda's army commander, Major-General Idi Amin staged a coup that ousted Milton Obote.

Telling of the affection that even some of his chief enemies held him in, during his first press conference, on January 26, 1971, Major-General Amin said: "Obote was a good man" but, according to Amin, had been surrounded by opportunists.

Far East trip

Obote, who was in the far eastern Asian island nation of Singapore attending the Commonwealth summit meeting flew straight to Kenya where at Embakasi International Airport – today known as Jomo Kenyatta International Airport – he was received by Kenyan Vice President Daniel arap Moi.

He later re-located to Dar es Salaam where his friend Nyerere accorded him what dignity and security could be given an ousted head of state whom Nyerere insisted on regarding as Uganda's legitimate leader.

His presence and shadow hang over the March 1979 Moshi unity conference in Tanzania as groups of exiled Ugandans prepared the way for a post-Amin era.

Obote returned to Uganda from a nine-year exile spell in Tanzania on May 27, 1980 aboard a Tanzanian Buffalo military transport plane and landed in the western Ugandan town of Mbarara, driving on to another western town Bushenyi where he delivered one of his trademark soaring speeches.

For all the neutral appearances kept up by Tanzania, Obote's return was widely regarded as a dress rehearsal for

387

his eventual return to power, which he did in December 1980 after one of the most controversial elections in Africa's post-independence history.

One of the unforgettable lines in his inaugural address on December 15, 1980 was his statement that this would be a "government by law and not by men."

During his second administration, a number of Ugandans left to start a guerrilla war. The two best-known were former presidential candidate Yoweri Museveni and a former minister in the first post-Amin government, Andrew Kayiira.

More than 20 years since leaving office, Obote continued to be a key player in Ugandan politics, his hold on the Uganda People's Congress party that he founded in 1960 never wavering.

He was at the centre of all the drama and high politics that informed Uganda and East Africa from the 1960s to the twenty-first century.

Kenyans would find Obote fascinating for the aforementioned history with Kenya and the nostalgic imagery of the heydays of the East African Community.

Tanzanians would be intrigued by Obote for these same reasons, in addition to the fact that he spent his entire first exile period in Dar es Salaam.

Zambians would recall the so-called "Mulungushi Club," a friendship between the then President Kenneth Kaunda, Nyerere, and Obote by which they met annually to exchange views and re-affirm their sense of pan-Africanism.

Ugandans would, of course, continue to be fascinated by this man who mentored both Idi Amin and Yoweri Museveni; Idi Amin he appointed as army commander and Yoweri Museveni worked as an intelligence agent in Obote's General Service Unit counterintelligence agency.

Appendix V:

Causes and consequences of the war in Acholiland

Professor Ogenga Otunnu

THE roots of the current war between the government of Uganda and the Lord's Resistance Army (LRA) in Acholiland are entwined with the history of conflicts in Uganda and the rise to power of the National Resistance Movement/National Resistance Army (NRM/A).

The conflict has persisted because of fragmented and divisive national politics, strategies and tactics adopted by the armed protagonists, and regional and international interests.

The harrowing war has claimed many innocent civilian

lives, forcefully displaced over 400,000 people and destroyed schools and health centres. In addition, the war has been characterized by widespread and systematic violations of human rights, including rapes, abductions of men, women and children, torture, increased economic decay, and national and regional insecurity.

Uganda: Land and People

Uganda lies along the Equator, between the great East African Rift Valleys. It is a landlocked country, bordered by Sudan in the north, Kenya in the east, Tanzania in the south, Rwanda in the southwest and the Democratic Republic of Congo in the west.

With a landmass of 241,139 square kilometres, its population is about 20 million.

Its territory includes Lake Victoria, Lake Albert, Lake Edward and Lake Kyoga. These lakes, together with several elaborate networks of river drainage, constitute the headwaters of the River Nile.

The country's economy is primarily agrarian, comprised mostly of smallholdings though pastoralism is dominant in Karamoja and Ankole.

Lake Kyoga forms both a physical and linguistic marker.

South of Kyoga is the so-called Bantu region, with the centralized pre-colonial states of Buganda, Toro, Ankole (Nkore) and Bunyoro the dominant territories.

North and east of Kyoga are the non-Bantu territories of the Acholi, Alur, Langi, Iteso and Karamojong.

The Acholi inhabit present-day northern Uganda and southern Sudan, where, in the pre-colonial era, they constructed decentralized states.

In the 1970s, the Acholi district of northern Uganda was divided into Gulu and Kitgum districts. In 2001, Kitgum was subdivided to create a third district of Pader. The three districts constitute an area commonly referred to as Acholiland.

Conflicts and fragmentation in colonial Uganda

Contemporary violent conflicts in the country are directly related to the profound crisis of legitimacy of the state, its institutions and their political incumbents.

This crisis, in part, reflects the way the state was constructed through European expansionist violence, manipulation of pre-existing differences, administrative policies of divide and rule and economic policies that further fractured the colonial entity.

These policies did not only undermine the faltering legitimacy of the state, but also impeded the emergence of a Ugandan nationalism and generated ethnic, religious and regional divisions that were to contribute in later years to instability and political violence.

One significant divide was along the lines of religious affiliation, which can be traced back to the arrival of Islam, Protestantism and Catholicism in Buganda.

These religious groups engaged in a ferocious conflict for dominance, and the Protestant faction emerged victorious after the Imperial British East Africa Company intervened in their favour.

Anglicans were to late dominate the top positions in the civil service, and this structural inequality was maintained after the colonial era. Consequently, religious beliefs and political party affiliations were to become entangled.

Conflicts in the colonial state were exacerbated by the partition of the country into economic zones. For example, while a large portion of the territory south of Lake Kyoga was designated as cash crop growing and industrial zones, the territory north of Lake Kyoga was designated as a labour reserve.

This partition, which was not dictated by development potentials, led to economic disparities between the south and the north.

The fragmentation of the society was compounded by the economic-cum-administrative policy that left the civil service largely in the hands of Baganda and the army largely in the hands of the Acholi and other northern ethnic groups.

These policies also widened the gulf between the socio-political south and the socio-political north. This was further sustained by the administrative policy that relied on the Baganda as colonial agents in other parts of the country.

The policy of divide and rule, which rested on so-called 'indirect rule', led to widespread anti-Buganda sentiment.

Conflicts and fragmentation in post-independent Uganda

The post-colonial regime inherited a fractured state. Milton Obote responded to this crisis of legitimacy by forming an alliance between his political party, the Uganda People's Congress (UPC) and the Buganda monarchy party (Kabaka Yekka).

With this marriage of convenience, Obote became the Executive Prime Minister and Kabaka Mutesa II became the President and Head of State. However, the alliance collapsed over a conflict over land (the 'lost counties') between Bunyoro and Buganda.

The 'divorce' led to widespread violence in Buganda. Obote responded by detaining five government ministers from the Bantu region, dismissing the President and Vice President and forcing President Mutesa into exile and suspending the 1962 constitution.

The government also imposed a state of emergency in Buganda, occupied Buganda's palace, following the flight of the Kabaka to England, and introduced a republican constitution.

Some Bantu-speaking groups perceived this struggle for legitimacy and power as a conflict between the Bantu south and the non-Bantu (Nilotic) north.

These difficulties overlapped with the instability generated in the region by the superpowers' quest for hegemony during the Cold War.

These crises were compounded by a conflict between Obote and his army commander, General Idi Amin.

In 1971, Amin seized power.

Immediately after he came to power, Amin ordered Acholi and Langi soldiers, who constituted the backbone of the army, to surrender their arms. The overwhelming majority of them did so. However, many were subsequently killed.

The government extended its conflict with the Acholi and Langi by arresting, detaining and killing highly educated and influential members of the ethnic groups.

Over time, Amin began to target people he perceived as disloyal from other parts of the county.

To protect the regime which lacked political legitimacy in the country, Amin recruited new soldiers into the national army from West Nile.

In addition, he appointed prominent Bantu to important positions in his government.

The regime, however, largely maintained the dominance of southerners in the civil service and commerce, while the northerners largely controlled the government and army.

In April 1979, the exiled rebels, who were overwhelmingly from Acholi and Langi, assisted by the Tanzanian army and Yoweri Museveni's Front for National Salvation (FRONASA), overthrew the Amin regime. Yusuf Lule assumed power.

However, ideological and ethnic conflicts within the Uganda National Liberation Front (UNLF) and the national army led to the collapse of the Lule administration within months. Godfrey Binaisa took over, but was himself deposed in May 1980 by Paulo Muwanga and his deputy Yoweri Museveni.

The new administration organized general elections in December 1980, which were won by Milton Obote and his Uganda People's Congress. But widespread irregularities and political violence undermined the legitimacy of the elections.

The main challenger, the Democratic Party (DP), rejected Obote's victory. Museveni also rejected the results.

Thereafter, a number of armed groups, including Lule's Uganda Freedom Fighters, Museveni's Popular Resistance Army (later they were to merge to form the National Resistance Movement/Army (NRM/A), and Dr Andrew Kayira's Uganda Freedom Movement/Army (UFM/A), declared war against the Obote government.

In West Nile, Brigadier Moses Ali's Uganda National Rescue Front (UNRF) and General Lumago's Former Uganda National Army (FUNA) also engaged the army and the UPC in bitter armed opposition.

Fighting was particularly intense in the Luwero triangle, where the mostly Baganda population was targeted for their perceived support of rebel groups. Many innocent civilians were tortured and murdered by the UNLA.

Although the UNLA was a national and multi-ethnic army, the NRM/A held the Acholi exclusively responsible for the atrocities committed, and this disputed perception was to shape subsequent attitudes toward the conflict.

In July 1985, conflict between some Langi and Acholi soldiers led to the overthrow of the Obote regime.

The coup, which brought General Tito Okello (an Acholi) to power, shattered the military alliance between the Acholi and Langi and escalated ethnic violence.

The Okello regime invited all fighting groups and political parties to join the military government.

Every armed group and political party, with the

exception of the NRA, joined the administration.

The NRA, however, engaged the regime in protracted peace negotiations held in Nairobi. In December 1985, the Nairobi Agreement was signed under the chairmanship of President Moi of Kenya.

However, the Agreement was never implemented and Museveni seized power on the 25th January 1986.

The NRA's seizure of power effectively meant that for the first time, socio-economic, political and military powers were all concentrated in the south.

The new administration, which absorbed political and military groups from the south and Moses Ali's UNRF group, engaged in intensive anti-northern propaganda.

The administration also discriminated against groups from eastern Uganda and West Nile.

This severe alienation and marginalization led to armed conflicts in Teso and West Nile.

After much destruction and displacement of the population in Teso, the government negotiated an end to the conflict in the east.

Emergence of the conflict in Acholiland

By April 1986, the Acholi had largely come to terms with the NRA victory.

The majority of former UNLA soldiers also heeded the appeal made by the government to hand over their arms and demobilize. The response by the Acholi ended the armed engagement in the territory.

However, after months of relative calm, anxieties escalated when the NRA began to commit human rights abuses in the name of crushing a nascent rebellion.

Over time NRA soldiers plundered the area and committed atrocities, including rape, abductions, confiscation of livestock, killing of unarmed civilians, and the destruction of granaries, schools, hospitals and bore holes escalated.

These atrocities in Acholiland were justified by some as revenge for the 'skulls of Luwero.'

Against this background of mistrust and violence, in May 1986 the government ordered all former UNLA soldiers to report to barracks.

The order was met with deep suspicion, in part, because it was reminiscent of Amin's edict that led to the 1971 massacre of Acholi soldiers.

Some ex-UNLA soldiers went into hiding; others fled to Sudan and some decided to take up arms.

Soon, these ex-soldiers were joined by a stream of youths fleeing from NRA operations.

During this period, the Sudan People's Liberation Army (SPLA), which was perceived by Acholi refugees as an ally of the Museveni government, attacked a refugee camp in southern Sudan.

On August 20, 1986, some Acholi refugee combatants, led by Brigadier Odong Latek, attacked the NRA. This armed group, known as the Uganda People's Democratic Army (UPDA), was later joined by the Holy Spirit Mobile Forces/Movement (HSMF/HSM), Severino Lukoya's Lord's Army, ultimately to be followed by the Lord's Resistance Army (LRA).

Why the war has persisted

The war has lasted for nearly sixteen years because of a number of interrelated factors.

To begin with, the war in Acholi has become an extension of regional and international power struggles.

On the regional front, Uganda provided military hardware and sanctuary to the SPLA. In retaliation, the Sudan government provided sanctuary and military hardware to the LRA.

On the international front, both the Uganda government and the SPLA received military and political support from the US, in part to curtail the influence of the Islamic government in Khartoum.

Another factor perpetuating the conflict has been that the war has become a lucrative source and cover for clandestine income for high-ranking military and government officials and other profiteers.

In addition, the unwillingness of the government and the LRA to genuinely pursue a negotiated settlement has sustained the war.

Lastly, atrocities committed by the LRA against unarmed civilians and the unwillingness of the rebel group to accept alternative political views on the conflict have prolonged the war.

Consequences of the war

The horrific and prolonged consequences of this war have devastated the society – a society that has been reduced to 'displaced camps', where people languish without assistance and protection.

The war has also destroyed the culture and social fabric of the Acholi society. Large numbers of orphans, who fend for themselves, illustrate this tragedy.

Furthermore, some children have been abducted by the LRA and forced to torture and kill. Thus, the Rt. Rev. Macleod Baker Ochola II summarized some of the effects the war on Acholiland as follows:

'Violent deaths of our people in the hands of various armed groups; arson perpetrated on mass scale in our land; rape and defilement of our women and girls; abduction of our young people; forced recruitment of our people into rebel ranks; the prevalence of a general atmosphere of fear and disenchantment amongst our people; mass displacement of our people; creation of protected villages which have become breeding grounds for malnutrition and deaths resulting from cholera, measles, and preventable diseases amongst our people; and destruction of our infrastructures and continuous decline in socio-economic growth.'(KM, 1997)

The war has also destabilized other parts of the country and contributed to other regional conflicts in the Great Lakes.

The multi-faceted and interrelated causes and consequences of the war should not, therefore, be seen as exclusively an Acholi issue. Nor should the war be treated as merely a humanitarian crisis.

It has many dimensions: political, social, economic and humanitarian. As such, durable solutions will need to respond to all of these challenges.

Dr. Ogenga Otunnu was Assistant Professor of African History, Refugee Studies and Contemporary Global Issues at DePaul University (Chicago) when he wrote this article in 2002.

He also taught African History and Refugee Studies at York University (Toronto) and has published on refugee crises, conflict resolution and genocide in Africa. Research for this article was partly done by Jane Laloyo.

Source:
Conciliation Resources, 173 Upper Street, London, UK.

Appendix VI:

Is it Time for Museveni to Go?

**Anne Perkins, *The Guardian*, London,
19 February 2009**

In his inaugural address 23 years ago, the Ugandan president, Yoweri Museveni, was cheered as he declared:

"The problems of Africa, and Uganda in particular, are caused by leaders who overstay in power, which breeds impunity, corruption and promotes patronage."

Museveni is still in power, and it looks very likely that he will fight for a fourth term in 2011. "He'll be another Mugabe" is the gloomy prediction among opposition politicians in Kampala.

Tim Allen, professor of development studies at the London School of Economics, sees the successful resolution of Zimbabwe's crisis as one of the most influencing events in African politics now. "If Mugabe goes, it would change the landscape," he says. "And if he is held to account, it would be very liberating."

There is no shortage of opposition to Museveni: Uganda has a splenetic, free-thinking, popular media. Radio programmes and newspapers uncover corruption, excoriate incompetence, poke fun at pomposity.

Since 2005, Museveni has permitted a multi-party democracy. His own National Resistance Movement (NRM), which for the previous 20 years simply co-opted its rivals, is dominant in parliament as he was in the first multi-party presidential election. His main opponent is the larger-than-life leader of the Forum for Democratic Change (FDC), Dr Kizza Besigye.

In the run-up to the 2006 election, Besigye was accused of both treason and rape. In his turn, he unsuccessfully contested the 2006 results, where Museveni claimed nearly 60% support to 37% for the FDC. Last month, as the country celebrated "liberation day," the FDC returned to the charge.

"The major cause of the liberation war was the injustice of vote rigging, but vice has become entrenched in the system. Corruption has also been institutionalised," the party's acting administrator, Boniface Toterebuka, claimed.

It is not only vote rigging that the opposition parties and the media complain about. Government ministers are mired in a scandal involving land sales at inflated values to other parts of the administration (Museveni looks likely to sack the ministers in an impending cabinet reshuffle), while the international disgrace over the disappearance of millions of Ugandan shillings intended for Aids relief lingers in public memory.

It is a subject Museveni returns to frequently. In his state of the nation last month, Museveni declared war on public corruption. The declaration only lacked authority because he made the same promises after his re-election two years ago - and because his more outspoken critics, like Andrew Mwenda in his *Independent* weekly magazine, allege that the entire Museveni family are beneficiaries of corruption.

But if they joke in Kampala bars that PAYE stands for Pay As Yoweri Enjoys, to many others, especially in the south, Museveni's 23 years in power at the head of the NRM have been a welcome period of stability after a generation of dictators who drove the economy to bankruptcy.

He has presided over a prolonged period of growth, which even last year was just under 10%. His administration is, mostly, still admired by the west. His enthusiasm for universal primary and secondary education, his poverty eradication programme and the new plan to target agriculture to boost output, all win international plaudits.

He woos the west in other ways too: he is strongly aligned with the war on terror, and there are nearly 2,000 Ugandan troops peacekeeping in Somalia. He has been a strong supporter of George Bush's abstinence message on HIV/Aids. "Relations with Washington are warm," a Congressional report concluded last year.

But, until recently, the north of Uganda has always been outside the pro-Museveni consensus, tainted by its association first with the country's colonial rulers and then with the disastrous years of Idi Amin and Milton Obote.

Katine is typical of much of the north in experiencing most of Museveni's rule as an era of terrible lawlessness and insurrection that has arrested development and led to the early deaths of hundreds of thousands of Ugandans, and the internment of many more in internally displaced people's camps.

Yet things are changing. Last summer, for the first time, Museveni toured the northern half of the country. He visited Soroti where he promised millions of Ugandan shillings for agricultural development. He even travelled further north, to the displaced people's camps of the region most devastated by the Lord's Resistance Army insurgency - and the Ugandan Defence Force's own controversial IDP camps.

Iteso voters are not Museveni enthusiasts: in common with many northerners they feel overlooked, left to suffer, by a president whose power base has always been in the south. At the last election they voted for Besigye.

But now another potential leader has emerged: Norbert Mao. Mao, once an MP who retreated to Gulu to head the council there, belongs to the tiny Democratic Party, which has stood apart from attempts to organise an anti-Museveni united front.

Mao is said to want to exploit both his charisma and strong northern credibility for the NRM. He has the unusual advantage, too, of a wife from the influential Buganda kingdom. His candidacy could offer a chance of national leadership.

Yet there is an appetite for change, and of growing disillusion in the man once widely regarded as the country's saviour. In a bitter editorial marking the NRM's 23 years in power, Andrew Mwenda wrote recently:

"Where NRM promised an independent, integrated and self-sustaining national economy, it has created a dependant (on foreign aid) disjointed economy. Instead of free and fair elections, we have rigged ones.

Respect for human rights died in torture chambers euphemistically called safe houses. Corruption has become a virtue, nepotism a way to run our nation and tribal bigotry the running philosophy of government. The rule of law took a beating when government organised hooded gangs who began attacking the courts and threatening judges."

Even his severest critics, though, admire Museveni's ability to exploit circumstance. During his 23rd anniversary celebrations last month, he even invited investors to report any government official who took a bribe.

But bloggers – and US Congress – fear opportunities for corruption are escalating with major oil discoveries around Lake Albert on the country's border with Congo. The terms of the deals so far signed have been kept secret on "commercial" grounds – the customary way of disguising backhanders to government ministers.

And, as Mwenda wrote, with more than 40% of Uganda's budget coming in the form of aid (a majority from the UK) it is not only Ugandan voters who might influence their country's future.

There are hints that the international community might be trying to engineer a way to ease Museveni out of direct power, to offer him an international position, "perhaps connected to the UN," according to Tim Allen, that would respect his status as an African president who had done much to promote peace and prosperity in his own country, and to aid the global war on terror.

There may be the prospect of a high-profile role that might offer Museveni, and his wider family, the money and status he has become accustomed to as the west's favourite African politician.

But he might also find – like Robert Mugabe – that too many Ugandan politicians and generals depend on him to allow him to leave the scene with honour.

Comments from readers of the article above:

ladiva, 19 February 2009:

You seem to take a benign view of Yoweri Museveni!

Why is he such a favourite with the West? He is just another dictator who has long overstayed his welcome. Unlike Mugabe, he oversees a country where a vicious and bloody war has been raging for years and thousands of people have died. Yet you give the impression that he is not so bad.

There are hints that the international community might be trying to engineer a way to ease Museveni out of direct power, to offer him an international position, "perhaps connected to the UN," according to Tim Allen, that would respect his status as an African president who had done much to promote peace and prosperity in his own country, and to aid the global war on terror.

"Respect his status...." – what nonsense! Such as statement just shows the double standards of the West.

HideousKinky, 19 February 2009:

I was born a year after Museveni became president and he is still president. He went fro being a visionary(refer to his inaugural speech), to being the president who, while millions die from being unable to buy something as simple as paracetamol, is now in possession of 2 private jets, one being one of the most expensive in the world. I watched a documentary a few years ago where the prime minister of Iceland flew with EasyJet.

Early this week, he made his wife a minister. For someone whose 1996 election tagline was ironically "No change," 13 years on, it seems likely he is achieving this.

Ugandans have come to accept institutionalised corruption, the rich literally get away with murder, the top crop of the police are military men, their tactics remain military like and it is obvious most of them haven't got a clue as to how to deal with civil affairs.

Ministers and MPs are openly bribed by the president to support questionable changes in the constitution, the most famous one being his removal of term limits for the president.

After his failure to 'create' development, he's turned to selling off public land to private foreign investors in hopes of outsiders creating the development for him.

The government of Uganda is an up and running business, have no doubt about it, corrupt ministers have their children studying in expensive boarding schools abroad while the average Ugandan family eats meat less than once a month out of sheer poverty.

Most of them have questionable sources of income, seeing as they are meant to have civil servants' salaries, driving very expensive cars, living in mansions,owning hotels....

Despite the free primary education, most families are unable to raise the fees to send their children beyond primary school. The main hospital is known to have doctors carrying out operations without surgical gloves, patients sleep in the corridors on the floor. The main university has started suspending day lectures due to lack of funding (read today's paper on Newvision.co.ug).

I'm disgusted by what this man and his cronies have done to the people of Uganda. While they fly 1st class to attend conferences abroad to pledge for more funds, or fly their daughters to Europe to have babies (Museveni has done this using his private jet, naturally paid for by poor Ugandans' taxes), the average Ugandan who works an 11 hour day and gets less than £30 a week has no car and 80% more likely to die in a road accident due to really appalling road conditions.

The government is not for the people, it never as been, it's for those that already have more wealth than you or I will ever encounter. I write this as a person who has lived in Uganda and talks to both the absolute poor and the filthy rich of the country.

I used to think wide spread corruption and borderline dictatorships existed everywhere else.

This is what the people of Uganda don't realise, that

405

the people they vote for are meant to do something for them, now most people see becoming a politician as the easiest route to riches.

kinyua, 19 February 2009:

There seems to be no mention of his fight against AIDS and how he has successfully managed to significantly lower the AIDS rate. Sure ol' man yoweri may be an egolomaniac but he has managed to keep his country in order.

The war that is mentioned is not his making but one that was spurred by the Lord's Resistance Army led by a Joseph Kony. Their aim was to form a breakaway state that would be governed by biblical principles. However, LRA soldiers have been implicated in rape and recruiting child soldiers and museveni has also managed to decrease their influence.

Secondly, is america really in a position to tell any1 else about oil deals. Who was it that was signing off fragile ecosystems in the southwest USA for oil drilling? Who was it that attacked a country purely on the basis of oil?

He took on a country that was maligned and suffering especially after the amin years. Uganda now has a vibrant democracy and a growing economy especially in the service sectors. I may not support all that museveni does but his achievements far outweigh his faults. For that at least you have to give him credit.

skeptomania, 20 February 2009:

Instead of asking us, perhaps the best person to answer would be your own journalist Victoria Brittain? She was a major Museveni cheerleader as he shot his way to power in 1985-1986, and moved journalistic heaven and earth to succesfully sell him in the western world.

We are long-memoried people. Stop trying to act all innocent and play more mind-games with us.

lutkot, 20 February 2009:

It is baffling the west's fascination with Museveni? The fact of the matter is that it seems the west have very low expectations when it comes to issues of democracy in Africa. Would the UK or US be happy with a leader the caliber of Museveni? I don't think so but some how they think he's ok for Uganda.

First of all Museveni was never elected by the Ugandan public to be their president. He seized power violently in the process murdering thousands of Ugandans. Since assuming power over twenty years ago he has failed to bring total peace to the entire country. Since 1986 hundreds of thousands have perished in northern Uganda due to insecurity and instability.

For the first twenty years since assuming power Uganda was a one party military dictatorship. All other political parties were banned from operating something which the west supported. Multi-party politics was only reintroduced in Uganda in 2006. Despite this the opposition parties are still harassed by the security forces who are loyal to Museveni and not Uganda.

2006 was supposed to be Museveni's last term in office as the Constitution did not permit him to continue as president at that point. He bribed members of parliament to change the constitution to allow him to become a life president.

The only people who have benefited from Musevni's rule are mostly his ethnic group. The rest have been excluded and subjected to biting poverty. Public services (hospitals, schools, roads, transports ... etc, are extremely run down or almost non existent in neglected areas like northern and eastern Uganda.

In conclusion. Museveni has been in power for a long

time. Twenty three years and counting. It is naive to think that he can improve the lives of Ugandans at this late hour. Twenty three years is long enough to make your mark and he has been a huge let appointment.

strugglingauthor, 20 February 2009:

I am astonished by this article. Having recently visited (southern) Uganda after a twelve-year absence, I found that support for Museveni had gone through the floor, and anxiety about lack of true democracy and increasing tribal tensions was sky-high. As for his support of education etc, he talks the talk but he doesn't walk the walk. Universal primary education may be a laudable aim but it isn't backed by proper funding. Sadly, even Uganda's previously exemplary record on AIDS has been threatened by his embracing of Bush's abstinence message. It's time for someone new, not just for the north but for everywhere.

Mukayuhi, 21 February 2009:

I visited Uganda last July and I was pleased with the progress and development Kaguta Museveni has achieved. Let's give credit where it is due. I walked in Kampala without fear of kidnapping and being robbed by security agents as was the case in the 70s and 80s. I travelled from Kampala to Kabale and Rukungiri without being hussled by soldiers on road blocks. Obviously some people have selective memory. How can anyone forget where Uganda has come from!!

I lived in Uganda during the brutal regimes of life president Field Marshal, Idi Amin and Dr. Milton Obote. I got beaten and robbed by the soldiers at road blocks and people disappeared day and night in Namanve forest and Nile Mansions torture chambers.

His Excellency Yoweri Museveni is the greatest leader

Africa has seen in a long time. He encourages Ugandans to be more innovative and self reliant. Every Ugandan child has a chance to go to school (universal primary education).

Why should Museveni's family not enjoy the priviledges that come with his job?

Yoweri Museveni is a man of vision, highly intelligent and courageous. He knows who the bad guys in NRM are, especially those who wanted to distabilise the movement using Temangalo land deal as cover. I am glad he's shown them where to get off lately. Why is Kahinda Otafiire so unhappy about his new role?

If you are not scared of hard work, there are lots of opportunities in Uganda.

Women in villages have become self sufficient and empowered.

As they say in Uganda, 'Museveni akyali mbooko' - long live Your Excellency Yoweri Kaguta Museveni. 'For God and my country'.

alexweir1949, 21 February 2009:

Musuveni is yet another of these pro-western dictators who litter the landscape of Africa, the Middle East, and the rest of the Third World. They steal big-time from their populations and collaborate with western corporations, governments and politicians. The West is very afraid of any voting system which cannot be frauded, since that would mean an end to these cronies who perpetuate Global Poverty. Let the people be free. The West must back down and embrace history, justice and an end to oppression and poverty. Mr Alex Weir, Harare, Zimbabwe.

JoePowell, 21 February 2009:

Interesting article.

You cannot underestimate the strength of American support for Museveni. The troops deployed in Somalia were in effect in exchange for a seat on the UN Security Council, marking the full international rehabilitation of Museveni after the farcical 2006 elections. Similarly the recent operations against the LRA in Eastern DRC where supported by American intelligence and funding. Simply put Uganda remains an island of stability in a region where even Kenya threatened to descend into civil war - the US does not want to risk that in Uganda.

Strugglingauthor - I think you'd find talking to rural farmers in Western and Southern Uganda that they are still among the biggest supporters of Museveni. This is in part because their expectations of Government are so low - security is all that matters.

Conversely opposition to the President has come among the groups that have actually benefited most from his neo-liberal management of the economy. The middle class and urban dwellers may be fed up of poor roads, high fuel prices, endemic corruption and load shedding but until the opposition manages to win the rural majority they will stay out of power. What I would like to see is the FDC really stepping up and providing robust opposition throughout the country, not only in their strongholds. It would also be good to hear Besigye talk more about his vision for the country, and not merely define himself as 'not Museveni'. There is certainly an appetite for change in the country. The next two years will be critical in deciding whether it is realised.

Joe - Kampala

AfricanSnowman, 21 February 2009:

What, an article about Uganda and Museveni that fails to mention its complicity in the Rwandan genocide and/or of its ongoing complicity in the deaths of millions in the DRC or of its role (like Kenya) as a "black site" for western inspired "extraordinary renditions"?

No surprises there.

JimToddMwanza, 21 February 2009:

An interesting article.

The assumption behind this article is that the only worthwhile contribution Museveni can make is as head of state. We must counter this asumption by showing that many people can, and do, make worthwhile contributions to their nation, and their people in other ways. In fact the most impressive people, in Africa and elsewhere are not heads of state, but ordinary people working for development and progress. The head of state must be the person most capable of leading the country, not the person with the biggest gun, or most efficient way of buying votes (or like Gordon Brown the slickest propaganda machine).

I too supported Museveni in the early 1980's, and he was better than other options at the time (I aslo supported Mugabe at that time). That does not mean to say he deserves my (or anyone else's) support indefinitely. Democratic countries need to embrace change, and diversity, and this should be the basis of any democracy. Without change the country cannot go forward and progress to new heights. It cannot deliver the aspirations of the people if only one person is in charge, and allows a single vision to predominate.

The failure may be placed at many people's doors, but ultimately we all have to decide how we deal with authoritarian leaders. The future of any country is too valuable to be left entirely, and solely to the people of that country. We should allow 'foreign interference', provided it is properly consistuted and subject to proper scrutiny. That would rid us of dictators like Mugabe, and would counterbalance extremism. I do not advocate any particular change, all I would wish is any change at all.

dswinder, 21 February 2009:

"The problems of Africa, and Uganda in particular, are caused by leaders who overstay in power, which breeds impunity, corruption and promotes patronage." – Museveni

That's sickly ironic.

"There are hints that the international community might be trying to engineer a way to ease Museveni out of direct power, to offer him an international position, 'perhaps connected to the UN,' according to Tim Allen, that would **respect his status as an African president who had done much to promote peace and prosperity in his own country**, and to aid the global war on terror."

ugandalife, 21 February 2009:

There are good reasons for disenchantment with Museveni. Senior people have diverted money with impunity, knowing they have had the protection of their leader. They justify it by stating how they fought to liberate the country.

Only recently has there been any movement against corruption and even then, its against the second tier of management, the scapegoats, so to speak.

Corruption is so ingrained, not only in the government but is businesses & other organizations, that it will take a jack hammer to break the surface.

Perhaps even a greater concern is the attitude portrayed by Museveni.

For those areas that did not or do not vote NRM, they will be ignored in any development according to his statement a few days ago.

He also stated that the opposition parties are the

412

"enemy"! This could also be the reason the LRA were able to operate with little opposition for 20 years. The north has never supported Museveni.

His record with AIDS has more to do with the NGO's that have worked endlessly to reduce exposure. The government is on record for failing to provide ARV's as well as other life-saving drugs. Huge stocks of drugs are destroyed because they expired while sitting in warehouses. AIDS cases, btw, are on the increase.

The UPE (universal primary education) program is seriously faulty. Teachers had a 30% absentee rate in 2007. Students are pushed ahead regardless how poorly they do. Less than 50% of children complete primary school.

Inflation is posted as 13.4% but in reality, its much higher. The prime bank rate is 20% and loans far exceed that.

There are constant power outages and chronic fuel supply problems that cripple the average person.

The courts are corrupt to the point where richest wins.

Give Museveni credit for stabilizing the country but his time is up. He and his buddies have become extremely rich. Now is the time to bow out gracefully but it won't happen.

Java1930, 22 February 2009:

The comments on this blog show you can't fool the public with a naive article such as this. We all know what Museveni is – its about time western governments admit that they also know where Museveni is heading and act before its too late. Uganda has suffered enough.

laidbackjay, 23 February 2009:

t is particulary interesting to read the comments of the relatively younger readers such as HideousKinky (pun, if any, not intended) who passionately points out the failures of Museveni's government.

HideousKinky, born in 1987, will be eligible to vote for the first time in 2011, and if you are reading this, please encourage your age group to vote in big numbers for the candidate you believe is the best for your country's future because the youth indeed, are the future. The younger, educated and informed Africans like Hideous Kinky are going to play an integral role in the future of African politics and the continent as a whole. Over the next 50 years, African leaders are going to be accountable to sharper, younger citizens who will not be fooled by empty promises.

Anne Perkin's article is quite factual regarding the positive contribution of the current Government, but many Africans are tired of settling for fourth and fifth best.

Our hope is that hopefuls like Nobert Mao and Kizza Besigye can start a healthy trend of democratic politics in Uganda, where serving one's country is a PROUD SERVICE and OBLIGATION as opposed to an ARROGANT display of POWER and GREED.

Kminor, 23 February 2009:

"Uganda now has a vibrant democracy."

No, it does not.

conditional, 24 February 2009:

I am impressed at the level of debate this article has generated and proud to note as a Ugandan that this is the kind of growth in attitude change.

It is absurd however to note that amidst all the praise that the west heaps on Museveni there is a section of Ugandans who have never understood what peace is and what all this praise is all about.

How can we have a generation of people in the same

country who are completely different in terms of access to social services (basic) education and health in the north and another that cannot define poverty in the west?

This is not democracy.

How can people be killed, butchered and live with the deformities in the same country as those from the western and southern parts of the country and one talks about peace in this country?

How can the country be lead by the president his wife, son, brother, cousins and friends and we call this democracy?

I love Museveni but you must go finally you have run out of new ideas!

Please go when we can still recall the vibrant, visionary you!

Appendix VII:

Museveni interviewed

Museveni has totally demeaned Uganda

M Suleman, *Uganda Correspondent,*
12 March 2012

There is no doubt that throughout his 26-year reign, Museveni has been the darling of both the international community and the international media. For all these years, the international media has portrayed him as pragmatic leader.

But if one is to go by the recent interview that Museveni had with Stephen Sucker of BBC Hardtalk, then there has been a dramatic change towards Museveni. This seems to be the hardest interview Museveni has ever had. It was short but it was prepared in such a way that Museveni was given no room to give his traditional confusing lectures.

The first question was based on Museveni's first public pronouncements of 1986 which, because of the sincerity he seemed to have had at the time, won him many supporters both internally and internationally. Museveni had very harsh words for leaders who overstay in power.

Today, Museveni is one of the longest leaders in Africa – longer than even Obote whom he waged war against. So Museveni had either to accept that he is now part of Africa's problem, or concoct a lie. He opted for the latter. He unashamedly lied not only to himself, but to the whole world when he said he meant leaders who overstay in power without being elected.

The second question was not easy either. Corruption has become endemic – and it has a long history. From the valley dams, DRC looting, ghost soldiers, arms/military procurements (helicopters/army uniforms) global Fund, Temangalo, Haba, Bassajjabalaba, to the recent oil concessions.

The gist of the question was: Is he not abating corruption – given that corruption seems to revolve around State House, the cabinet, and his family and friends. His brother Salim Saleh for example, was forced to return kickbacks that he received in the junk helicopter deal. The Global Fund embezzlement on the other hand implicated his family members.

Ministers who are found guilty of corruption are merely sacked and later rehabilitated. State House is not only operating like an Estates Agent's office that specialises in selling government property; it is also doubling as a clearing house for the all government procurement deals!

The government is not only full of a certain tribe or ethnic groups, it is also has Museveni's wife serving as cabinet Minister. All this points to the fact that all institutions have collapsed and he is the only institution! In Museveni's eyes, the fact that many corruption scandals are being unearthed shows that state institutions are functioning well. The truth however is that institutions simply can't conceal the thousands of corruption scandal spilling over.

The other question was on Museveni's militarism. It is well known that in addition to the 16-year northern war, the NRA/Ugandan soldiers have been in Rwanda, DRC, Sudan, Central African Republic, Kenya, and now in Somalia. Since 1986, the country has been on a permanent war footing. How then does Uganda fund Museveni's adventures and meet her subsistence development demands at the same time?

In his reply, Museveni said like the frontline states during apartheid, it is his obligation to liberate other African states! The salient question in all this is this: Isn't Museveni's overstay in power, his government's corruption, and his militarism, which has brought Uganda to the social and economic meltdown it is experiencing today?

In short, it was indeed Hardtalk. The interview portrayed Museveni as a man whose word cannot be trusted. And, since the president of a country is the custodian of its national values and pride, Museveni totally demeaned Uganda.

Appendix VIII:

The Asian Question Again: A Reflection

Mahmood Mamdani
Sunday Vision, **Kampala, Uganda, 28 April 2007**

I have been trying to make sense of the events of April 12 from the distance of New York and with the help of the Internet and the telephone.

Some say these events are an unfortunate breakdown in law and order, best forgotten and put behind us. Common sense, however, tells me that larger issues are at stake and, if not addressed, have the potential of fuelling further popular outrage. The surest public indication of this is growing reference to the 1972 Asian expulsion in discussions of April 12.

I was a teaching assistant at Makerere at the time of the 1972 Asian expulsion, and was among the last to leave in early November.

I had finished my O'Levels in 1962 at Senior Secondary School, Old Kampala, and was one of over 20 students who received scholarships to study in the US. The scholarships were part of America's Independence gift to Uganda. In the language of that period, I was among those who could claim to have literally eaten the fruit of Independence. Certainly, without a successful struggle for independence, I would not have got the higher education that I did.

Student activist

One of my first activities as a student was to participate in the civil rights movement in the US. In less than a year, I was among busloads of students going from northern universities to march in Birmingham, Alabama, in the south. We marched through secondary schools, singing songs like 'Which side are you on, boys, which side are you on?' and 'We shall overcome', and asking students to leave classes and join us.

As we moved downtown, police on horseback and motorcycles, wielding metal-studded batons, jumped at us. I and scores of other students were thrown in jail. Allowed to make one phone call from jail, I called the Uganda ambassador in Washington DC.

"What are you doing interfering in the internal affairs of a foreign country?" he asked. "This is not an internal affair. This is a freedom struggle. How can you forget? We just got our freedom last year," was my response. I had learnt that freedom knew no boundary, certainly not that of colour or country.

I returned home in early 1972 as a convinced Pan-African nationalist, but was thrown out later in the year as an Asian.

Early in November, I flew to London and was admitted to a refugee camp. The British press was full of stories about Amin and the Asian expulsion. Every story talked of Amin not as a dictator, but as a black dictator. With few exceptions, the British press racialised Amin. His blackness was offered as the primary explanation for his brutality. Fresh from civil rights struggles in the American south, and anti-Vietnam war struggles in the American north, I had seen brutality in the white and was unwilling to accept this explanation.

Partly for that reason, I left London within nine months and took up my first job at the University of Dar-es-Salaam.

Although my physical being was in Dar-es-Salaam where both my parents had been born, my mind was preoccupied with Uganda: Why Amin? Why the support for Amin? The years that followed confirmed that Amin was a demagogue and brutal at that. But that still did not explain the support for Amin. It was painful for me to realise that if Amin was originally popular because he had removed the Obote dictatorship, the reason for his continued popularity had to do with the fact that he, more than any other leader, had put the Asian Question at the forefront of the political agenda.

Every Ugandan understood in his or her guts that the secret of Asian business success lay not just in hard work, but also in a racially unjust colonial system which made it difficult for black people to enter trade, thereby confirming Asian dominance in trade. Handicapped in the marketplace, those aspiring to business turned to political organisation. It is through repeated political action — in 1945, then 1949, and then again 1959 — that they were able to gain entry into the marketplace. The demand for political independence went alongside another — that for social justice for those who had been the victims of colonial racial discrimination.

423

A decade of independence increased this demand for one reason: it seemed Asian businessmen had been able to turn national independence to private advantage. Not only had independence liberated them like everyone else from the limits placed by colonial rule, Asian business tycoons seemed to have developed a comfortable alliance with big bureaucrats and top politicians who gave them political protection (what is today called 'no change') in return for lucrative bribes.

With its paan and sari shops, and cinema houses showing Bollywood movies, Kampala's population got browner as the sun set and its black workforce left for satellite communities on the edge of town. Pointing to this informal apartheid in a complacent post-Independence Uganda, Amin asked uncomfortable questions, even if in a coarse and racist language: "If Uganda is independent, why does its capital city look like Bombay on a Sunday?" I realised that Amin spoke the language of justice, however crudely, and that was the reason he was able to ride the crest of a historic wave of popular protest.

I returned to Uganda in 1979 when Amin was thrown out. It is difficult to forget the shock of returning to a city where I had grown up and knew just about every street, but could no longer recognise a soul. There were also other shocks in store. Most people I met supported Amin's decision to expel Asians, though they disagreed on the details: the time given to wind up family and business affairs, the limits on what each family could take out, and so on. Listening to them, I realised that even though they saw Amin as a brutal dictator, many also saw him as a nationalist. Even if they disagreed with his methods, they applauded his goal, a Uganda for Ugandans, particularly black Ugandans.

Could this new Uganda be a home for me? Determined to make a second beginning, I rejoined Makerere University. I recall the decade that followed 1979 as one of coming to political age for a second time. Even if ravaged by civil war and dictators, the new Uganda seemed a healthier society, less marked by the racial distortions of a colonial experience and Ugandans were proud of it. As a person of Asian background, I felt more comfortable, even safer, in the new Uganda than, for example, did Asians in neighbouring Kenya. I was not the only one. The few Asian businesspersons I knew also seemed to realise that they were more secure in a society where businesspersons were no longer a racially identifiable minority.

The new Uganda began to change under the NRM. The new President was determined to reverse the legacy of Idi Amin and return Uganda to his notion of a normal society. Two big government-initiated changes followed. The first was the decision to return previously confiscated properties to its former Asian owners. Asked by the Law Society to speak on the issue, I argued against a return of properties and spoke in favour of compensation. I said a return of properties would result in either absentee ownership or concentration of property in few hands, or both; in either case, it will be socially unhealthy. But the return of properties was part of a larger IMF package and it was the President's wish, so nobody listened.

Once it faced opposition, the NRM too discovered the advantages of dealing with a business class which had few links within the country and could easily be isolated and kept on a short leash. Once again, close links began to develop between individual Asian tycoons and prominent politicians in the Government, as they had in the Obote period.

The second big change was born of this corruption and was more the result of unofficial than formal decisions. Though the network of corruption focused on government departments that handled immigration and was clandestine, its effects were publicly visible.

The number of Asian residents of Uganda began to multiply, from less than 5,000 when the NRM came to power to an estimated 20,000 today. Of these, only 2,000 came from the pre-1972 generation. The largest section was brought in to service big Asian businesses which preferred to hire their core employees from outside, so it would be easier to keep them on a short leash. Not surprisingly, the new arrivals were mainly petty traders and semi-skilled employees.

The new official terminology that identified just about every person of Asian origin as an 'investor' could not hide this fact. Neither was the change confined to the capital city, Kampala. It was even more visible in smaller market towns, such as Lugazi, Kakira, Kamuli, or Iganga, or other places where the number of traders of Asian origin mushroomed in just a few years from just a handful to many more.

Ominous signs

Even before the scandal around Mabira came to light, signs of rising tension were evident on the social and political landscape of Uganda. Mabira turned into a major scandal because it symbolised a collusion between an increasingly unaccountable President and an arrogant tycoon from a racialised minority.

The President had taken to treating the country as his private preserve; the grant of Mabira was simply the latest in a series of grants (of a school in one case or an information ministry facility in another) by the president, always claiming that his personal will represented the interests of 'development'. The tycoon too claimed to be doing the country a favour — once again, 'development' — rather than lining his own pockets. Mabira outraged just about everyone, from the Kabaka to the mukopi, the mwami to the muyaye.

No doubt both the political opposition and the muyaye on the street took full advantage of this public outrage. And yet, it is a mistake to hold them responsible for creating the issue and the grievance of which they took

426

advantage. Nor was the April 12 demonstration mainly a protest about Mabira. It wasn't, which is why public protest on the Asian Question will continue even when the Mabira issue is resolved.

The Asian Question

So what is this Asian Question? It is a different question for different groups of Ugandans. For those in urban and peri-urban areas looking to join commerce, it has to do with the crowding of the market place by immigrant traders, even hawkers — Indian and Chinese — often entitled as 'investors'.

For the middle and the lower-middle classes who have put their energies and assets in secondary and even higher education in the hope of securing their children a white-collar job, it is about the ease with which immigrants seem to be able to get residence and work permits at the expense of jobless nationals. For businesspersons of substance, it is about unfair competition and unequal access to officially sanctioned resources and connections. All of them complain of unfair treatment, and all expect preferential treatment for nationals in an independent country. For all of them, this is a question of nationalism, of meaningful independence.

In their conscience and sometimes in private conversations, most Asian residents of Uganda realise that these grievances are just, for these aspirations are not confined to Uganda and Ugandans, but are common throughout the formerly colonised countries in Africa and Asia.

For ordinary Asian residents, it makes sense to demand that tycoons in the community respect the aspirations of ordinary Ugandans, and to disassociate themselves publicly from those who fail to do so.

All the talk about 'the Asian community' should not hide the fact that not all Asians have the same interest. Of particular importance is the difference between those who see Uganda as home and those who don't.

Many of this latter group are essentially carpetbaggers (in the Asian community, they are known as 'rockets' that land and take off at will). Whereas it makes sense for these temporary sojourners to rely on the Police for protection, such a strategy would be foolish indeed for those who see Uganda as home. This group, the Ugandan Asians, need to think of how to build a future as part of the Ugandan majority.

If we can draw one lesson from the Amin period, it is this: how the Asian Question is defined and resolved will affect not only the Asian minority, but all Ugandans. The Asian Question can be defined in a racist and exclusive way, as it was by Amin, so that the fact of colour blurs that of citizenship and commitment. Or it can be defined in a non-racial and inclusive way so that we make a distinction between different types of Asian residents in today's Uganda, legally between citizens and non-citizens, and socially between those for whom Uganda is no more than a transit facility (the 'rockets') and those for whom Uganda is a home for generations.

Wake-up call

April 12 is a wake-up call that we are dealing with a social question of national dimensions, one that will critically shape Uganda's politics over the coming period. For one, it is rapidly undermining the unity of the government in power. The NRM, including its MPs and members in the Cabinet, are already split on this issue. Should the presidency continue to disregard popular opinion on this question, it is sure to find itself further isolated.

The more popular agitation grows, the more it will teach the electorate that democracy is less about elections than about holding those elected accountable to the citizenry on a day-to-day basis.

Political accountability has to begin with the right to simple information. Whether it is the transfer of public resources (such as in the case of Mabira) to private persons or the issue of residence and work permits to non-nationals, all relevant information must be made public, and done so regularly. The first principle of democracy is that every policy be open to public debate and scrutiny.

The demonstrations have also brought to the fore a key weakness in the opposition. Even if it has the capacity to organise demonstrations, the opposition clearly lacks the foresight and the capacity to give it direction.

The real significance of April 12 is that it has ushered in a period of open competition on who will lead the opposition to an unaccountable presidency. The cutting edge of this competition is likely to be the Asian Question. More than any other, it will set apart demagogues from democrats, and pose a challenge to Ugandans, black and brown, as to whether or not we have the foresight and the capacity to forge a tolerant and inclusive society.

431

CPSIA information can be obtained at www.ICGtesting.com
Printed in the USA
LVOW05s1230300914

406553LV00001B/439/P